Australia Business Law

Handbook

Just The

facts101

Textbook Key Facts

by Cram101

Table of Contents

Index: Answers

Just The Facts101

Exam Prep for

Australia Business Law Handbook

Just The Facts101 Exam Prep is your link from
the textbook and lecture to your exams.

**Just The Facts101 Exam Preps are unauthorized and comprehensive reviews
of your textbooks.**

All material provided by CTI Publications (c) 2019

Textbook publishers and textbook authors do not participate in or contribute to these reviews.

Just The Facts101 Exam Prep

eAIN 444344

Foundations of Business

A business, also known as an enterprise, agency or a firm, is an entity involved in the provision of goods and/or services to consumers. Businesses are prevalent in capitalist economies, where most of them are privately owned and provide goods and services to customers in exchange for other goods, services, or money.

:: Credit cards ::

The _____ Company, also known as Amex, is an American multinational financial services corporation headquartered in Three World Financial Center in New York City. The company was founded in 1850 and is one of the 30 components of the Dow Jones Industrial Average. The company is best known for its charge card, credit card, and traveler's cheque businesses.

Exam Probability: **Medium**

1. *Answer choices:*

(see index for correct answer)

- a. SecurityMetrics
- b. Diners Club International
- c. The Everything Card
- d. American Express

Guidance: level 1

:: Classification systems ::

_____ is the practice of comparing business processes and performance metrics to industry bests and best practices from other companies. Dimensions typically measured are quality, time and cost.

Exam Probability: **Medium**

2. *Answer choices:*

(see index for correct answer)

- a. Benchmarking
- b. British undergraduate degree classification
- c. Stellar classification
- d. Linnaean taxonomy

Guidance: level 1

:: Retailing ::

_____ is the process of selling consumer goods or services to customers through multiple channels of distribution to earn a profit. _____ ers satisfy demand identified through a supply chain. The term "_____ er" is typically applied where a service provider fills the small orders of a large number of individuals, who are end-users, rather than large orders of a small number of wholesale, corporate or government clientele. Shopping generally refers to the act of buying products. Sometimes this is done to obtain final goods, including necessities such as food and clothing; sometimes it takes place as a recreational activity. Recreational shopping often involves window shopping and browsing: it does not always result in a purchase.

Exam Probability: **High**

3. *Answer choices:*

(see index for correct answer)

- a. Selena Etc.
- b. Video game store

- c. Garage sale
- d. Retail

Guidance: level 1

:: Business law ::

_____ is where a person's financial liability is limited to a fixed sum, most commonly the value of a person's investment in a company or partnership. If a company with _____ is sued, then the claimants are suing the company, not its owners or investors. A shareholder in a limited company is not personally liable for any of the debts of the company, other than for the amount already invested in the company and for any unpaid amount on the shares in the company, if any. The same is true for the members of a _____ partnership and the limited partners in a limited partnership. By contrast, sole proprietors and partners in general partnerships are each liable for all the debts of the business .

Exam Probability: **Medium**

4. *Answer choices:*

(see index for correct answer)

- a. Ordinary course of business
- b. De facto corporation and corporation by estoppel
- c. Advertising regulation
- d. Limited liability

Guidance: level 1

:: Land value taxation ::

_____ , sometimes referred to as dry _____ , is the solid surface of Earth that is not permanently covered by water. The vast majority of human activity throughout history has occurred in _____ areas that support agriculture, habitat, and various natural resources. Some life forms have developed from predecessor species that lived in bodies of water.

Exam Probability: **Medium**

5. *Answer choices:*
(see index for correct answer)

- a. Lands Valuation Appeal Court
- b. Land
- c. Land value tax
- d. Henry George

Guidance: level 1

:: Accounting terminology ::

_____ is a legally enforceable claim for payment held by a business for goods supplied and/or services rendered that customers/clients have ordered but not paid for. These are generally in the form of invoices raised by a business and delivered to the customer for payment within an agreed time frame. _____ is shown in a balance sheet as an asset. It is one of a series of accounting transactions dealing with the billing of a customer for goods and services that the customer has ordered. These may be distinguished from notes receivable, which are debts created through formal legal instruments called promissory notes.

Exam Probability: **High**

6. *Answer choices:*

(see index for correct answer)

- a. Accrual
- b. double-entry bookkeeping
- c. Accounts receivable
- d. Share premium

Guidance: level 1

:: Workplace ::

_____ is a systematic determination of a subject's merit, worth and significance, using criteria governed by a set of standards. It can assist an organization, program, design, project or any other intervention or initiative to assess any aim, realisable concept/proposal, or any alternative, to help in decision-making; or to ascertain the degree of achievement or value in regard to the aim and objectives and results of any such action that has been completed. The primary purpose of _____ , in addition to gaining insight into prior or existing initiatives, is to enable reflection and assist in the identification of future change.

Exam Probability: **Medium**

7. *Answer choices:*

(see Index for correct answer)

- a. Evaluation
- b. Feminisation of the workplace
- c. Workplace democracy
- d. Workplace revenge

Guidance: level 1

:: ::

_____ is a means of protection from financial loss. It is a form of risk management, primarily used to hedge against the risk of a contingent or uncertain loss

8. *Answer choices:*

(see index for correct answer)

- a. information systems assessment
- b. Insurance
- c. similarity-attraction theory
- d. cultural

Guidance: level 1

:: Financial markets ::

A _____ is a financial market in which long-term debt or equity-backed securities are bought and sold. _____ s channel the wealth of savers to those who can put it to long-term productive use, such as companies or governments making long-term investments. Financial regulators like the Bank of England and the U.S. Securities and Exchange Commission oversee _____ s to protect investors against fraud, among other duties.

Exam Probability: **High**

9. *Answer choices:*

(see index for correct answer)

- a. GEOS
- b. Capital market

- c. Limits to arbitrage
- d. Market depth

Guidance: level 1

:: Management accounting ::

_____ s are costs that change as the quantity of the good or service that a business produces changes. _____ s are the sum of marginal costs over all units produced. They can also be considered normal costs. Fixed costs and _____ s make up the two components of total cost. Direct costs are costs that can easily be associated with a particular cost object. However, not all _____ s are direct costs. For example, variable manufacturing overhead costs are _____ s that are indirect costs, not direct costs. _____ s are sometimes called unit-level costs as they vary with the number of units produced.

Exam Probability: **High**

10. *Answer choices:*

(see index for correct answer)

- a. Variable cost
- b. Financial statement analysis
- c. Hedge accounting
- d. Management accounting

Guidance: level 1

:: Unemployment ::

In economics, a _____ is a business cycle contraction when there is a general decline in economic activity. Macroeconomic indicators such as GDP , investment spending, capacity utilization, household income, business profits, and inflation fall, while bankruptcies and the unemployment rate rise. In the United Kingdom, it is defined as a negative economic growth for two consecutive quarters.

Exam Probability: **Low**

11. *Answer choices:*

(see index for correct answer)

- a. Recession
- b. Outplacement
- c. Unemployment Provision Convention, 1934
- d. Male unemployment

Guidance: level 1

:: Problem solving ::

In other words, _____ is a situation where a group of people meet to generate new ideas and solutions around a specific domain of interest by removing inhibitions. People are able to think more freely and they suggest as many spontaneous new ideas as possible. All the ideas are noted down and those ideas are not criticized and after _____ session the ideas are evaluated. The term was popularized by Alex Faickney Osborn in the 1953 book Applied Imagination.

Exam Probability: **Medium**

12. *Answer choices:*

(see index for correct answer)

- a. Problem shaping
- b. Unified structured inventive thinking
- c. Brainstorming
- d. Curiosity

Guidance: level 1

:: Customs duties ::

A _____ is a tax on imports or exports between sovereign states. It is a form of regulation of foreign trade and a policy that taxes foreign products to encourage or safeguard domestic industry. _____ s are the simplest and oldest instrument of trade policy. Traditionally, states have used them as a source of income. Now, they are among the most widely used instruments of protection, along with import and export quotas.

13. *Answer choices:*

(see index for correct answer)

- a. World Customs Organization
- b. Malaysian motor vehicle import duties
- c. Customs racketeering
- d. Tariff

Guidance: level 1

:: Labour relations ::

_____ is a field of study that can have different meanings depending on the context in which it is used. In an international context, it is a subfield of labor history that studies the human relations with regard to work – in its broadest sense – and how this connects to questions of social inequality. It explicitly encompasses unregulated, historical, and non-Western forms of labor. Here, _____ define "for or with whom one works and under what rules. These rules determine the type of work, type and amount of remuneration, working hours, degrees of physical and psychological strain, as well as the degree of freedom and autonomy associated with the work."

Exam Probability: **Low**

14. *Answer choices:*

(see index for correct answer)

- a. Disciplinary counseling
- b. Open shop
- c. Inflatable rat
- d. Comprehensive campaign

Guidance: level 1

:: Debt ::

_____ is when something, usually money, is owed by one party, the borrower or _____ or, to a second party, the lender or creditor. _____ is a deferred payment, or series of payments, that is owed in the future, which is what differentiates it from an immediate purchase. The _____ may be owed by sovereign state or country, local government, company, or an individual. Commercial _____ is generally subject to contractual terms regarding the amount and timing of repayments of principal and interest. Loans, bonds, notes, and mortgages are all types of _____ . The term can also be used metaphorically to cover moral obligations and other interactions not based on economic value. For example, in Western cultures, a person who has been helped by a second person is sometimes said to owe a " _____ of gratitude" to the second person.

Exam Probability: **Low**

15. *Answer choices:*

(see index for correct answer)

- a. Compulsive buying disorder
- b. Debt

- c. Perpetual subordinated debt
- d. Phantom debt

Guidance: level 1

:: Project management ::

In political science, an _____ is a means by which a petition signed by a certain minimum number of registered voters can force a government to choose to either enact a law or hold a public vote in parliament in what is called indirect _____, or under direct _____, the proposition is immediately put to a plebiscite or referendum, in what is called a Popular initiated Referendum or citizen-initiated referendum).

Exam Probability: **Low**

16. *Answer choices:*

(see index for correct answer)

- a. Initiative
- b. Project sponsorship
- c. Total project control
- d. Project cycle management

Guidance: level 1

:: Currency ::

A _____ , in the most specific sense is money in any form when in use or circulation as a medium of exchange, especially circulating banknotes and coins. A more general definition is that a _____ is a system of money in common use, especially for people in a nation. Under this definition, US dollars , pounds sterling , Australian dollars , European euros , Russian rubles and Indian Rupees are examples of currencies. These various currencies are recognized as stores of value and are traded between nations in foreign exchange markets, which determine the relative values of the different currencies. Currencies in this sense are defined by governments, and each type has limited boundaries of acceptance.

Exam Probability: **High**

17. *Answer choices:*

(see index for correct answer)

- a. Redenomination
- b. Commodity currency
- c. Currency
- d. Medium of exchange

Guidance: level 1

:: ::

_____ is an abstract concept of management of complex systems according to a set of rules and trends. In systems theory, these types of rules exist in various fields of biology and society, but the term has slightly different meanings according to context. For example.

18. *Answer choices:*

(see index for correct answer)

- a. Regulation
- b. Character
- c. process perspective
- d. corporate values

Guidance: level 1

:: Competition regulators ::

The _____ is an independent agency of the United States government, established in 1914 by the _____ Act. Its principal mission is the promotion of consumer protection and the elimination and prevention of anticompetitive business practices, such as coercive monopoly. It is headquartered in the _____ Building in Washington, D.C.

Exam Probability: **Low**

19. *Answer choices:*

(see index for correct answer)

- a. Fair Trade Commission
- b. Office of Fair Trading

- c. Federal Trade Commission
- d. Jersey Competition Regulatory Authority

Guidance: level 1

:: Accounting software ::

_____ is any item or verifiable record that is generally accepted as payment for goods and services and repayment of debts, such as taxes, in a particular country or socio-economic context. The main functions of _____ are distinguished as: a medium of exchange, a unit of account, a store of value and sometimes, a standard of deferred payment. Any item or verifiable record that fulfils these functions can be considered as _____ .

Exam Probability: **Medium**

20. *Answer choices:*
(see index for correct answer)

- a. National Software
- b. XBRL
- c. Procurify
- d. POS solutions

Guidance: level 1

:: Project management ::

Some scenarios associate "this kind of planning" with learning "life skills".
_____ s are necessary, or at least useful, in situations where individuals need to know what time they must be at a specific location to receive a specific service, and where people need to accomplish a set of goals within a set time period.

Exam Probability: **Low**

21. *Answer choices:*

(see index for correct answer)

- a. Front-end loading
- b. Project Management Institute
- c. Product-based planning
- d. Schedule

Guidance: level 1

:: Free trade agreements ::

A _____ is a wide-ranging taxes, tariff and trade treaty that often includes investment guarantees. It exists when two or more countries agree on terms that helps them trade with each other. The most common _____ s are of the preferential and free trade types are concluded in order to reduce tariffs, quotas and other trade restrictions on items traded between the signatories.

Exam Probability: **High**

22. *Answer choices:*

(see index for correct answer)

- a. Ouchy Convention
- b. Comprehensive Economic Partnership Agreement
- c. New West Partnership
- d. African Free Trade Zone

Guidance: level 1

:: Stock market ::

_____ is a form of corporate equity ownership, a type of security. The terms voting share and ordinary share are also used frequently in other parts of the world; " _____ " being primarily used in the United States. They are known as Equity shares or Ordinary shares in the UK and other Commonwealth realms. This type of share gives the stockholder the right to share in the profits of the company, and to vote on matters of corporate policy and the composition of the members of the board of directors.

Exam Probability: **Low**

23. *Answer choices:*

(see index for correct answer)

- a. Underweight
- b. Common stock
- c. WeSeed

- d. Issued shares

Guidance: level 1

:: Survey methodology ::

An _____ is a conversation where questions are asked and answers are given. In common parlance, the word " _____ " refers to a one-on-one conversation between an _____ er and an _____ ee. The _____ er asks questions to which the _____ ee responds, usually so information may be transferred from _____ ee to _____ er . Sometimes, information can be transferred in both directions. It is a communication, unlike a speech, which produces a one-way flow of information.

Exam Probability: **High**

24. *Answer choices:*
(see index for correct answer)

- a. Public opinion
- b. Interview
- c. Survey sampling
- d. Total survey error

Guidance: level 1

:: Marketing ::

A _____ is a group of customers within a business's serviceable available market at which a business aims its marketing efforts and resources. A _____ is a subset of the total market for a product or service. The _____ typically consists of consumers who exhibit similar characteristics and are considered most likely to buy a business's market offerings or are likely to be the most profitable segments for the business to service.

Exam Probability: **Low**

25. *Answer choices:*

(see index for correct answer)

- a. Target market
- b. Movie packaging
- c. Customer acquisition cost
- d. Kano model

Guidance: level 1

:: Data management ::

_____ is a form of intellectual property that grants the creator of an original creative work an exclusive legal right to determine whether and under what conditions this original work may be copied and used by others, usually for a limited term of years. The exclusive rights are not absolute but limited by limitations and exceptions to _____ law, including fair use. A major limitation on _____ on ideas is that _____ protects only the original expression of ideas, and not the underlying ideas themselves.

26. *Answer choices:*

(see index for correct answer)

- a. Copyright
- b. Wiping
- c. Data warehouse
- d. Storage area network

Guidance: level 1

:: Rhetoric ::

_____ is the pattern of narrative development that aims to make vivid a place, object, character, or group. _____ is one of four rhetorical modes , along with exposition, argumentation, and narration. In practice it would be difficult to write literature that drew on just one of the four basic modes.

Exam Probability: **Low**

27. *Answer choices:*

(see index for correct answer)

- a. Euphuism
- b. Parrhesia
- c. Parade of horribles

- d. Description

Guidance: level 1

:: ::

_____ is the study and management of exchange relationships. _____ is the business process of creating relationships with and satisfying customers. With its focus on the customer, _____ is one of the premier components of business management.

Exam Probability: **Medium**

28. *Answer choices:*

(see index for correct answer)

- a. personal values
- b. Sarbanes-Oxley act of 2002
- c. functional perspective
- d. imperative

Guidance: level 1

:: Regression analysis ::

A _____ often refers to a set of documented requirements to be satisfied by a material, design, product, or service. A _____ is often a type of technical standard.

29. *Answer choices:*

(see index for correct answer)

- a. Residual sum of squares
- b. Zero-inflated model
- c. Hat matrix
- d. Nonlinear regression

Guidance: level 1

:: Production and manufacturing ::

_____ is a set of techniques and tools for process improvement. Though as a shortened form it may be found written as 6S, it should not be confused with the methodology known as 6S .

30. *Answer choices:*

(see index for correct answer)

- a. Nondestructive testing
- b. Value-added agriculture
- c. Fieldbus Foundation
- d. MAPICS

Guidance: level 1

:: Reputation management ::

_____ or image of a social entity is an opinion about that entity, typically as a result of social evaluation on a set of criteria.

Exam Probability: **Low**

31. *Answer choices:*

(see index for correct answer)

- a. TrustedSource
- b. Get Satisfaction
- c. Reputation
- d. Advogato

Guidance: level 1

:: Economic globalization ::

_____ is an agreement in which one company hires another company to be responsible for a planned or existing activity that is or could be done internally,and sometimes involves transferring employees and assets from one firm to another.

Exam Probability: **High**

32. *Answer choices:*
(see index for correct answer)

- a. Outsourcing
- b. reshoring

Guidance: level 1

:: Human resource management ::

_____ encompasses values and behaviors that contribute to the unique social and psychological environment of a business. The _____ influences the way people interact, the context within which knowledge is created, the resistance they will have towards certain changes, and ultimately the way they share knowledge. _____ represents the collective values, beliefs and principles of organizational members and is a product of factors such as history, product, market, technology, strategy, type of employees, management style, and national culture; culture includes the organization's vision, values, norms, systems, symbols, language, assumptions, environment, location, beliefs and habits.

Exam Probability: **Medium**

33. *Answer choices:*

(see index for correct answer)

- a. Expense management
- b. Reward management
- c. Management by objectives
- d. Organizational culture

Guidance: level 1

:: ::

_____ is the administration of an organization, whether it is a business, a not-for-profit organization, or government body. _____ includes the activities of setting the strategy of an organization and coordinating the efforts of its employees to accomplish its objectives through the application of available resources, such as financial, natural, technological, and human resources. The term " _____ " may also refer to those people who manage an organization.

Exam Probability: **Low**

34. *Answer choices:*

(see index for correct answer)

- a. open system
- b. hierarchical
- c. Management

- d. cultural

Guidance: level 1

:: Mereology ::

_____ , in the abstract, is what belongs to or with something, whether as an attribute or as a component of said thing. In the context of this article, it is one or more components , whether physical or incorporeal, of a person's estate; or so belonging to, as in being owned by, a person or jointly a group of people or a legal entity like a corporation or even a society. Depending on the nature of the _____ , an owner of _____ has the right to consume, alter, share, redefine, rent, mortgage, pawn, sell, exchange, transfer, give away or destroy it, or to exclude others from doing these things, as well as to perhaps abandon it; whereas regardless of the nature of the _____ , the owner thereof has the right to properly use it , or at the very least exclusively keep it.

Exam Probability: **Low**

35. *Answer choices:*

(see index for correct answer)

- a. Meronomy
- b. Gunk
- c. Mereological essentialism
- d. Mereotopology

Guidance: level 1

:: Goods ::

In most contexts, the concept of _____ denotes the conduct that should be preferred when posed with a choice between possible actions. _____ is generally considered to be the opposite of evil, and is of interest in the study of morality, ethics, religion and philosophy. The specific meaning and etymology of the term and its associated translations among ancient and contemporary languages show substantial variation in its inflection and meaning depending on circumstances of place, history, religious, or philosophical context.

Exam Probability: **Medium**

36. *Answer choices:*

(see index for correct answer)

- a. Refined goods
- b. Private good
- c. Rivalry
- d. Speciality goods

Guidance: level 1

:: Product management ::

A _____ , trade mark, or trade-mark is a recognizable sign, design, or expression which identifies products or services of a particular source from those of others, although _____ s used to identify services are usually called service marks. The _____ owner can be an individual, business organization, or any legal entity. A _____ may be located on a package, a label, a voucher, or on the product itself. For the sake of corporate identity, _____ s are often displayed on company buildings. It is legally recognized as a type of intellectual property.

Exam Probability: **Medium**

37. *Answer choices:*

(see index for correct answer)

- a. Scarcity Development Cycle
- b. business name
- c. Swing tag
- d. Trademark look

Guidance: level 1

:: Financial statements ::

In financial accounting, a _____ or statement of financial position or statement of financial condition is a summary of the financial balances of an individual or organization, whether it be a sole proprietorship, a business partnership, a corporation, private limited company or other organization such as Government or not-for-profit entity. Assets, liabilities and ownership equity are listed as of a specific date, such as the end of its financial year. A _____ is often described as a "snapshot of a company's financial condition". Of the four basic financial statements, the _____ is the only statement which applies to a single point in time of a business' calendar year.

Exam Probability: **Low**

38. *Answer choices:*

(see index for correct answer)

- a. Balance sheet
- b. Clean surplus accounting
- c. Statements on auditing standards
- d. Statement on Auditing Standards No. 55

Guidance: level 1

:: Management ::

_____ is the practice of initiating, planning, executing, controlling, and closing the work of a team to achieve specific goals and meet specific success criteria at the specified time.

39. *Answer choices:*

(see index for correct answer)

- a. Project management
- b. Balanced scorecard
- c. Performance indicator
- d. Lead scoring

Guidance: level 1

:: Asset ::

In financial accounting, an _____ is any resource owned by the business. Anything tangible or intangible that can be owned or controlled to produce value and that is held by a company to produce positive economic value is an _____ . Simply stated, _____ s represent value of ownership that can be converted into cash . The balance sheet of a firm records the monetary value of the _____ s owned by that firm. It covers money and other valuables belonging to an individual or to a business.

Exam Probability: **High**

40. *Answer choices:*

(see index for correct answer)

- a. Fixed asset

- b. Current asset

:: Critical thinking ::

In psychology, _____ is regarded as the cognitive process resulting in the selection of a belief or a course of action among several alternative possibilities. Every _____ process produces a final choice, which may or may not prompt action.

Exam Probability: **High**

41. *Answer choices:*

(see index for correct answer)

- a. TregoED
- b. Decision-making
- c. Project Reason
- d. Merseyside Skeptics Society

:: Social security ::

_____ is "any government system that provides monetary assistance to people with an inadequate or no income." In the United States, this is usually called welfare or a social safety net, especially when talking about Canada and European countries.

Exam Probability: **Medium**

42. *Answer choices:*

(see index for correct answer)

- a. Social security
- b. Social Security Agency
- c. Social Security Board
- d. Employees%27 State Insurance

Guidance: level 1

:: Banking ::

A _____ is a financial institution that accepts deposits from the public and creates credit. Lending activities can be performed either directly or indirectly through capital markets. Due to their importance in the financial stability of a country, _____ s are highly regulated in most countries. Most nations have institutionalized a system known as fractional reserve _____ ing under which _____ s hold liquid assets equal to only a portion of their current liabilities. In addition to other regulations intended to ensure liquidity, _____ s are generally subject to minimum capital requirements based on an international set of capital standards, known as the Basel Accords.

43. *Answer choices:*

(see index for correct answer)

- a. Financial inclusion
- b. Banq
- c. Bank
- d. Joint account

Guidance: level 1

:: Health promotion ::

_____ , as defined by the World _____ Organization , is "a state of complete physical, mental and social well-being and not merely the absence of disease or infirmity." This definition has been subject to controversy, as it may have limited value for implementation. _____ may be defined as the ability to adapt and manage physical, mental and social challenges throughout life.

Exam Probability: **Low**

44. *Answer choices:*

(see index for correct answer)

- a. Haven Institute
- b. Unwarranted variation

- c. Social marketing
- d. Health

Guidance: level 1

:: Office administration ::

An _____ is generally a room or other area where an organization's employees perform administrative work in order to support and realize objects and goals of the organization. The word " _____ " may also denote a position within an organization with specific duties attached to it ; the latter is in fact an earlier usage, _____ as place originally referring to the location of one's duty. When used as an adjective, the term " _____ " may refer to business-related tasks. In law, a company or organization has _____ s in any place where it has an official presence, even if that presence consists of a storage silo rather than an establishment with desk-and-chair. An _____ is also an architectural and design phenomenon: ranging from a small _____ such as a bench in the corner of a small business of extremely small size , through entire floors of buildings, up to and including massive buildings dedicated entirely to one company. In modern terms an _____ is usually the location where white-collar workers carry out their functions. As per James Stephenson, " _____ is that part of business enterprise which is devoted to the direction and co-ordination of its various activities."

Exam Probability: **Low**

45. *Answer choices:*

(see index for correct answer)

- a. Office

- b. Office administration
- c. Fish! Philosophy
- d. Inter departmental communication

Guidance: level 1

:: Stock market ::

_____ is freedom from, or resilience against, potential harm caused by others. Beneficiaries of _____ may be of persons and social groups, objects and institutions, ecosystems or any other entity or phenomenon vulnerable to unwanted change by its environment.

Exam Probability: **Low**

46. *Answer choices:*

(see index for correct answer)

- a. Earnings call
- b. All or none
- c. Security
- d. Delivery versus payment

Guidance: level 1

:: Non-profit technology ::

Instituto del Tercer Mundo is a Non-Governmental Organization that performs information, communication and education activities. _____ , which was established in 1989, shares the same secretariat and coordinating personnel as Social Watch and is based in Montevideo, Uruguay.

Exam Probability: **High**

47. *Answer choices:*

(see index for correct answer)

- a. Aplos Software
- b. ITeM
- c. World Information Society Day
- d. Red Wing Software

Guidance: level 1

:: Financial crises ::

A _____ is any of a broad variety of situations in which some financial assets suddenly lose a large part of their nominal value. In the 19th and early 20th centuries, many financial crises were associated with banking panics, and many recessions coincided with these panics. Other situations that are often called financial crises include stock market crashes and the bursting of other financial bubbles, currency crises, and sovereign defaults. Financial crises directly result in a loss of paper wealth but do not necessarily result in significant changes in the real economy .

48. *Answer choices:*

(see index for correct answer)

- a. Panic of 1847
- b. Currency crisis
- c. The Panic of 1819
- d. The Vienna Initiative

Guidance: level 1

:: Export and import control ::

" _____ " means the Government Service which is responsible for the administration of _____ law and the collection of duties and taxes and which also has the responsibility for the application of other laws and regulations relating to the importation, exportation, movement or storage of goods.

Exam Probability: **Medium**

49. *Answer choices:*

(see index for correct answer)

- a. Customs
- b. VNIIS Exemption Letter

- c. United States Munitions List
- d. Animal and Plant Health Inspection Service

Guidance: level 1

:: ::

Culture is the social behavior and norms found in human societies. Culture is considered a central concept in anthropology, encompassing the range of phenomena that are transmitted through social learning in human societies. _____ universals are found in all human societies; these include expressive forms like art, music, dance, ritual, religion, and technologies like tool usage, cooking, shelter, and clothing. The concept of material culture covers the physical expressions of culture, such as technology, architecture and art, whereas the immaterial aspects of culture such as principles of social organization , mythology, philosophy, literature , and science comprise the intangible _____ heritage of a society.

Exam Probability: **Medium**

50. *Answer choices:*

(see index for correct answer)

- a. similarity-attraction theory
- b. corporate values
- c. deep-level diversity
- d. levels of analysis

Guidance: level 1

:: Financial accounting ::

_____ is a financial metric which represents operating liquidity available to a business, organisation or other entity, including governmental entities. Along with fixed assets such as plant and equipment, _____ is considered a part of operating capital. Gross _____ is equal to current assets. _____ is calculated as current assets minus current liabilities. If current assets are less than current liabilities, an entity has a _____ deficiency, also called a _____ deficit.

Exam Probability: **Medium**

51. *Answer choices:*

(see index for correct answer)

- a. Asset swap
- b. Book value
- c. Hidden asset
- d. Advance payment

Guidance: level 1

:: Marketing ::

A _____ is something that is necessary for an organism to live a healthy life. _____ s are distinguished from wants in that, in the case of a _____ , a deficiency causes a clear adverse outcome: a dysfunction or death. In other words, a _____ is something required for a safe, stable and healthy life while a want is a desire, wish or aspiration. When _____ s or wants are backed by purchasing power, they have the potential to become economic demands.

Exam Probability: **High**

52. *Answer choices:*

(see index for correct answer)

- a. Price skimming
- b. Marchitecture
- c. Ben Franklin effect
- d. Need

Guidance: level 1

:: Private equity ::

_____ is a type of private equity, a form of financing that is provided by firms or funds to small, early-stage, emerging firms that are deemed to have high growth potential, or which have demonstrated high growth . _____ firms or funds invest in these early-stage companies in exchange for equity, or an ownership stake, in the companies they invest in. _____ ists take on the risk of financing risky start-ups in the hopes that some of the firms they support will become successful. Because startups face high uncertainty, VC investments do have high rates of failure. The start-ups are usually based on an innovative technology or business model and they are usually from the high technology industries, such as information technology , clean technology or biotechnology.

Exam Probability: **Medium**

53. *Answer choices:*

(see index for correct answer)

- a. Angel investor
- b. Venture capital
- c. Junk bond
- d. Private equity in the 1990s

Guidance: level 1

:: Management occupations ::

_____ is the process of designing, launching and running a new business, which is often initially a small business. The people who create these businesses are called entrepreneurs.

54. *Answer choices:*

(see index for correct answer)

- a. Entrepreneurship
- b. Apparatchik
- c. Comptroller
- d. Chief customer officer

Guidance: level 1

:: ::

An _____ is the production of goods or related services within an economy. The major source of revenue of a group or company is the indicator of its relevant _____ . When a large group has multiple sources of revenue generation, it is considered to be working in different industries. Manufacturing _____ became a key sector of production and labour in European and North American countries during the Industrial Revolution, upsetting previous mercantile and feudal economies. This came through many successive rapid advances in technology, such as the production of steel and coal.

55. *Answer choices:*

(see index for correct answer)

- a. process perspective
- b. open system
- c. Industry
- d. cultural

Guidance: level 1

:: International trade ::

_____ involves the transfer of goods or services from one person or entity to another, often in exchange for money. A system or network that allows _____ is called a market.

Exam Probability: **High**

56. *Answer choices:*
(see index for correct answer)

- a. Trade
- b. International trade law
- c. Trade creation
- d. New International Economic Order

Guidance: level 1

:: Costs ::

In microeconomic theory, the _____ , or alternative cost, of making a particular choice is the value of the most valuable choice out of those that were not taken. In other words, opportunity that will require sacrifices.

Exam Probability: **Medium**

57. *Answer choices:*

(see index for correct answer)

- a. Direct materials cost
- b. Prospective costs
- c. Opportunity cost
- d. Cost reduction

Guidance: level 1

:: Evaluation ::

_____ solving consists of using generic or ad hoc methods in an orderly manner to find solutions to _____ s. Some of the _____ -solving techniques developed and used in philosophy, artificial intelligence, computer science, engineering, mathematics, or medicine are related to mental _____ -solving techniques studied in psychology.

Exam Probability: **Low**

58. *Answer choices:*

(see index for correct answer)

- a. Impact assessment
- b. Technology assessment
- c. Quality assurance
- d. Common Criteria Testing Laboratory

Guidance: level 1

:: ::

A _____ is any person who contracts to acquire an asset in return for some form of consideration.

Exam Probability: **High**

59. *Answer choices:*

(see index for correct answer)

- a. co-culture
- b. Buyer
- c. personal values
- d. surface-level diversity

Guidance: level 1

Management

Management is the administration of an organization, whether it is a business, a not-for-profit organization, or government body. Management includes the activities of setting the strategy of an organization and coordinating the efforts of its employees (or of volunteers) to accomplish its objectives through the application of available resources, such as financial, natural, technological, and human resources.

:: Business models ::

_____ es are privately owned corporations, partnerships, or sole proprietorships that have fewer employees and/or less annual revenue than a regular-sized business or corporation. Businesses are defined as "small" in terms of being able to apply for government support and qualify for preferential tax policy varies depending on the country and industry. _____ es range from fifteen employees under the Australian Fair Work Act 2009, fifty employees according to the definition used by the European Union, and fewer than five hundred employees to qualify for many U.S. _____ Administration programs. While _____ es can also be classified according to other methods, such as annual revenues, shipments, sales, assets, or by annual gross or net revenue or net profits, the number of employees is one of the most widely used measures.

Exam Probability: **Medium**

1. *Answer choices:*

(see index for correct answer)

- a. IASME
- b. Lemonade stand
- c. Data as a service
- d. Gratis

Guidance: level 1

:: Project management ::

In political science, an _____ is a means by which a petition signed by a certain minimum number of registered voters can force a government to choose to either enact a law or hold a public vote in parliament in what is called indirect _____ , or under direct _____ , the proposition is immediately put to a plebiscite or referendum, in what is called a Popular initiated Referendum or citizen-initiated referendum).

Exam Probability: **Medium**

2. *Answer choices:*

(see index for correct answer)

- a. Graphical path method
- b. PM Declaration of Interdependence
- c. Risk register
- d. Point of total assumption

Guidance: level 1

:: Management ::

The term _____ refers to measures designed to increase the degree of autonomy and self-determination in people and in communities in order to enable them to represent their interests in a responsible and self-determined way, acting on their own authority. It is the process of becoming stronger and more confident, especially in controlling one's life and claiming one's rights.

_____ as action refers both to the process of self-_____ and to professional support of people, which enables them to overcome their sense of powerlessness and lack of influence, and to recognize and use their resources. To do work with power.

Exam Probability: **Medium**

3. *Answer choices:*

(see index for correct answer)

- a. Empowerment
- b. Change advisory board
- c. Event management
- d. Control limits

Guidance: level 1

:: ::

In production, research, retail, and accounting, a _____ is the value of money that has been used up to produce something or deliver a service, and hence is not available for use anymore. In business, the _____ may be one of acquisition, in which case the amount of money expended to acquire it is counted as _____ . In this case, money is the input that is gone in order to acquire the thing. This acquisition _____ may be the sum of the _____ of production as incurred by the original producer, and further _____ s of transaction as incurred by the acquirer over and above the price paid to the producer. Usually, the price also includes a mark-up for profit over the _____ of production.

Exam Probability: **High**

4. *Answer choices:*

(see index for correct answer)

- a. information systems assessment
- b. interpersonal communication
- c. Cost
- d. hierarchical perspective

Guidance: level 1

:: Operations research ::

_____ is a method to achieve the best outcome in a mathematical model whose requirements are represented by linear relationships. _____ is a special case of mathematical programming .

5. *Answer choices:*

(see index for correct answer)

- a. Algorithm design
- b. K-medians clustering
- c. Linear programming
- d. mathematical programming

Guidance: level 1

:: ::

_____ is the process of making predictions of the future based on past and present data and most commonly by analysis of trends. A commonplace example might be estimation of some variable of interest at some specified future date. Prediction is a similar, but more general term. Both might refer to formal statistical methods employing time series, cross-sectional or longitudinal data, or alternatively to less formal judgmental methods. Usage can differ between areas of application: for example, in hydrology the terms "forecast" and "_____" are sometimes reserved for estimates of values at certain specific future times, while the term "prediction" is used for more general estimates, such as the number of times floods will occur over a long period.

Exam Probability: **High**

6. *Answer choices:*

(see index for correct answer)

- a. surface-level diversity
- b. functional perspective
- c. Forecasting
- d. Character

Guidance: level 1

:: Rhetoric ::

_____ is the pattern of narrative development that aims to make vivid a place, object, character, or group. _____ is one of four rhetorical modes , along with exposition, argumentation, and narration. In practice it would be difficult to write literature that drew on just one of the four basic modes.

Exam Probability: **High**

7. *Answer choices:*

(see index for correct answer)

- a. Description
- b. Nasreddin
- c. Narrative criticism
- d. Think of the children

Guidance: level 1

In mathematics, a _____ is a relationship between two numbers indicating how many times the first number contains the second. For example, if a bowl of fruit contains eight oranges and six lemons, then the _____ of oranges to lemons is eight to six . Similarly, the _____ of lemons to oranges is 6:8 and the _____ of oranges to the total amount of fruit is 8:14 .

Exam Probability: **High**

8. *Answer choices:*

(see index for correct answer)

- a. imperative
- b. deep-level diversity
- c. co-culture
- d. similarity-attraction theory

Guidance: level 1

The _____ is an intergovernmental organization that is concerned with the regulation of international trade between nations. The WTO officially commenced on 1 January 1995 under the Marrakesh Agreement, signed by 124 nations on 15 April 1994, replacing the General Agreement on Tariffs and Trade , which commenced in 1948. It is the largest international economic organization in the world.

Exam Probability: **High**

9. *Answer choices:*

(see index for correct answer)

- a. empathy
- b. functional perspective
- c. World Trade Organization
- d. hierarchical

Guidance: level 1

:: Leadership ::

_____ Theory, or the _____ Model, is a model created by Paul Hersey and Ken Blanchard, developed while working on Management of Organizational Behavior. The theory was first introduced in 1969 as "life cycle theory of leadership". During the mid-1970s, life cycle theory of leadership was renamed " _____ Theory."

Exam Probability: **Medium**

10. *Answer choices:*

(see index for correct answer)

- a. Motivational Leadership
- b. Spirit of Enniskillen Trust
- c. Inspired Leadership Award
- d. Situational leadership

Guidance: level 1

:: Marketing ::

_____ , in marketing, manufacturing, call centres and management, is the use of flexible computer-aided manufacturing systems to produce custom output. Such systems combine the low unit costs of mass production processes with the flexibility of individual customization.

Exam Probability: **High**

11. *Answer choices:*

(see index for correct answer)

- a. Online ethnography
- b. Purchase funnel
- c. John Neeson
- d. Mass customization

:: Data analysis ::

In statistics, the _____ is a measure that is used to quantify the amount of variation or dispersion of a set of data values. A low _____ indicates that the data points tend to be close to the mean of the set, while a high _____ indicates that the data points are spread out over a wider range of values.

Exam Probability: **Low**

12. *Answer choices:*

(see index for correct answer)

- a. Lincoln index
- b. Lulu smoothing
- c. Standard deviation
- d. German tank problem

:: Management ::

_____ is the identification, evaluation, and prioritization of risks followed by coordinated and economical application of resources to minimize, monitor, and control the probability or impact of unfortunate events or to maximize the realization of opportunities.

Exam Probability: **Medium**

13. *Answer choices:*

(see index for correct answer)

- a. Product Development and Systems Engineering Consortium
- b. Target culture
- c. Organizational hologram
- d. Risk management

Guidance: level 1

:: ::

_____ is the collection of mechanisms, processes and relations by which corporations are controlled and operated. Governance structures and principles identify the distribution of rights and responsibilities among different participants in the corporation and include the rules and procedures for making decisions in corporate affairs. _____ is necessary because of the possibility of conflicts of interests between stakeholders, primarily between shareholders and upper management or among shareholders.

Exam Probability: **High**

14. *Answer choices:*

(see index for correct answer)

- a. hierarchical
- b. functional perspective
- c. Corporate governance
- d. personal values

Guidance: level 1

:: Production economics ::

In microeconomics, _____ are the cost advantages that enterprises obtain due to their scale of operation , with cost per unit of output decreasing with increasing scale.

Exam Probability: **Medium**

15. *Answer choices:*

(see index for correct answer)

- a. short run
- b. Industrial production index
- c. Product pipeline
- d. Diminishing returns

Guidance: level 1

:: Time management ::

_____ is the process of planning and exercising conscious control of time spent on specific activities, especially to increase effectiveness, efficiency, and productivity. It involves a juggling act of various demands upon a person relating to work, social life, family, hobbies, personal interests and commitments with the finiteness of time. Using time effectively gives the person "choice" on spending/managing activities at their own time and expediency.

Exam Probability: **Low**

16. *Answer choices:*

(see index for correct answer)

- a. Getting Things Done
- b. waiting room
- c. Maestro concept
- d. Time management

Guidance: level 1

:: Stochastic processes ::

_____ in its modern meaning is a "new idea, creative thoughts, new imaginations in form of device or method". _____ is often also viewed as the application of better solutions that meet new requirements, unarticulated needs, or existing market needs. Such _____ takes place through the provision of more-effective products, processes, services, technologies, or business models that are made available to markets, governments and society. An _____ is something original and more effective and, as a consequence, new, that "breaks into" the market or society. _____ is related to, but not the same as, invention, as _____ is more apt to involve the practical implementation of an invention to make a meaningful impact in the market or society, and not all _____ s require an invention. _____ often manifests itself via the engineering process, when the problem being solved is of a technical or scientific nature. The opposite of _____ is exnovation.

Exam Probability: **Medium**

17. *Answer choices:*

(see index for correct answer)

- a. Increasing process
- b. Path space
- c. Innovation
- d. Random function

Guidance: level 1

:: Employee relations ::

_____ ownership, or employee share ownership, is an ownership interest in a company held by the company's workforce. The ownership interest may be facilitated by the company as part of employees' remuneration or incentive compensation for work performed, or the company itself may be employee owned.

Exam Probability: **Low**

18. *Answer choices:*

(see index for correct answer)

- a. Employee stock
- b. Employee handbook
- c. Fringe benefit
- d. Employee engagement

Guidance: level 1

:: Management ::

A _____ is an idea of the future or desired result that a person or a group of people envisions, plans and commits to achieve. People endeavor to reach _____ s within a finite time by setting deadlines.

Exam Probability: **High**

19. *Answer choices:*

(see index for correct answer)

- a. Visual learning
- b. Control limits
- c. Shrinkage
- d. Instruction creep

Guidance: level 1

:: ::

_____ is the moral stance, political philosophy, ideology, or social outlook that emphasizes the moral worth of the individual. Individualists promote the exercise of one's goals and desires and so value independence and self-reliance and advocate that interests of the individual should achieve precedence over the state or a social group, while opposing external interference upon one's own interests by society or institutions such as the government. _____ is often defined in contrast to totalitarianism, collectivism, and more corporate social forms.

Exam Probability: **Low**

20. *Answer choices:*

(see index for correct answer)

- a. Individualism
- b. personal values
- c. open system
- d. process perspective

:: ::

A _____ is a leader's method of providing direction, implementing
plans, and motivating people. Various authors have proposed identifying many
different _____ s as exhibited by leaders in the political, business or
other fields. Studies on _____ are conducted in the military field,
expressing an approach that stresses a holistic view of leadership, including
how a leader's physical presence determines how others perceive that leader.
The factors of physical presence in this context include military bearing,
physical fitness, confidence, and resilience. The leader's intellectual
capacity helps to conceptualize solutions and to acquire knowledge to do the
job. A leader's conceptual abilities apply agility, judgment, innovation,
interpersonal tact, and domain knowledge. Domain knowledge encompasses tactical
and technical knowledge as well as cultural and geopolitical awareness. Daniel
Goleman in his article "Leadership that Gets Results" talks about six styles
of leadership.

Exam Probability: **Low**

21. *Answer choices:*

(see index for correct answer)

- a. surface-level diversity
- b. Leadership style
- c. Character
- d. interpersonal communication

:: Legal terms ::

_____ , a form of alternative dispute resolution , is a way to resolve disputes outside the courts. The dispute will be decided by one or more persons , which renders the " _____ award". An _____ award is legally binding on both sides and enforceable in the courts.

Exam Probability: **High**

22. *Answer choices:*

(see index for correct answer)

- a. Confession of judgment
- b. Arbitration
- c. Pain and suffering
- d. Nominal party

Guidance: level 1

:: Reputation management ::

_____ or image of a social entity is an opinion about that entity, typically as a result of social evaluation on a set of criteria.

Exam Probability: **High**

23. *Answer choices:*

(see index for correct answer)

- a. Slashdot
- b. The Economy of Esteem
- c. 123people
- d. BrandYourself

Guidance: level 1

:: ::

_____ or standardisation is the process of implementing and developing technical standards based on the consensus of different parties that include firms, users, interest groups, standards organizations and governments. _____ can help maximize compatibility, interoperability, safety, repeatability, or quality. It can also facilitate commoditization of formerly custom processes. In social sciences, including economics, the idea of _____ is close to the solution for a coordination problem, a situation in which all parties can realize mutual gains, but only by making mutually consistent decisions. This view includes the case of "spontaneous _____ processes", to produce de facto standards.

Exam Probability: **Medium**

24. *Answer choices:*

(see index for correct answer)

- a. surface-level diversity

- b. information systems assessment
- c. Standardization
- d. Sarbanes-Oxley act of 2002

Guidance: level 1

:: Life skills ::

_____ , emotional leadership , emotional quotient and _____ quotient , is the capability of individuals to recognize their own emotions and those of others, discern between different feelings and label them appropriately, use emotional information to guide thinking and behavior, and manage and/or adjust emotions to adapt to environments or achieve one's goal.

Exam Probability: **High**

25. *Answer choices:*

(see index for correct answer)

- a. emotion work
- b. Emotional intelligence
- c. Social intelligence
- d. multiple intelligence

Guidance: level 1

:: Marketing ::

_____ is based on a marketing concept which can be adopted by an organization as a strategy for business expansion. Where implemented, a franchisor licenses its know-how, procedures, intellectual property, use of its business model, brand, and rights to sell its branded products and services to a franchisee. In return the franchisee pays certain fees and agrees to comply with certain obligations, typically set out in a Franchise Agreement.

Exam Probability: **High**

26. *Answer choices:*

(see index for correct answer)

- a. Horizontal integration
- b. Franchising
- c. Franchise fee
- d. Bass diffusion model

Guidance: level 1

:: ::

_____ is a kind of action that occur as two or more objects have an effect upon one another. The idea of a two-way effect is essential in the concept of _____ , as opposed to a one-way causal effect. A closely related term is interconnectivity, which deals with the _____ s of _____ s within systems: combinations of many simple _____ s can lead to surprising emergent phenomena. _____ has different tailored meanings in various sciences. Changes can also involve _____ .

Exam Probability: **Low**

27. *Answer choices:*

(see index for correct answer)

- a. functional perspective
- b. interpersonal communication
- c. open system
- d. Interaction

Guidance: level 1

:: Product management ::

_____ s, also known as Shewhart charts or process-behavior charts, are a statistical process control tool used to determine if a manufacturing or business process is in a state of control.

Exam Probability: **Low**

28. *Answer choices:*

(see index for correct answer)

- a. Diffusion of innovations
- b. Visual brand language
- c. Control chart
- d. Trademark

Guidance: level 1

:: ::

The _____ or just chief executive , is the most senior corporate, executive, or administrative officer in charge of managing an organization especially an independent legal entity such as a company or nonprofit institution. CEOs lead a range of organizations, including public and private corporations, non-profit organizations and even some government organizations . The CEO of a corporation or company typically reports to the board of directors and is charged with maximizing the value of the entity, which may include maximizing the share price, market share, revenues or another element. In the non-profit and government sector, CEOs typically aim at achieving outcomes related to the organization`s mission, such as reducing poverty, increasing literacy, etc.

Exam Probability: **Medium**

29. *Answer choices:*

(see index for correct answer)

- a. co-culture
- b. levels of analysis
- c. hierarchical perspective
- d. open system

Guidance: level 1

:: Generally Accepted Accounting Principles ::

In accounting, _____ is the income that a business have from its normal business activities, usually from the sale of goods and services to customers. _____ is also referred to as sales or turnover. Some companies receive _____ from interest, royalties, or other fees. _____ may refer to business income in general, or it may refer to the amount, in a monetary unit, earned during a period of time, as in "Last year, Company X had _____ of $42 million". Profits or net income generally imply total _____ minus total expenses in a given period. In accounting, in the balance statement it is a subsection of the Equity section and _____ increases equity, it is often referred to as the "top line" due to its position on the income statement at the very top. This is to be contrasted with the "bottom line" which denotes net income .

Exam Probability: **High**

30. *Answer choices:*

(see index for correct answer)

- a. Normal balance
- b. Engagement letter

- c. Deferral
- d. Revenue

Guidance: level 1

:: ::

_____ is the process of collecting, analyzing and/or reporting information regarding the performance of an individual, group, organization, system or component. _____ is not a new concept, some of the earliest records of human activity relate to the counting or recording of activities.

Exam Probability: **Medium**

31. *Answer choices:*

(see index for correct answer)

- a. cultural
- b. process perspective
- c. Performance measurement
- d. hierarchical

Guidance: level 1

:: Regression analysis ::

A _____ often refers to a set of documented requirements to be satisfied by a material, design, product, or service. A _____ is often a type of technical standard.

Exam Probability: **Medium**

32. *Answer choices:*

(see index for correct answer)

- a. Specification
- b. Multivariate adaptive regression splines
- c. Tobit model
- d. Ordinal regression

Guidance: level 1

:: ::

Some scenarios associate "this kind of planning" with learning "life skills".Schedules are necessary, or at least useful, in situations where individuals need to know what time they must be at a specific location to receive a specific service, and where people need to accomplish a set of goals within a set time period.

Exam Probability: **High**

33. *Answer choices:*

(see index for correct answer)

- a. surface-level diversity
- b. Character
- c. empathy
- d. information systems assessment

Guidance: level 1

:: ::

_____ , known in Europe as research and technological development , refers to innovative activities undertaken by corporations or governments in developing new services or products, or improving existing services or products. _____ constitutes the first stage of development of a potential new service or the production process.

Exam Probability: **Medium**

34. *Answer choices:*
(see index for correct answer)

- a. hierarchical
- b. Research and development
- c. corporate values
- d. functional perspective

:: Employment compensation ::

_____ refers to various incentive plans introduced by businesses that provide direct or indirect payments to employees that depend on company's profitability in addition to employees' regular salary and bonuses. In publicly traded companies these plans typically amount to allocation of shares to employees. One of the earliest pioneers of _____ was Englishman Theodore Cooke Taylor, who is known to have introduced the practice in his woollen mills during the late 1800s .

Exam Probability: **Low**

35. *Answer choices:*

(see index for correct answer)

- a. Equal pay for equal work
- b. Annual leave
- c. Severance package
- d. Profit sharing

:: Human resource management ::

_____ , executive management, upper management, or a management team is generally a team of individuals at the highest level of management of an organization who have the day-to-day tasks of managing that organization — sometimes a company or a corporation.

Exam Probability: **Low**

36. *Answer choices:*

(see index for correct answer)

- a. Senior management
- b. Leadership development
- c. Randstad Holding
- d. Organizational orientations

Guidance: level 1

:: Organizational behavior ::

In organizational behavior and industrial and organizational psychology, _____ is an individual's psychological attachment to the organization. The basis behind many of these studies was to find ways to improve how workers feel about their jobs so that these workers would become more committed to their organizations. _____ predicts work variables such as turnover, organizational citizenship behavior, and job performance. Some of the factors such as role stress, empowerment, job insecurity and employability, and distribution of leadership have been shown to be connected to a worker's sense of _____ .

37. *Answer choices:*

(see index for correct answer)

- a. Affective events theory
- b. Managerial grid model
- c. Micro-initiative
- d. Organizational commitment

Guidance: level 1

:: Logistics ::

_____ is generally the detailed organization and implementation of a complex operation. In a general business sense, _____ is the management of the flow of things between the point of origin and the point of consumption in order to meet requirements of customers or corporations. The resources managed in _____ may include tangible goods such as materials, equipment, and supplies, as well as food and other consumable items. The _____ of physical items usually involves the integration of information flow, materials handling, production, packaging, inventory, transportation, warehousing, and often security.

Exam Probability: **High**

38. *Answer choices:*

(see index for correct answer)

- a. Phase jitter modulation
- b. Tracking number
- c. Hubs and Nodes
- d. Center for Transportation and Logistics Neuer Adler

Guidance: level 1

:: Belief ::

_____ is the study of general and fundamental questions about existence, knowledge, values, reason, mind, and language. Such questions are often posed as problems to be studied or resolved. The term was probably coined by Pythagoras . Philosophical methods include questioning, critical discussion, rational argument, and systematic presentation. Classic philosophical questions include: Is it possible to know anything and to prove it What is most real Philosophers also pose more practical and concrete questions such as: Is there a best way to live Is it better to be just or unjust Do humans have free will

Exam Probability: **Low**

39. *Answer choices:*

(see index for correct answer)

- a. Philosophy of happiness
- b. Persuasion
- c. Philosophy
- d. Basic belief

:: Budgets ::

A _____ is a financial plan for a defined period, often one year. It may also include planned sales volumes and revenues, resource quantities, costs and expenses, assets, liabilities and cash flows. Companies, governments, families and other organizations use it to express strategic plans of activities or events in measurable terms.

Exam Probability: **Low**

40. *Answer choices:*

(see index for correct answer)

- a. Budgeted cost of work scheduled
- b. Performance-based budgeting
- c. Link budget
- d. Programme budgeting

:: ::

The _____ is a political and economic union of 28 member states that are located primarily in Europe. It has an area of 4,475,757 km2 and an estimated population of about 513 million. The EU has developed an internal single market through a standardised system of laws that apply in all member states in those matters, and only those matters, where members have agreed to act as one. EU policies aim to ensure the free movement of people, goods, services and capital within the internal market, enact legislation in justice and home affairs and maintain common policies on trade, agriculture, fisheries and regional development. For travel within the Schengen Area, passport controls have been abolished. A monetary union was established in 1999 and came into full force in 2002 and is composed of 19 EU member states which use the euro currency.

Exam Probability: **Low**

41. *Answer choices:*

(see index for correct answer)

- a. process perspective
- b. co-culture
- c. empathy
- d. European Union

Guidance: level 1

:: Evaluation ::

_____ is a way of preventing mistakes and defects in manufactured products and avoiding problems when delivering products or services to customers; which ISO 9000 defines as "part of quality management focused on providing confidence that quality requirements will be fulfilled". This defect prevention in _____ differs subtly from defect detection and rejection in quality control and has been referred to as a shift left since it focuses on quality earlier in the process .

Exam Probability: **Medium**

42. *Answer choices:*

(see index for correct answer)

- a. Program evaluation
- b. Immanent evaluation
- c. Quality assurance
- d. Defence Evaluation and Research Agency

Guidance: level 1

:: ::

_____ refers to the confirmation of certain characteristics of an object, person, or organization. This confirmation is often, but not always, provided by some form of external review, education, assessment, or audit. Accreditation is a specific organization's process of _____ . According to the National Council on Measurement in Education, a _____ test is a credentialing test used to determine whether individuals are knowledgeable enough in a given occupational area to be labeled "competent to practice" in that area.

Exam Probability: **Medium**

43. *Answer choices:*

(see index for correct answer)

- a. deep-level diversity
- b. Character
- c. Sarbanes-Oxley act of 2002
- d. process perspective

Guidance: level 1

:: ::

_____ is the amount of time someone works beyond normal working hours. The term is also used for the pay received for this time. Normal hours may be determined in several ways.

Exam Probability: **Low**

44. *Answer choices:*

(see index for correct answer)

- a. Sarbanes-Oxley act of 2002
- b. surface-level diversity
- c. Overtime
- d. cultural

Guidance: level 1

:: ::

_____ , in its broadest context, includes both the attainment of that which is just and the philosophical discussion of that which is just. The concept of _____ is based on numerous fields, and many differing viewpoints and perspectives including the concepts of moral correctness based on ethics, rationality, law, religion, equity and fairness. Often, the general discussion of _____ is divided into the realm of social _____ as found in philosophy, theology and religion, and, procedural _____ as found in the study and application of the law.

Exam Probability: **Medium**

45. *Answer choices:*

(see index for correct answer)

- a. cultural
- b. Justice

- c. hierarchical perspective
- d. co-culture

Guidance: level 1

:: Project management ::

_____ is the right to exercise power, which can be formalized by a state and exercised by way of judges, appointed executives of government, or the ecclesiastical or priestly appointed representatives of a God or other deities.

Exam Probability: **High**

46. *Answer choices:*
(see index for correct answer)

- a. Structured data analysis
- b. Project planning
- c. Master of Science in Project Management
- d. Authority

Guidance: level 1

:: Production economics ::

_____ is the joint use of a resource or space. It is also the process of dividing and distributing. In its narrow sense, it refers to joint or alternating use of inherently finite goods, such as a common pasture or a shared residence. Still more loosely, "_____" can actually mean giving something as an outright gift: for example, to "share" one's food really means to give some of it as a gift. _____ is a basic component of human interaction, and is responsible for strengthening social ties and ensuring a person's well-being.

Exam Probability: **High**

47. *Answer choices:*

(see index for correct answer)

- a. Isoquant
- b. Choice of techniques
- c. Production theory
- d. Foundations of Economic Analysis

Guidance: level 1

:: Human resource management ::

_____ involves improving the effectiveness of organizations and the individuals and teams within them. Training may be viewed as related to immediate changes in organizational effectiveness via organized instruction, while development is related to the progress of longer-term organizational and employee goals. While _____ technically have differing definitions, the two are oftentimes used interchangeably and/or together. _____ has historically been a topic within applied psychology but has within the last two decades become closely associated with human resources management, talent management, human resources development, instructional design, human factors, and knowledge management.

Exam Probability: **High**

48. *Answer choices:*

(see index for correct answer)

- a. Training and development
- b. Competency-based job description
- c. Workplace mentoring
- d. Workforce sciences

Guidance: level 1

:: ::

A _____ or sample _____ is a single measure of some attribute of a sample . It is calculated by applying a function to the values of the items of the sample, which are known together as a set of data.

49. *Answer choices:*

(see index for correct answer)

- a. deep-level diversity
- b. Statistic
- c. similarity-attraction theory
- d. functional perspective

Guidance: level 1

:: Packaging ::

In work place, _____ or job _____ means good ranking with the hypothesized conception of requirements of a role. There are two types of job _____ s: contextual and task. Task _____ is related to cognitive ability while contextual _____ is dependent upon personality. Task _____ are behavioral roles that are recognized in job descriptions and by remuneration systems, they are directly related to organizational _____ , whereas, contextual _____ are value based and additional behavioral roles that are not recognized in job descriptions and covered by compensation; they are extra roles that are indirectly related to organizational _____ . Citizenship _____ like contextual _____ means a set of individual activity/contribution that supports the organizational culture.

50. *Answer choices:*

(see index for correct answer)

- a. Performance
- b. Shelf-ready packaging
- c. Ullage
- d. Sustainable packaging

Guidance: level 1

:: ::

An _____ is a person temporarily or permanently residing in a country other than their native country. In common usage, the term often refers to professionals, skilled workers, or artists taking positions outside their home country, either independently or sent abroad by their employers, who can be companies, universities, governments, or non-governmental organisations. Effectively migrant workers, they usually earn more than they would at home, and less than local employees. However, the term ` _____ ` is also used for retirees and others who have chosen to live outside their native country. Historically, it has also referred to exiles.

Exam Probability: **Medium**

51. *Answer choices:*

(see index for correct answer)

- a. Expatriate
- b. Sarbanes-Oxley act of 2002
- c. deep-level diversity

- d. co-culture

:: Leadership ::

_____ is a theory of leadership where a leader works with teams to identify needed change, creating a vision to guide the change through inspiration, and executing the change in tandem with committed members of a group; it is an integral part of the Full Range Leadership Model. _____ serves to enhance the motivation, morale, and job performance of followers through a variety of mechanisms; these include connecting the follower's sense of identity and self to a project and to the collective identity of the organization; being a role model for followers in order to inspire them and to raise their interest in the project; challenging followers to take greater ownership for their work, and understanding the strengths and weaknesses of followers, allowing the leader to align followers with tasks that enhance their performance.

Exam Probability: **High**

52. *Answer choices:*
(see index for correct answer)

- a. The Saint, the Surfer, and the CEO
- b. Outstanding leadership theory
- c. Motivational Leadership
- d. Transformational leadership

:: Employment ::

The _____ is an individual's metaphorical "journey" through learning, work and other aspects of life. There are a number of ways to define _____ and the term is used in a variety of ways.

Exam Probability: **Low**

53. *Answer choices:*

(see index for correct answer)

- a. Labor geography
- b. Attendance allowance
- c. Career
- d. Digital nomad

Guidance: level 1

:: Production economics ::

_____ is the creation of a whole that is greater than the simple sum of its parts. The term _____ comes from the Attic Greek word sea synergia from synergos, , meaning "working together".

54. *Answer choices:*

(see index for correct answer)

- a. Learning-by-doing
- b. Productivity Alpha
- c. Specialization
- d. Synergy

Guidance: level 1

:: Income ::

In business and accounting, net income is an entity's income minus cost of goods sold, expenses and taxes for an accounting period. It is computed as the residual of all revenues and gains over all expenses and losses for the period, and has also been defined as the net increase in shareholders' equity that results from a company's operations. In the context of the presentation of financial statements, the IFRS Foundation defines net income as synonymous with profit and loss. The difference between revenue and the cost of making a product or providing a service, before deducting overheads, payroll, taxation, and interest payments. This is different from operating income .

Exam Probability: **High**

55. *Answer choices:*

(see index for correct answer)

- a. Passive income
- b. Pay grade
- c. Implied level of government service
- d. Aggregate income

Guidance: level 1

:: ::

An _____ is a process where candidates are examined to determine their suitability for specific types of employment, especially management or military command. The candidates' personality and aptitudes are determined by techniques including interviews, group exercises, presentations, examinations and psychometric testing.

Exam Probability: **Medium**

56. *Answer choices:*

(see index for correct answer)

- a. open system
- b. Character
- c. Assessment center
- d. hierarchical perspective

Guidance: level 1

:: Goods ::

In most contexts, the concept of _____ denotes the conduct that should be preferred when posed with a choice between possible actions. _____ is generally considered to be the opposite of evil, and is of interest in the study of morality, ethics, religion and philosophy. The specific meaning and etymology of the term and its associated translations among ancient and contemporary languages show substantial variation in its inflection and meaning depending on circumstances of place, history, religious, or philosophical context.

Exam Probability: **High**

57. *Answer choices:*

(see index for correct answer)

- a. Club good
- b. Durable good
- c. Good
- d. Private good

Guidance: level 1

:: Materials ::

A _____ , also known as a feedstock, unprocessed material, or primary commodity, is a basic material that is used to produce goods, finished products, energy, or intermediate materials which are feedstock for future finished products. As feedstock, the term connotes these materials are bottleneck assets and are highly important with regard to producing other products. An example of this is crude oil, which is a _____ and a feedstock used in the production of industrial chemicals, fuels, plastics, and pharmaceutical goods; lumber is a _____ used to produce a variety of products including all types of furniture. The term "_____" denotes materials in minimally processed or unprocessed in states; e.g., raw latex, crude oil, cotton, coal, raw biomass, iron ore, air, logs, or water i.e. "...any product of agriculture, forestry, fishing and any other mineral that is in its natural form or which has undergone the transformation required to prepare it for internationally marketing in substantial volumes."

Exam Probability: **High**

58. *Answer choices:*

(see index for correct answer)

- a. Raw material
- b. Microporous material
- c. Salisbury screen
- d. Drawdown chart

Guidance: level 1

:: ::

According to Torrington, a _____ is usually developed by conducting a job analysis, which includes examining the tasks and sequences of tasks necessary to perform the job. The analysis considers the areas of knowledge and skills needed for the job. A job usually includes several roles. According to Hall, the _____ might be broadened to form a person specification or may be known as "terms of reference". The person/job specification can be presented as a stand-alone document, but in practice it is usually included within the _____ . A _____ is often used by employers in the recruitment process.

Exam Probability: **Medium**

59. *Answer choices:*

(see index for correct answer)

- a. Job description
- b. hierarchical
- c. levels of analysis
- d. empathy

Guidance: level 1

Business law

Corporate law (also known as business law) is the body of law governing the rights, relations, and conduct of persons, companies, organizations and businesses. It refers to the legal practice relating to, or the theory of corporations. Corporate law often describes the law relating to matters which derive directly from the life-cycle of a corporation. It thus encompasses the formation, funding, governance, and death of a corporation.

:: Commercial item transport and distribution ::

A _____ is a commitment or expectation to perform some action in general or if certain circumstances arise. A _____ may arise from a system of ethics or morality, especially in an honor culture. Many duties are created by law, sometimes including a codified punishment or liability for non-performance. Performing one`s _____ may require some sacrifice of self-interest.

Exam Probability: **Low**

1. *Answer choices:*

(see index for correct answer)

- a. Duty
- b. Roll-on/roll-off
- c. Currency adjustment factor
- d. Tractor unit

Guidance: level 1

:: Business models ::

A _____ , _____ company or daughter company is a company that is owned or controlled by another company, which is called the parent company, parent, or holding company. The _____ can be a company, corporation, or limited liability company. In some cases it is a government or state-owned enterprise. In some cases, particularly in the music and book publishing industries, subsidiaries are referred to as imprints.

Exam Probability: **Low**

2. *Answer choices:*

(see index for correct answer)

- a. Home business
- b. Subsidiary
- c. Business-agile enterprise
- d. Data as a service

:: ::

Advertising is a marketing communication that employs an openly sponsored, non-personal message to promote or sell a product, service or idea. Sponsors of advertising are typically businesses wishing to promote their products or services. Advertising is differentiated from public relations in that an advertiser pays for and has control over the message. It differs from personal selling in that the message is non-personal, i.e., not directed to a particular individual. Advertising is communicated through various mass media, including traditional media such as newspapers, magazines, television, radio, outdoor advertising or direct mail; and new media such as search results, blogs, social media, websites or text messages. The actual presentation of the message in a medium is referred to as an _____ , or "ad" or advert for short.

Exam Probability: **Medium**

3. *Answer choices:*

(see index for correct answer)

- a. Advertisement
- b. Character
- c. interpersonal communication
- d. deep-level diversity

:: Manufactured goods ::

A _____ or final good is any commodity that is produced or consumed by the consumer to satisfy current wants or needs. _____ s are ultimately consumed, rather than used in the production of another good. For example, a microwave oven or a bicycle that is sold to a consumer is a final good or _____ , but the components that are sold to be used in those goods are intermediate goods. For example, textiles or transistors can be used to make some further goods.

Exam Probability: **Low**

4. *Answer choices:*

(see index for correct answer)

- a. Final good
- b. Bespoke
- c. Household goods
- d. Tarpaulin

Guidance: level 1

:: ::

_____ Motor Company is an American multinational automaker that has its main headquarter in Dearborn, Michigan, a suburb of Detroit. It was founded by Henry _____ and incorporated on June 16, 1903. The company sells automobiles and commercial vehicles under the _____ brand and most luxury cars under the Lincoln brand. _____ also owns Brazilian SUV manufacturer Troller, an 8% stake in Aston Martin of the United Kingdom and a 32% stake in Jiangling Motors. It also has joint-ventures in China , Taiwan , Thailand , Turkey , and Russia . The company is listed on the New York Stock Exchange and is controlled by the _____ family; they have minority ownership but the majority of the voting power.

Exam Probability: **Medium**

5. *Answer choices:*

(see index for correct answer)

- a. interpersonal communication
- b. personal values
- c. co-culture
- d. process perspective

Guidance: level 1

:: Film production ::

_____ is a legal term more comprehensive and of higher import than either warranty or "security". It most commonly designates a private transaction by means of which one person, to obtain some trust, confidence or credit for another, engages to be answerable for him. It may also designate a treaty through which claims, rights or possessions are secured. It is to be differentiated from the colloquial "personal _____" in that a _____ is a legal concept which produces an economic effect. A personal _____ by contrast is often used to refer to a promise made by an individual which is supported by, or assured through, the word of the individual. In the same way, a _____ produces a legal effect wherein one party affirms the promise of another by promising to themselves pay if default occurs.

Exam Probability: **High**

6. *Answer choices:*

(see index for correct answer)

- a. Read-through
- b. Premise
- c. Redress
- d. Guarantee

Guidance: level 1

:: Shareholders ::

A _____ is a payment made by a corporation to its shareholders, usually as a distribution of profits. When a corporation earns a profit or surplus, the corporation is able to re-invest the profit in the business and pay a proportion of the profit as a _____ to shareholders. Distribution to shareholders may be in cash or, if the corporation has a _____ reinvestment plan, the amount can be paid by the issue of further shares or share repurchase. When _____ s are paid, shareholders typically must pay income taxes, and the corporation does not receive a corporate income tax deduction for the _____ payments.

Exam Probability: **High**

7. *Answer choices:*

(see index for correct answer)

- a. Dividend
- b. Say on pay
- c. Shotgun clause
- d. UK Shareholders Association

Guidance: level 1

:: Monopoly (economics) ::

A _____ is a form of intellectual property that gives its owner the legal right to exclude others from making, using, selling, and importing an invention for a limited period of years, in exchange for publishing an enabling public disclosure of the invention. In most countries _____ rights fall under civil law and the _____ holder needs to sue someone infringing the _____ in order to enforce his or her rights. In some industries _____ s are an essential form of competitive advantage; in others they are irrelevant.

Exam Probability: **Low**

8. *Answer choices:*

(see index for correct answer)

- a. Electricity liberalization
- b. Price-cap regulation
- c. Demonopolization
- d. Patent

Guidance: level 1

:: Business law ::

A _____ is an offer that will remain open for a certain period or until a certain time or occurrence of a certain event, during which it is incapable of being revoked. As a general rule, all offers are revocable at any time prior to acceptance, even those offers that purport to be irrevocable on their face.

9. *Answer choices:*

(see index for correct answer)

- a. Legal tender
- b. Statutory authority
- c. Firm offer
- d. Teck Corp. Ltd. v. Millar

Guidance: level 1

:: Money market instruments ::

_____ , in the global financial market, is an unsecured promissory note with a fixed maturity of not more than 270 days.

Exam Probability: **Medium**

10. *Answer choices:*

(see index for correct answer)

- a. Commercial paper in India
- b. Banker's acceptance

Guidance: level 1

:: Finance ::

_____ is the investigation or exercise of care that a reasonable business or person is expected to take before entering into an agreement or contract with another party, or an act with a certain standard of care.

Exam Probability: **Medium**

11. *Answer choices:*

(see index for correct answer)

- a. Hamilton Community Foundation
- b. Liquid Tradable Securities
- c. Due diligence
- d. Unsecured creditor

Guidance: level 1

:: United States corporate law ::

In tort law, a _____ is a legal obligation which is imposed on an individual requiring adherence to a standard of reasonable care while performing any acts that could foreseeably harm others. It is the first element that must be established to proceed with an action in negligence. The claimant must be able to show a _____ imposed by law which the defendant has breached. In turn, breaching a duty may subject an individual to liability. The _____ may be imposed by operation of law between individuals who have no current direct relationship but eventually become related in some manner, as defined by common law .

Exam Probability: **High**

12. *Answer choices:*

(see index for correct answer)

- a. Model Nonprofit Corporation Act
- b. Corporate law in the United States
- c. Duty of care
- d. NYSE Listed Company Manual

Guidance: level 1

:: Decision theory ::

A _____ is a deliberate system of principles to guide decisions and achieve rational outcomes. A _____ is a statement of intent, and is implemented as a procedure or protocol. Policies are generally adopted by a governance body within an organization. Policies can assist in both subjective and objective decision making. Policies to assist in subjective decision making usually assist senior management with decisions that must be based on the relative merits of a number of factors, and as a result are often hard to test objectively, e.g. work-life balance _____ . In contrast policies to assist in objective decision making are usually operational in nature and can be objectively tested, e.g. password _____ .

Exam Probability: **High**

13. *Answer choices:*

(see index for correct answer)

- a. Value of information
- b. Mental accounting
- c. Clarity test
- d. Policy

Guidance: level 1

:: Stock market ::

_____ is freedom from, or resilience against, potential harm caused by others. Beneficiaries of _____ may be of persons and social groups, objects and institutions, ecosystems or any other entity or phenomenon vulnerable to unwanted change by its environment.

14. *Answer choices:*

(see index for correct answer)

- a. Stock promoter
- b. Monthly income preferred stock
- c. Secondary shares
- d. Security

Guidance: level 1

:: Utilitarianism ::

_____ is a family of consequentialist ethical theories that promotes actions that maximize happiness and well-being for the majority of a population. Although different varieties of _____ admit different characterizations, the basic idea behind all of them is to in some sense maximize utility, which is often defined in terms of well-being or related concepts. For instance, Jeremy Bentham, the founder of _____ , described utility as

Exam Probability: **Medium**

15. *Answer choices:*

(see index for correct answer)

- a. Preference utilitarianism

- b. Hedonism
- c. Utilitarianism
- d. Utilitarian bioethics

Guidance: level 1

:: ::

A _____ loan or, simply, _____ is used either by purchasers of real property to raise funds to buy real estate, or alternatively by existing property owners to raise funds for any purpose, while putting a lien on the property being _____ d. The loan is "secured" on the borrower's property through a process known as _____ origination. This means that a legal mechanism is put into place which allows the lender to take possession and sell the secured property to pay off the loan in the event the borrower defaults on the loan or otherwise fails to abide by its terms. The word _____ is derived from a Law French term used in Britain in the Middle Ages meaning "death pledge" and refers to the pledge ending when either the obligation is fulfilled or the property is taken through foreclosure. A _____ can also be described as "a borrower giving consideration in the form of a collateral for a benefit ".

Exam Probability: **Medium**

16. *Answer choices:*

(see index for correct answer)

- a. Mortgage
- b. similarity-attraction theory
- c. interpersonal communication

- d. Character

Guidance: level 1

:: ::

_____ is a process under which executive or legislative actions are subject to review by the judiciary. A court with authority for _____ may invalidate laws, acts and governmental actions that are incompatible with a higher authority: an executive decision may be invalidated for being unlawful or a statute may be invalidated for violating the terms of a constitution. _____ is one of the checks and balances in the separation of powers: the power of the judiciary to supervise the legislative and executive branches when the latter exceed their authority. The doctrine varies between jurisdictions, so the procedure and scope of _____ may differ between and within countries.

Exam Probability: **Medium**

17. *Answer choices:*

(see index for correct answer)

- a. corporate values
- b. hierarchical
- c. Judicial review
- d. interpersonal communication

Guidance: level 1

_____ is property that is movable. In common law systems, _____ may also be called chattels or personalty. In civil law systems, _____ is often called movable property or movables – any property that can be moved from one location to another.

Exam Probability: **High**

18. *Answer choices:*

(see index for correct answer)

- a. empathy
- b. cultural
- c. interpersonal communication
- d. Personal property

Guidance: level 1

:: Business law ::

A _____ is a form of security interest granted over an item of property to secure the payment of a debt or performance of some other obligation. The owner of the property, who grants the _____ , is referred to as the _____ ee and the person who has the benefit of the _____ is referred to as the _____ or or _____ holder.

19. *Answer choices:*

(see index for correct answer)

- a. Examinership
- b. Articles of partnership
- c. Lien
- d. Refusal to deal

Guidance: level 1

:: ::

A _____ is the party who initiates a lawsuit before a court. By doing so, the _____ seeks a legal remedy; if this search is successful, the court will issue judgment in favor of the _____ and make the appropriate court order . " _____ " is the term used in civil cases in most English-speaking jurisdictions, the notable exception being England and Wales, where a _____ has, since the introduction of the Civil Procedure Rules in 1999, been known as a "claimant", but that term also has other meanings. In criminal cases, the prosecutor brings the case against the defendant, but the key complaining party is often called the "complainant".

20. *Answer choices:*

(see index for correct answer)

- a. functional perspective
- b. Plaintiff
- c. surface-level diversity
- d. hierarchical perspective

:: ::

_____ is a type of government support for the citizens of that society. _____ may be provided to people of any income level, as with social security , but it is usually intended to ensure that the poor can meet their basic human needs such as food and shelter. _____ attempts to provide poor people with a minimal level of well-being, usually either a free- or a subsidized-supply of certain goods and social services, such as healthcare, education, and vocational training.

Exam Probability: **Low**

21. *Answer choices:*

(see index for correct answer)

- a. information systems assessment
- b. cultural
- c. similarity-attraction theory
- d. functional perspective

:: Contract law ::

_____ , in human interactions, is a sincere intention to be fair, open, and honest, regardless of the outcome of the interaction. While some Latin phrases lose their literal meaning over centuries, this is not the case with bona fides; it is still widely used and interchangeable with its generally accepted modern-day English translation of _____ . It is an important concept within law and business. The opposed concepts are bad faith, mala fides and perfidy . In contemporary English, the usage of bona fides is synonymous with credentials and identity. The phrase is sometimes used in job advertisements, and should not be confused with the bona fide occupational qualifications or the employer`s _____ effort, as described below.

Exam Probability: **High**

22. *Answer choices:*

(see index for correct answer)

- a. Flexible contracts
- b. Terms of service
- c. Firm commitment
- d. Good faith

Guidance: level 1

:: ::

_____ is a process whereby a person assumes the parenting of another, usually a child, from that person's biological or legal parent or parents. Legal _____ s permanently transfers all rights and responsibilities, along with filiation, from the biological parent or parents.

Exam Probability: **Low**

23. *Answer choices:*

(see index for correct answer)

- a. deep-level diversity
- b. functional perspective
- c. imperative
- d. Adoption

Guidance: level 1

:: Insurance law ::

_____ exists when an insured person derives a financial or other kind of benefit from the continuous existence, without repairment or damage, of the insured object . A person has an _____ in something when loss of or damage to that thing would cause the person to suffer a financial or other kind of loss.Normally, _____ is established by ownership, possession, or direct relationship. For example, people have _____ s in their own homes and vehicles, but not in their neighbors' homes and vehicles, and almost certainly not those of strangers.

24. *Answer choices:*

(see index for correct answer)

- a. Marine Insurance Act 1906
- b. National Flood Insurance Program
- c. Insurable interest
- d. QC clause

Guidance: level 1

:: Legal doctrines and principles ::

_____ , land acquisition , compulsory purchase , resumption , resumption/compulsory acquisition , or expropriation is the power of a state, provincial, or national government to take private property for public use. However, this power can be legislatively delegated by the state to municipalities, government subdivisions, or even to private persons or corporations, when they are authorized by the legislature to exercise the functions of public character.

Exam Probability: **Low**

25. *Answer choices:*

(see index for correct answer)

- a. Duty to rescue

- b. Contributory negligence
- c. Eminent domain
- d. Res ipsa loquitur

Guidance: level 1

:: Psychometrics ::

_____ is a dynamic, structured, interactive process where a neutral third party assists disputing parties in resolving conflict through the use of specialized communication and negotiation techniques. All participants in _____ are encouraged to actively participate in the process. _____ is a "party-centered" process in that it is focused primarily upon the needs, rights, and interests of the parties. The mediator uses a wide variety of techniques to guide the process in a constructive direction and to help the parties find their optimal solution. A mediator is facilitative in that she/he manages the interaction between parties and facilitates open communication. _____ is also evaluative in that the mediator analyzes issues and relevant norms , while refraining from providing prescriptive advice to the parties .

Exam Probability: **Medium**

26. *Answer choices:*

(see index for correct answer)

- a. William H. Tucker
- b. Standards for Educational and Psychological Testing
- c. Normal curve equivalent
- d. Objective test

:: ::

_____ is the production of products for use or sale using labour and machines, tools, chemical and biological processing, or formulation. The term may refer to a range of human activity, from handicraft to high tech, but is most commonly applied to industrial design, in which raw materials are transformed into finished goods on a large scale. Such finished goods may be sold to other manufacturers for the production of other, more complex products, such as aircraft, household appliances, furniture, sports equipment or automobiles, or sold to wholesalers, who in turn sell them to retailers, who then sell them to end users and consumers.

Exam Probability: **Low**

27. *Answer choices:*

(see index for correct answer)

- a. Manufacturing
- b. information systems assessment
- c. similarity-attraction theory
- d. imperative

:: Actuarial science ::

_____ is the possibility of losing something of value. Values can be gained or lost when taking _____ resulting from a given action or inaction, foreseen or unforeseen. _____ can also be defined as the intentional interaction with uncertainty. Uncertainty is a potential, unpredictable, and uncontrollable outcome; _____ is a consequence of action taken in spite of uncertainty.

Exam Probability: **Low**

28. *Answer choices:*

(see index for correct answer)

- a. Actuarial control cycle
- b. Risk
- c. Maximum life span
- d. Actuarial exam

Guidance: level 1

:: Business law ::

A _____ is a document guaranteeing the payment of a specific amount of money, either on demand, or at a set time, with the payer usually named on the document. More specifically, it is a document contemplated by or consisting of a contract, which promises the payment of money without condition, which may be paid either on demand or at a future date. The term can have different meanings, depending on what law is being applied and what country and context it is used in.

29. *Answer choices:*

(see index for correct answer)

- a. Board of directors
- b. Negotiable instrument
- c. United Kingdom commercial law
- d. Trading while insolvent

Guidance: level 1

:: ::

_____ or accountancy is the measurement, processing, and communication of financial information about economic entities such as businesses and corporations. The modern field was established by the Italian mathematician Luca Pacioli in 1494. _____ , which has been called the "language of business", measures the results of an organization's economic activities and conveys this information to a variety of users, including investors, creditors, management, and regulators. Practitioners of _____ are known as accountants. The terms "_____" and "financial reporting" are often used as synonyms.

Exam Probability: **Medium**

30. *Answer choices:*

(see index for correct answer)

- a. co-culture
- b. levels of analysis
- c. Accounting
- d. surface-level diversity

Guidance: level 1

:: Contract law ::

A _____ is a legally-binding agreement which recognises and governs the rights and duties of the parties to the agreement. A _____ is legally enforceable because it meets the requirements and approval of the law. An agreement typically involves the exchange of goods, services, money, or promises of any of those. In the event of breach of _____ , the law awards the injured party access to legal remedies such as damages and cancellation.

Exam Probability: **High**

31. *Answer choices:*

(see index for correct answer)

- a. Bonus clause
- b. Memorandum of understanding
- c. Contract
- d. Invitation to treat

Guidance: level 1

:: Mortgage ::

_____ is a legal process in which a lender attempts to recover the balance of a loan from a borrower who has stopped making payments to the lender by forcing the sale of the asset used as the collateral for the loan.

Exam Probability: **High**

32. *Answer choices:*

(see index for correct answer)

- a. Loss mitigation
- b. Mortgageport
- c. Foreclosure
- d. Seller financing

Guidance: level 1

:: Mereology ::

_____ , in the abstract, is what belongs to or with something, whether as an attribute or as a component of said thing. In the context of this article, it is one or more components , whether physical or incorporeal, of a person's estate; or so belonging to, as in being owned by, a person or jointly a group of people or a legal entity like a corporation or even a society. Depending on the nature of the _____ , an owner of _____ has the right to consume, alter, share, redefine, rent, mortgage, pawn, sell, exchange, transfer, give away or destroy it, or to exclude others from doing these things, as well as to perhaps abandon it; whereas regardless of the nature of the _____ , the owner thereof has the right to properly use it , or at the very least exclusively keep it.

Exam Probability: **High**

33. *Answer choices:*

(see index for correct answer)

- a. Mereological essentialism
- b. Mereology
- c. Meronomy
- d. Property

Guidance: level 1

:: ::

A _____ is an organization, usually a group of people or a company, authorized to act as a single entity and recognized as such in law. Early incorporated entities were established by charter . Most jurisdictions now allow the creation of new _____ s through registration.

Exam Probability: **Medium**

34. *Answer choices:*

(see index for correct answer)

- a. imperative
- b. interpersonal communication
- c. personal values
- d. Corporation

Guidance: level 1

:: Industrial agreements ::

_____ is a process of negotiation between employers and a group of employees aimed at agreements to regulate working salaries, working conditions, benefits, and other aspects of workers' compensation and rights for workers. The interests of the employees are commonly presented by representatives of a trade union to which the employees belong. The collective agreements reached by these negotiations usually set out wage scales, working hours, training, health and safety, overtime, grievance mechanisms, and rights to participate in workplace or company affairs.

35. *Answer choices:*

(see index for correct answer)

- a. Industrial arbitration
- b. Workplace Authority
- c. Collective bargaining
- d. Australian Industrial Relations Commission

Guidance: level 1

:: ::

_____ is the consumption and saving opportunity gained by an entity within a specified timeframe, which is generally expressed in monetary terms. For households and individuals, " _____ is the sum of all the wages, salaries, profits, interest payments, rents, and other forms of earnings received in a given period of time."

Exam Probability: **High**

36. *Answer choices:*

(see index for correct answer)

- a. Income
- b. information systems assessment

- c. functional perspective
- d. empathy

Guidance: level 1

:: ::

In English law, a _____ or _____ absolute is an estate in land, a form of freehold ownership. It is a way that real estate and land may be owned in common law countries, and is the highest possible ownership interest that can be held in real property. Allodial title is reserved to governments under a civil law structure. The rights of the _____ owner are limited by government powers of taxation, compulsory purchase, police power, and escheat, and it could also be limited further by certain encumbrances or conditions in the deed, such as, for example, a condition that required the land to be used as a public park, with a reversion interest in the grantor if the condition fails; this is a _____ conditional.

Exam Probability: **High**

37. *Answer choices:*

(see index for correct answer)

- a. Fee simple
- b. personal values
- c. Sarbanes-Oxley act of 2002
- d. levels of analysis

Guidance: level 1

A _____ is a formal presentation of a matter such as a complaint, indictment or bill of exchange. In early-medieval England, juries of _____ would hear inquests in order to establish whether someone should be presented for a crime.

Exam Probability: **High**

38. *Answer choices:*

(see index for correct answer)

- a. hierarchical
- b. levels of analysis
- c. Presentment
- d. functional perspective

Guidance: level 1

:: Decision theory ::

Within economics the concept of _____ is used to model worth or value, but its usage has evolved significantly over time. The term was introduced initially as a measure of pleasure or satisfaction within the theory of utilitarianism by moral philosophers such as Jeremy Bentham and John Stuart Mill. But the term has been adapted and reapplied within neoclassical economics, which dominates modern economic theory, as a _____ function that represents a consumer's preference ordering over a choice set. As such, it is devoid of its original interpretation as a measurement of the pleasure or satisfaction obtained by the consumer from that choice.

Exam Probability: **Medium**

39. *Answer choices:*

(see index for correct answer)

- a. Utility
- b. Feasible region
- c. Ambiguity aversion
- d. Choquet integral

Guidance: level 1

:: Information technology audit ::

_____ is the act of using a computer to take or alter electronic data, or to gain unlawful use of a computer or system. In the United States, _____ is specifically proscribed by the _____ and Abuse Act, which criminalizes computer-related acts under federal jurisdiction. Types of _____ include.

40. *Answer choices:*

(see index for correct answer)

- a. Statement on Auditing Standards No. 99: Consideration of Fraud
- b. SekChek Local
- c. Computer fraud
- d. David Coderre

Guidance: level 1

:: Legal terms ::

An _____ is a legal and equitable remedy in the form of a special court order that compels a party to do or refrain from specific acts. "When a court employs the extraordinary remedy of _____ , it directs the conduct of a party, and does so with the backing of its full coercive powers." A party that fails to comply with an _____ faces criminal or civil penalties, including possible monetary sanctions and even imprisonment. They can also be charged with contempt of court. Counter _____ s are _____ s that stop or reverse the enforcement of another _____ .

Exam Probability: **Low**

41. *Answer choices:*

(see index for correct answer)

- a. Condonation
- b. European Authorized Representative
- c. Injunction
- d. False pretenses

Guidance: level 1

:: Real estate valuation ::

_____ or OMV is the price at which an asset would trade in a competitive auction setting. _____ is often used interchangeably with open _____, fair value or fair _____, although these terms have distinct definitions in different standards, and may or may not differ in some circumstances.

Exam Probability: **Medium**

42. *Answer choices:*

(see index for correct answer)

- a. Sales comparison approach
- b. Highest and best use
- c. ZipRealty
- d. Real estate benchmarking

Guidance: level 1

:: Contract law ::

A _____ cannot be enforced by law. _____ s are different from voidable contracts, which are contracts that may be nullified. However, when a contract is being written and signed, there is no automatic mechanism available in every situation that can be utilized to detect the validity or enforceability of that contract. Practically, a contract can be declared to be void by a court of law. So the main question is that under what conditions can a contract be deemed as void

Exam Probability: **Medium**

43. *Answer choices:*

(see index for correct answer)

- a. Complete contract
- b. Impossibility
- c. Warranty tolling
- d. Condition precedent

Guidance: level 1

:: False advertising law ::

The Lanham Act is the primary federal trademark statute of law in the United States. The Act prohibits a number of activities, including trademark infringement, trademark dilution, and false advertising.

44. *Answer choices:*

(see index for correct answer)

- a. Rebecca Tushnet
- b. POM Wonderful LLC v. Coca-Cola Co.

Guidance: level 1

:: Business law ::

The term is used to designate a range of diverse, if often kindred, concepts. These have historically been addressed in a number of discrete disciplines, notably mathematics, physics, chemistry, ethics, aesthetics, ontology, and theology.

Exam Probability: **Low**

45. *Answer choices:*

(see index for correct answer)

- a. Principal
- b. Perfection
- c. Managed service company
- d. Wrongful trading

:: ::

An _____ is a contingent motivator. Traditional _____ s are extrinsic motivators which reward actions to yield a desired outcome. The effectiveness of traditional _____ s has changed as the needs of Western society have evolved. While the traditional _____ model is effective when there is a defined procedure and goal for a task, Western society started to require a higher volume of critical thinkers, so the traditional model became less effective. Institutions are now following a trend in implementing strategies that rely on intrinsic motivations rather than the extrinsic motivations that the traditional _____ s foster.

Exam Probability: **Low**

46. *Answer choices:*

(see index for correct answer)

- a. process perspective
- b. Sarbanes-Oxley act of 2002
- c. imperative
- d. Incentive

:: United States federal public corruption crime ::

Mail fraud and _____ are federal crimes in the United States that involve mailing or electronically transmitting something associated with fraud. Jurisdiction is claimed by the federal government if the illegal activity crosses interstate or international borders.

Exam Probability: **High**

47. *Answer choices:*

(see index for correct answer)

- a. RICO Act
- b. Racketeer Influenced and Corrupt Organizations Act

Guidance: level 1

:: ::

An _____ is a criminal accusation that a person has committed a crime. In jurisdictions that use the concept of felonies, the most serious criminal offence is a felony; jurisdictions that do not use the felonies concept often use that of an indictable offence, an offence that requires an _____ .

Exam Probability: **High**

48. *Answer choices:*

(see index for correct answer)

- a. surface-level diversity
- b. imperative
- c. Indictment
- d. cultural

Guidance: level 1

:: ::

_____ is that part of a civil law legal system which is part of the jus commune that involves relationships between individuals, such as the law of contracts or torts , and the law of obligations . It is to be distinguished from public law, which deals with relationships between both natural and artificial persons and the state, including regulatory statutes, penal law and other law that affects the public order. In general terms, _____ involves interactions between private citizens, whereas public law involves interrelations between the state and the general population.

Exam Probability: **Medium**

49. *Answer choices:*

(see index for correct answer)

- a. personal values
- b. Character
- c. Private law
- d. cultural

:: Forgery ::

_____ is a white-collar crime that generally refers to the false making or material alteration of a legal instrument with the specific intent to defraud anyone . Tampering with a certain legal instrument may be forbidden by law in some jurisdictions but such an offense is not related to _____ unless the tampered legal instrument was actually used in the course of the crime to defraud another person or entity. Copies, studio replicas, and reproductions are not considered forgeries, though they may later become forgeries through knowing and willful misrepresentations.

Exam Probability: **Medium**

50. *Answer choices:*

(see index for correct answer)

- a. Archaeological forgery
- b. Counterfeit electronic components
- c. False evidence
- d. Forgery

:: ::

An _____ , commonly called an appeals court, court of appeals , appeal court , court of second instance or second instance court, is any court of law that is empowered to hear an appeal of a trial court or other lower tribunal. In most jurisdictions, the court system is divided into at least three levels: the trial court, which initially hears cases and reviews evidence and testimony to determine the facts of the case; at least one intermediate _____ ; and a supreme court which primarily reviews the decisions of the intermediate courts. A jurisdiction's supreme court is that jurisdiction's highest _____ . _____ s nationwide can operate under varying rules.

Exam Probability: **Low**

51. *Answer choices:*

(see index for correct answer)

- a. interpersonal communication
- b. corporate values
- c. Sarbanes-Oxley act of 2002
- d. process perspective

Guidance: level 1

:: Corporate finance ::

_____ is a contract law concept about the purchase of the release from a debt obligation. It is one of the methods by which parties to a contract may terminate their agreement. The release is completed by the transfer of valuable consideration that must not be the actual performance of the obligation itself. The accord is the agreement to discharge the obligation and the satisfaction is the legal "consideration" which binds the parties to the agreement. A valid accord does not discharge the prior contract; instead it suspends the right to enforce it in accordance with the terms of the accord contract, in which satisfaction, or performance of the contract will discharge both contracts . If the creditor breaches the accord, then the debtor will be able to bring up the existence of the accord in order to enjoin any action against him.

Exam Probability: **High**

52. *Answer choices:*

(see index for correct answer)

- a. E-invoicing
- b. Accord and satisfaction
- c. Permanent interest bearing shares
- d. Master limited partnership

Guidance: level 1

:: ::

The _____ is one of the several United States Uniform Acts proposed by the National Conference of Commissioners on Uniform State Laws . Forty-seven states, the District of Columbia, and the U.S. Virgin Islands have adopted the UETA. Its purpose is to harmonize state laws concerning retention of paper records and the validity of electronic signatures.

Exam Probability: **Medium**

53. *Answer choices:*

(see index for correct answer)

- a. hierarchical
- b. Uniform Electronic Transactions Act
- c. Character
- d. corporate values

Guidance: level 1

:: Anti-competitive behaviour ::

Restraints of trade is a common law doctrine relating to the enforceability of contractual restrictions on freedom to conduct business. It is a precursor of modern competition law. In an old leading case of Mitchel v Reynolds Lord Smith LC said,

Exam Probability: **Low**

54. *Answer choices:*

(see index for correct answer)

- a. Byrd Amendment
- b. Anti-siphoning laws in Australia
- c. Resale price maintenance
- d. Group boycott

Guidance: level 1

:: ::

An _____ is a formal or official change made to a law, contract, constitution, or other legal document. It is based on the verb to amend, which means to change for better. _____ s can add, remove, or update parts of these agreements. They are often used when it is better to change the document than to write a new one.

Exam Probability: **High**

55. *Answer choices:*

(see index for correct answer)

- a. functional perspective
- b. similarity-attraction theory
- c. imperative
- d. process perspective

:: ::

_____ is a marketing communication that employs an openly sponsored, non-personal message to promote or sell a product, service or idea. Sponsors of _____ are typically businesses wishing to promote their products or services. _____ is differentiated from public relations in that an advertiser pays for and has control over the message. It differs from personal selling in that the message is non-personal, i.e., not directed to a particular individual. _____ is communicated through various mass media, including traditional media such as newspapers, magazines, television, radio, outdoor _____ or direct mail; and new media such as search results, blogs, social media, websites or text messages. The actual presentation of the message in a medium is referred to as an advertisement, or "ad" or advert for short.

Exam Probability: **Low**

56. *Answer choices:*

(see index for correct answer)

- a. Character
- b. Advertising
- c. interpersonal communication
- d. imperative

:: Finance ::

A _____ , in the law of the United States, is a contract that governs the relationship between the parties to a kind of financial transaction known as a secured transaction. In a secured transaction, the Grantor assigns, grants and pledges to the grantee a security interest in personal property which is referred to as the collateral. Examples of typical collateral are shares of stock, livestock, and vehicles. A _____ is not used to transfer any interest in real property , only personal property. The document used by lenders to obtain a lien on real property is a mortgage or deed of trust.

Exam Probability: **Low**

57. *Answer choices:*

(see index for correct answer)

- a. Target benefit plan
- b. Security agreement
- c. Creative director
- d. Specialized investment fund

Guidance: level 1

:: ::

The _____ Act of 1890 was a United States antitrust law that regulates competition among enterprises, which was passed by Congress under the presidency of Benjamin Harrison.

58. *Answer choices:*

(see index for correct answer)

- a. personal values
- b. open system
- c. levels of analysis
- d. process perspective

Guidance: level 1

:: ::

The _____ is the highest court within the hierarchy of courts in many legal jurisdictions. Other descriptions for such courts include court of last resort, apex court, and high court of appeal. Broadly speaking, the decisions of a _____ are not subject to further review by any other court. _____s typically function primarily as appellate courts, hearing appeals from decisions of lower trial courts, or from intermediate-level appellate courts.

Exam Probability: **High**

59. *Answer choices:*

(see index for correct answer)

- a. surface-level diversity

- b. Supreme Court
- c. hierarchical
- d. functional perspective

Guidance: level 1

Finance

Finance is a field that is concerned with the allocation (investment) of assets and liabilities over space and time, often under conditions of risk or uncertainty. Finance can also be defined as the science of money management. Participants in the market aim to price assets based on their risk level, fundamental value, and their expected rate of return. Finance can be split into three sub-categories: public finance, corporate finance and personal finance.

:: Hazard analysis ::

Broadly speaking, a _____ is the combined effort of 1. identifying and analyzing potential events that may negatively impact individuals, assets, and/or the environment ; and 2. making judgments "on the tolerability of the risk on the basis of a risk analysis" while considering influencing factors . Put in simpler terms, a _____ analyzes what can go wrong, how likely it is to happen, what the potential consequences are, and how tolerable the identified risk is. As part of this process, the resulting determination of risk may be expressed in a quantitative or qualitative fashion. The _____ is an inherent part of an overall risk management strategy, which attempts to, after a _____ , "introduce control measures to eliminate or reduce" any potential risk-related consequences.

Exam Probability: **Low**

1. *Answer choices:*

(see index for correct answer)

- a. Risk assessment
- b. Hazard identification
- c. Swiss cheese model

Guidance: level 1

:: Financial markets ::

The _____ , also called the aftermarket and follow on public offering is the financial market in which previously issued financial instruments such as stock, bonds, options, and futures are bought and sold. Another frequent usage of " _____ " is to refer to loans which are sold by a mortgage bank to investors such as Fannie Mae and Freddie Mac.

Exam Probability: **Medium**

2. *Answer choices:*

(see index for correct answer)

- a. Systematic trading
- b. Ultra-low latency direct market access
- c. Secondary market
- d. Holy grail distribution

Guidance: level 1

:: Banking ::

A _____ is a financial institution that accepts deposits from the public and creates credit. Lending activities can be performed either directly or indirectly through capital markets. Due to their importance in the financial stability of a country, _____ s are highly regulated in most countries. Most nations have institutionalized a system known as fractional reserve _____ ing under which _____ s hold liquid assets equal to only a portion of their current liabilities. In addition to other regulations intended to ensure liquidity, _____ s are generally subject to minimum capital requirements based on an international set of capital standards, known as the Basel Accords.

Exam Probability: **High**

3. *Answer choices:*

(see index for correct answer)

- a. Variance risk premium
- b. Wholesale banking
- c. Asset-based lending
- d. Tier 2 capital

Guidance: level 1

:: ::

_____ is a means of protection from financial loss. It is a form of risk management, primarily used to hedge against the risk of a contingent or uncertain loss

4. *Answer choices:*

(see index for correct answer)

- a. Sarbanes-Oxley act of 2002
- b. Insurance
- c. functional perspective
- d. imperative

Guidance: level 1

:: Data analysis ::

In statistics, the _____ is a measure that is used to quantify the amount of variation or dispersion of a set of data values. A low _____ indicates that the data points tend to be close to the mean of the set, while a high _____ indicates that the data points are spread out over a wider range of values.

Exam Probability: **Medium**

5. *Answer choices:*

(see index for correct answer)

- a. Training set
- b. Strictly standardized mean difference

- c. Standard deviation
- d. Combinatorial data analysis

Guidance: level 1

:: Financial ratios ::

_____ is a measure of how revenue growth translates into growth in operating income. It is a measure of leverage, and of how risky, or volatile, a company's operating income is.

Exam Probability: **High**

6. *Answer choices:*
(see index for correct answer)

- a. PE ratio
- b. Debt service ratio
- c. PEG ratio
- d. CROCI

Guidance: level 1

:: Generally Accepted Accounting Principles ::

_____, or non-current liabilities, are liabilities that are due beyond a year or the normal operation period of the company. The normal operation period is the amount of time it takes for a company to turn inventory into cash. On a classified balance sheet, liabilities are separated between current and _____ to help users assess the company's financial standing in short-term and long-term periods. _____ give users more information about the long-term prosperity of the company, while current liabilities inform the user of debt that the company owes in the current period. On a balance sheet, accounts are listed in order of liquidity, so _____ come after current liabilities. In addition, the specific long-term liability accounts are listed on the balance sheet in order of liquidity. Therefore, an account due within eighteen months would be listed before an account due within twenty-four months. Examples of _____ are bonds payable, long-term loans, capital leases, pension liabilities, post-retirement healthcare liabilities, deferred compensation, deferred revenues, deferred income taxes, and derivative liabilities.

Exam Probability: **High**

7. *Answer choices:*

(see index for correct answer)

- a. Insurance asset management
- b. Long-term liabilities
- c. Gross income
- d. Management accounting principles

Guidance: level 1

:: Accounting terminology ::

Total _____ is a method of Accounting cost which entails the full cost of manufacturing or providing a service. TAC includes not just the costs of materials and labour, but also of all manufacturing overheads . The cost of each cost center can be direct or indirect. The direct cost can be easily identified with individual cost centers. Whereas indirect cost cannot be easily identified with the cost center. The distribution of overhead among the departments is called apportionment.

Exam Probability: **Low**

8. *Answer choices:*

(see index for correct answer)

- a. double-entry bookkeeping
- b. Adjusting entries
- c. Absorption costing
- d. Mark-to-market

Guidance: level 1

:: Land value taxation ::

_____ , sometimes referred to as dry _____ , is the solid surface of Earth that is not permanently covered by water. The vast majority of human activity throughout history has occurred in _____ areas that support agriculture, habitat, and various natural resources. Some life forms have developed from predecessor species that lived in bodies of water.

9. *Answer choices:*

(see index for correct answer)

- a. Harry Gunnison Brown
- b. Lands Valuation Appeal Court
- c. Land
- d. Henry George

Guidance: level 1

:: Global systemically important banks ::

The _____ Corporation is an American multinational investment bank and financial services company based in Charlotte, North Carolina with central hubs in New York City, London, Hong Kong, Minneapolis, and Toronto. _____ was formed through NationsBank's acquisition of BankAmerica in 1998. It is the second largest banking institution in the United States, after JP Morgan Chase. As a part of the Big Four, it services approximately 10.73% of all American bank deposits, in direct competition with Citigroup, Wells Fargo, and JPMorgan Chase. Its primary financial services revolve around commercial banking, wealth management, and investment banking.

Exam Probability: **High**

10. *Answer choices:*

(see index for correct answer)

- a. The Bank of Tokyo-Mitsubishi UFJ
- b. The Bank of New York Mellon
- c. Nordea
- d. The Royal Bank of Scotland

Guidance: level 1

:: Goods ::

In most contexts, the concept of _____ denotes the conduct that should be preferred when posed with a choice between possible actions. _____ is generally considered to be the opposite of evil, and is of interest in the study of morality, ethics, religion and philosophy. The specific meaning and etymology of the term and its associated translations among ancient and contemporary languages show substantial variation in its inflection and meaning depending on circumstances of place, history, religious, or philosophical context.

Exam Probability: **Medium**

11. *Answer choices:*

(see index for correct answer)

- a. Club good
- b. Bad
- c. Veblen good
- d. Anti-rival good

:: Accounting in the United States ::

_____ is the title of qualified accountants in numerous countries in the English-speaking world. In the United States, the CPA is a license to provide accounting services to the public. It is awarded by each of the 50 states for practice in that state. Additionally, almost every state has passed mobility laws to allow CPAs from other states to practice in their state. State licensing requirements vary, but the minimum standard requirements include passing the Uniform _____ Examination, 150 semester units of college education, and one year of accounting related experience.

Exam Probability: **High**

12. *Answer choices:*

(see index for correct answer)

- a. Certified Government Financial Manager
- b. Accounting Principles Board
- c. Certified Public Accountant
- d. Public Company Accounting Oversight Board

:: Actuarial science ::

_____ is the addition of interest to the principal sum of a loan or deposit, or in other words, interest on interest. It is the result of reinvesting interest, rather than paying it out, so that interest in the next period is then earned on the principal sum plus previously accumulated interest. _____ is standard in finance and economics.

Exam Probability: **High**

13. *Answer choices:*

(see index for correct answer)

- a. Confidence weighting
- b. Fictional actuaries
- c. Compound interest
- d. Compound annual growth rate

Guidance: level 1

:: Financial ratios ::

The _____ is a financial ratio indicating the relative proportion of shareholders' equity and debt used to finance a company's assets. Closely related to leveraging, the ratio is also known as risk, gearing or leverage. The two components are often taken from the firm's balance sheet or statement of financial position , but the ratio may also be calculated using market values for both, if the company's debt and equity are publicly traded, or using a combination of book value for debt and market value for equity financially.

14. *Answer choices:*

(see index for correct answer)

- a. Cost accrual ratio
- b. PE ratio
- c. Net capital outflow
- d. Return on capital employed

Guidance: level 1

:: ::

In business, economics or investment, market _____ is a market's feature whereby an individual or firm can quickly purchase or sell an asset without causing a drastic change in the asset's price. _____ is about how big the trade-off is between the speed of the sale and the price it can be sold for. In a liquid market, the trade-off is mild: selling quickly will not reduce the price much. In a relatively illiquid market, selling it quickly will require cutting its price by some amount.

Exam Probability: **High**

15. *Answer choices:*

(see index for correct answer)

- a. hierarchical

- b. Liquidity
- c. deep-level diversity
- d. empathy

Guidance: level 1

:: Finance ::

_____ , in finance and accounting, means stated value or face value. From this come the expressions at par , over par and under par .

Exam Probability: **Medium**

16. *Answer choices:*
(see index for correct answer)

- a. Par value
- b. Performance attribution
- c. Rate of profit
- d. Financial audit

Guidance: level 1

:: ::

_____ is the field of accounting concerned with the summary, analysis and reporting of financial transactions related to a business. This involves the preparation of financial statements available for public use. Stockholders, suppliers, banks, employees, government agencies, business owners, and other stakeholders are examples of people interested in receiving such information for decision making purposes.

Exam Probability: **Low**

17. *Answer choices:*

(see index for correct answer)

- a. surface-level diversity
- b. deep-level diversity
- c. personal values
- d. Financial accounting

Guidance: level 1

:: Business ethics ::

In accounting and in most Schools of economic thought, _____ is a rational and unbiased estimate of the potential market price of a good, service, or asset. It takes into account such objectivity factors as.

Exam Probability: **High**

18. *Answer choices:*

(see index for correct answer)

- a. Conflict-of-interest editing on Wikipedia
- b. United Nations Global Compact
- c. Fair value
- d. Corporate crime

Guidance: level 1

:: International taxation ::

_____ is the levying of tax by two or more jurisdictions on the same declared income , asset , or financial transaction . Double liability is mitigated in a number of ways, for example.

Exam Probability: **Low**

19. *Answer choices:*

(see index for correct answer)

- a. Robin Hood tax
- b. Arm's-length transaction
- c. European Union withholding tax
- d. Double taxation

Guidance: level 1

In the field of analysis of algorithms in computer science, the _____ is a method of amortized analysis based on accounting. The _____ often gives a more intuitive account of the amortized cost of an operation than either aggregate analysis or the potential method. Note, however, that this does not guarantee such analysis will be immediately obvious; often, choosing the correct parameters for the _____ requires as much knowledge of the problem and the complexity bounds one is attempting to prove as the other two methods.

Exam Probability: **High**

20. *Answer choices:*

(see index for correct answer)

- a. cultural
- b. interpersonal communication
- c. Character
- d. levels of analysis

Guidance: level 1

_____ is the process whereby a business sets the price at which it will sell its products and services, and may be part of the business's marketing plan. In setting prices, the business will take into account the price at which it could acquire the goods, the manufacturing cost, the market place, competition, market condition, brand, and quality of product.

Exam Probability: **Low**

21. *Answer choices:*

(see index for correct answer)

- a. hierarchical
- b. Character
- c. co-culture
- d. Pricing

Guidance: level 1

:: ::

In marketing, a _____ is a ticket or document that can be redeemed for a financial discount or rebate when purchasing a product.

Exam Probability: **Low**

22. *Answer choices:*

(see index for correct answer)

- a. surface-level diversity
- b. interpersonal communication
- c. Coupon
- d. similarity-attraction theory

Guidance: level 1

:: Generally Accepted Accounting Principles ::

A _____ or reacquired stock is stock which is bought back by the issuing company, reducing the amount of outstanding stock on the open market .

Exam Probability: **Medium**

23. *Answer choices:*

(see index for correct answer)

- a. Treasury stock
- b. Operating statement
- c. Goodwill
- d. Matching principle

Guidance: level 1

:: Stock market ::

A share price is the price of a single share of a number of saleable stocks of a company, derivative or other financial asset. In layman's terms, the _____ is the highest amount someone is willing to pay for the stock, or the lowest amount that it can be bought for.

Exam Probability: **Low**

24. *Answer choices:*

(see index for correct answer)

- a. Stop price
- b. Whisper number
- c. Green chip
- d. Stock price

Guidance: level 1

:: Actuarial science ::

_____ is the possibility of losing something of value. Values can be gained or lost when taking _____ resulting from a given action or inaction, foreseen or unforeseen . _____ can also be defined as the intentional interaction with uncertainty. Uncertainty is a potential, unpredictable, and uncontrollable outcome; _____ is a consequence of action taken in spite of uncertainty.

25. *Answer choices:*

(see index for correct answer)

- a. Underwriting
- b. Force of mortality
- c. Credibility theory
- d. Enterprise risk management

Guidance: level 1

:: ::

In production, research, retail, and accounting, a _____ is the value of money that has been used up to produce something or deliver a service, and hence is not available for use anymore. In business, the _____ may be one of acquisition, in which case the amount of money expended to acquire it is counted as _____ . In this case, money is the input that is gone in order to acquire the thing. This acquisition _____ may be the sum of the _____ of production as incurred by the original producer, and further _____ s of transaction as incurred by the acquirer over and above the price paid to the producer. Usually, the price also includes a mark-up for profit over the _____ of production.

26. *Answer choices:*

(see index for correct answer)

- a. Cost
- b. Sarbanes-Oxley act of 2002
- c. personal values
- d. process perspective

Guidance: level 1

:: Finance ::

A _____ , publicly-traded company, publicly-held company, publicly-listed company, or public limited company is a corporation whose ownership is dispersed among the general public in many shares of stock which are freely traded on a stock exchange or in over-the-counter markets. In some jurisdictions, public companies over a certain size must be listed on an exchange. A _____ can be listed or unlisted .

Exam Probability: **Low**

27. *Answer choices:*

(see index for correct answer)

- a. Public company
- b. OnDeck
- c. Asset purchase agreement
- d. Asset tracking

Guidance: level 1

:: Accounting terminology ::

_____ of something is, in finance, the adding together of interest or different investments over a period of time. It holds specific meanings in accounting, where it can refer to accounts on a balance sheet that represent liabilities and non-cash-based assets used in _____ -based accounting. These types of accounts include, among others, accounts payable, accounts receivable, goodwill, deferred tax liability and future interest expense.

28. *Answer choices:*

(see index for correct answer)

- a. Accounts receivable
- b. Accrual
- c. outstanding balance
- d. double-entry bookkeeping

Guidance: level 1

:: Generally Accepted Accounting Principles ::

In accounting, _____ is the income that a business have from its normal business activities, usually from the sale of goods and services to customers. _____ is also referred to as sales or turnover. Some companies receive _____ from interest, royalties, or other fees. _____ may refer to business income in general, or it may refer to the amount, in a monetary unit, earned during a period of time, as in "Last year, Company X had _____ of $42 million". Profits or net income generally imply total _____ minus total expenses in a given period. In accounting, in the balance statement it is a subsection of the Equity section and _____ increases equity, it is often referred to as the "top line" due to its position on the income statement at the very top. This is to be contrasted with the "bottom line" which denotes net income .

Exam Probability: **Medium**

29. *Answer choices:*

(see index for correct answer)

- a. Expense
- b. Shares outstanding
- c. Gross profit
- d. Revenue

Guidance: level 1

:: Capital gains taxes ::

A _____ refers to profit that results from a sale of a capital asset, such as stock, bond or real estate, where the sale price exceeds the purchase price. The gain is the difference between a higher selling price and a lower purchase price. Conversely, a capital loss arises if the proceeds from the sale of a capital asset are less than the purchase price.

Exam Probability: **High**

30. *Answer choices:*

(see index for correct answer)

- a. Capital gains tax
- b. Capital cost tax factor
- c. Capital gain

Guidance: level 1

:: Insolvency ::

_____ is the process in accounting by which a company is brought to an end in the United Kingdom, Republic of Ireland and United States. The assets and property of the company are redistributed. _____ is also sometimes referred to as winding-up or dissolution, although dissolution technically refers to the last stage of _____ . The process of _____ also arises when customs, an authority or agency in a country responsible for collecting and safeguarding customs duties, determines the final computation or ascertainment of the duties or drawback accruing on an entry.

31. *Answer choices:*

(see index for correct answer)

- a. Personal Insolvency Arrangement
- b. Liquidation
- c. Liquidator
- d. Conservatorship

Guidance: level 1

:: Stock market ::

_____ is a form of corporate equity ownership, a type of security. The terms voting share and ordinary share are also used frequently in other parts of the world; "_____" being primarily used in the United States. They are known as Equity shares or Ordinary shares in the UK and other Commonwealth realms. This type of share gives the stockholder the right to share in the profits of the company, and to vote on matters of corporate policy and the composition of the members of the board of directors.

Exam Probability: **Medium**

32. *Answer choices:*

(see index for correct answer)

- a. Common stock

- b. Security
- c. Barbell strategy
- d. Tech Buzz

Guidance: level 1

:: ::

A _____ is an individual or institution that legally owns one or more shares of stock in a public or private corporation. _____ s may be referred to as members of a corporation. Legally, a person is not a _____ in a corporation until their name and other details are entered in the corporation's register of _____ s or members.

Exam Probability: **Low**

33. *Answer choices:*

(see index for correct answer)

- a. open system
- b. empathy
- c. hierarchical
- d. hierarchical perspective

Guidance: level 1

:: Actuarial science ::

_____ services are provided by some large financial institutions, such as banks, or insurance or investment houses, whereby they guarantee payment in case of damage or financial loss and accept the financial risk for liability arising from such guarantee. An _____ arrangement may be created in a number of situations including insurance, issue of securities in a public offering, and bank lending, among others. The person or institution that agrees to sell a minimum number of securities of the company for commission is called the underwriter.

Exam Probability: **High**

34. *Answer choices:*

(see index for correct answer)

- a. Solvency ratio
- b. Disease
- c. Financial modeling
- d. Late-life mortality deceleration

Guidance: level 1

:: Business economics ::

_____ is one of the constituents of a leasing calculus or operation. It describes the future value of a good in terms of absolute value in monetary terms and it is sometimes abbreviated into a percentage of the initial price when the item was new.

Exam Probability: **High**

35. *Answer choices:*

(see index for correct answer)

- a. Residual value
- b. Disclosed fees
- c. Cost object
- d. Real net output ratio

Guidance: level 1

:: ::

_____ is a concept of English common law and is a necessity for simple contracts but not for special contracts . The concept has been adopted by other common law jurisdictions, including the US.

Exam Probability: **High**

36. *Answer choices:*

(see index for correct answer)

- a. Consideration
- b. Sarbanes-Oxley act of 2002
- c. empathy
- d. deep-level diversity

Guidance: level 1

:: Costs ::

In microeconomic theory, the _____ , or alternative cost, of making a particular choice is the value of the most valuable choice out of those that were not taken. In other words, opportunity that will require sacrifices.

Exam Probability: **Low**

37. *Answer choices:*

(see index for correct answer)

- a. Direct materials cost
- b. Cost curve
- c. Cost reduction
- d. Opportunity cost of capital

Guidance: level 1

:: Loans ::

In finance, a _____ is the lending of money by one or more individuals, organizations, or other entities to other individuals, organizations etc. The recipient incurs a debt, and is usually liable to pay interest on that debt until it is repaid, and also to repay the principal amount borrowed.

Exam Probability: **High**

38. *Answer choices:*

(see index for correct answer)

- a. Loan
- b. Commercial and industrial loan
- c. Asset-based loan
- d. Unpaid principal balance

Guidance: level 1

:: Generally Accepted Accounting Principles ::

_____ , also referred to as the bottom line, net income, or net earnings is a measure of the profitability of a venture after accounting for all costs and taxes. It is the actual profit, and includes the operating expenses that are excluded from gross profit.

Exam Probability: **High**

39. *Answer choices:*

(see index for correct answer)

- a. Earnings before interest and taxes
- b. Income statement
- c. Petty cash
- d. Net profit

Guidance: level 1

:: Accounting terminology ::

In accounting/accountancy, _____ are journal entries usually made at the end of an accounting period to allocate income and expenditure to the period in which they actually occurred. The revenue recognition principle is the basis of making _____ that pertain to unearned and accrued revenues under accrual-basis accounting. They are sometimes called Balance Day adjustments because they are made on balance day.

Exam Probability: **Low**

40. *Answer choices:*

(see index for correct answer)

- a. Basis of accounting
- b. Adjusting entries
- c. Capital surplus
- d. Share premium

:: Management accounting ::

_____ is the process of recording, classifying, analyzing, summarizing, and allocating costs associated with a process, after that developing various courses of action to control the costs. Its goal is to advise the management on how to optimize business practices and processes based on cost efficiency and capability. _____ provides the detailed cost information that management needs to control current operations and plan for the future.

Exam Probability: **Low**

41. *Answer choices:*

(see index for correct answer)

- a. activity based costing
- b. Cost accounting
- c. Responsibility center
- d. Dual overhead rate

:: Manufacturing ::

_____ s are goods that have completed the manufacturing process but have not yet been sold or distributed to the end user.

Exam Probability: **Low**

42. *Answer choices:*

(see index for correct answer)

- a. Finished good
- b. Cymbal making
- c. Microfactory
- d. Supplier Risk Management

Guidance: level 1

:: Leasing ::

A finance lease is a type of lease in which a finance company is typically the legal owner of the asset for the duration of the lease, while the lessee not only has operating control over the asset, but also has a some share of the economic risks and returns from the change in the valuation of the underlying asset.

Exam Probability: **Medium**

43. *Answer choices:*

(see index for correct answer)

- a. Capital lease
- b. Farmout agreement

Guidance: level 1

:: Project management ::

Some scenarios associate "this kind of planning" with learning "life skills".
_____ s are necessary, or at least useful, in situations where individuals
need to know what time they must be at a specific location to receive a
specific service, and where people need to accomplish a set of goals within a
set time period.

Exam Probability: **High**

44. *Answer choices:*

(see index for correct answer)

- a. Schedule
- b. Task
- c. Deliverable
- d. Karol Adamiecki

Guidance: level 1

:: Global systemically important banks ::

_____ Inc. or Citi is an American multinational investment bank and financial services corporation headquartered in New York City. The company was formed by the merger of banking giant Citicorp and financial conglomerate Travelers Group in 1998; Travelers was subsequently spun off from the company in 2002. _____ owns Citicorp, the holding company for Citibank, as well as several international subsidiaries.

Exam Probability: **Medium**

45. *Answer choices:*

(see index for correct answer)

- a. UniCredit
- b. Banco Bilbao Vizcaya Argentaria
- c. The Bank of New York Mellon
- d. The Royal Bank of Scotland

Guidance: level 1

:: Market research ::

_____ , an acronym for Information through Disguised Experimentation is an annual market research fair conducted by the students of IIM-Lucknow. Students create games and use various other simulated environments to capture consumers' subconscious thoughts. This innovative method of market research removes the sensitization effect that might bias peoples answers to questions. This ensures that the most truthful answers are captured to research questions. The games are designed in such a way that the observers can elicit all the required information just by observing and noting down the behaviour and the responses of the participants.

Exam Probability: **Medium**

46. *Answer choices:*

(see index for correct answer)

- a. Monroe Mendelsohn Research
- b. Market research and opinion polling in China
- c. INDEX
- d. LRMR

Guidance: level 1

:: Legal terms ::

_____ s may be governments, corporations or investment trusts.
_____ s are legally responsible for the obligations of the issue and for reporting financial conditions, material developments and any other operational activities as required by the regulations of their jurisdictions.

47. *Answer choices:*

(see index for correct answer)

- a. Fair competition
- b. Intangible property
- c. Fact-finding
- d. Issuer

Guidance: level 1

:: ::

An _____ is the production of goods or related services within an economy. The major source of revenue of a group or company is the indicator of its relevant _____ . When a large group has multiple sources of revenue generation, it is considered to be working in different industries. Manufacturing _____ became a key sector of production and labour in European and North American countries during the Industrial Revolution, upsetting previous mercantile and feudal economies. This came through many successive rapid advances in technology, such as the production of steel and coal.

Exam Probability: **Medium**

48. *Answer choices:*

(see index for correct answer)

- a. levels of analysis
- b. open system
- c. corporate values
- d. co-culture

Guidance: level 1

:: Cash flow ::

In corporate finance, _____ or _____ to firm is a way of looking at a business's cash flow to see what is available for distribution among all the securities holders of a corporate entity. This may be useful to parties such as equity holders, debt holders, preferred stock holders, and convertible security holders when they want to see how much cash can be extracted from a company without causing issues to its operations.

Exam Probability: **High**

49. *Answer choices:*

(see index for correct answer)

- a. Discounted cash flow
- b. Cash flow loan
- c. Free cash flow
- d. Cash flow hedge

Guidance: level 1

:: Government bonds ::

A _____ or sovereign bond is a bond issued by a national government, generally with a promise to pay periodic interest payments called coupon payments and to repay the face value on the maturity date. The aim of a _____ is to support government spending. _____ s are usually denominated in the country's own currency, in which case the government cannot be forced to default, although it may choose to do so. If a government is close to default on its debt the media often refer to this as a sovereign debt crisis.

Exam Probability: **Low**

50. *Answer choices:*

(see index for correct answer)

- a. War bond
- b. Risk-free bond
- c. Government bond
- d. Gilt-edged

Guidance: level 1

:: ::

A _____ is any person who contracts to acquire an asset in return for some form of consideration.

51. *Answer choices:*

(see index for correct answer)

- a. co-culture
- b. Buyer
- c. interpersonal communication
- d. imperative

Guidance: level 1

:: bad_topic ::

_____ refers to systematic approach to the governance and realization of value from the things that a group or entity is responsible for, over their whole life cycles. It may apply both to tangible assets and to intangible assets . _____ is a systematic process of developing, operating, maintaining, upgrading, and disposing of assets in the most cost-effective manner .

Exam Probability: **Low**

52. *Answer choices:*

(see index for correct answer)

- a. Web advertising
- b. conative

- c. incorrect
- d. Asset management

Guidance: level 1

:: Expense ::

_____ relates to the cost of borrowing money. It is the price that a lender charges a borrower for the use of the lender's money. On the income statement, _____ can represent the cost of borrowing money from banks, bond investors, and other sources. _____ is different from operating expense and CAPEX, for it relates to the capital structure of a company, and it is usually tax-deductible.

Exam Probability: **High**

53. *Answer choices:*

(see index for correct answer)

- a. Freight expense
- b. Interest expense
- c. Accretion expense
- d. Business overhead expense disability insurance

Guidance: level 1

:: Income ::

_____ is a ratio between the net profit and cost of investment resulting from an investment of some resources. A high ROI means the investment's gains favorably to its cost. As a performance measure, ROI is used to evaluate the efficiency of an investment or to compare the efficiencies of several different investments. In purely economic terms, it is one way of relating profits to capital invested. _____ is a performance measure used by businesses to identify the efficiency of an investment or number of different investments.

Exam Probability: **Low**

54. *Answer choices:*

(see index for correct answer)

- a. Return on investment
- b. Aggregate income
- c. Passive income
- d. Implied level of government service

Guidance: level 1

:: ::

An _____ is a person that allocates capital with the expectation of a future financial return. Types of investments include: equity, debt securities, real estate, currency, commodity, token, derivatives such as put and call options, futures, forwards, etc. This definition makes no distinction between the _____ s in the primary and secondary markets. That is, someone who provides a business with capital and someone who buys a stock are both _____ s. An _____ who owns a stock is a shareholder.

Exam Probability: **Low**

55. *Answer choices:*

(see index for correct answer)

- a. Investor
- b. hierarchical
- c. personal values
- d. imperative

Guidance: level 1

:: Financial markets ::

In economics and finance, _____ is the practice of taking advantage of a price difference between two or more markets: striking a combination of matching deals that capitalize upon the imbalance, the profit being the difference between the market prices. When used by academics, an _____ is a transaction that involves no negative cash flow at any probabilistic or temporal state and a positive cash flow in at least one state; in simple terms, it is the possibility of a risk-free profit after transaction costs. For example, an _____ opportunity is present when there is the opportunity to instantaneously buy something for a low price and sell it for a higher price.

Exam Probability: **Low**

56. *Answer choices:*

(see index for correct answer)

- a. Price-weighted index
- b. QuickFIX
- c. Arbitrage
- d. Thomson Reuters league tables

Guidance: level 1

:: Data management ::

_____ is a form of intellectual property that grants the creator of an original creative work an exclusive legal right to determine whether and under what conditions this original work may be copied and used by others, usually for a limited term of years. The exclusive rights are not absolute but limited by limitations and exceptions to _____ law, including fair use. A major limitation on _____ on ideas is that _____ protects only the original expression of ideas, and not the underlying ideas themselves.

Exam Probability: **Medium**

57. *Answer choices:*

(see index for correct answer)

- a. single sourcing
- b. Information governance
- c. SQL programming tool
- d. Copyright

Guidance: level 1

:: ::

_____ is the study and management of exchange relationships. _____ is the business process of creating relationships with and satisfying customers. With its focus on the customer, _____ is one of the premier components of business management.

Exam Probability: **High**

58. *Answer choices:*

(see index for correct answer)

- a. hierarchical
- b. Marketing
- c. information systems assessment
- d. empathy

Guidance: level 1

:: Debt ::

_____ , in finance and economics, is payment from a borrower or deposit-taking financial institution to a lender or depositor of an amount above repayment of the principal sum , at a particular rate. It is distinct from a fee which the borrower may pay the lender or some third party. It is also distinct from dividend which is paid by a company to its shareholders from its profit or reserve, but not at a particular rate decided beforehand, rather on a pro rata basis as a share in the reward gained by risk taking entrepreneurs when the revenue earned exceeds the total costs.

Exam Probability: **Low**

59. *Answer choices:*

(see index for correct answer)

- a. Default
- b. Bailout

- c. Cohort default rate
- d. Asset protection

Guidance: level 1

Human resource management

Human resource (HR) management is the strategic approach to the effective management of organization workers so that they help the business gain a competitive advantage. It is designed to maximize employee performance in service of an employer's strategic objectives. HR is primarily concerned with the management of people within organizations, focusing on policies and on systems. HR departments are responsible for overseeing employee-benefits design, employee recruitment, training and development, performance appraisal, and rewarding (e.g., managing pay and benefit systems). HR also concerns itself with organizational change and industrial relations, that is, the balancing of organizational practices with requirements arising from collective bargaining and from governmental laws.

:: Human resource management ::

_____ , also known as management by results , was first popularized by Peter Drucker in his 1954 book The Practice of Management. _____ is the process of defining specific objectives within an organization that management can convey to organization members, then deciding on how to achieve each objective in sequence. This process allows managers to take work that needs to be done one step at a time to allow for a calm, yet productive work environment. This process also helps organization members to see their accomplishments as they achieve each objective, which reinforces a positive work environment and a sense of achievement. An important part of MBO is the measurement and comparison of an employee's actual performance with the standards set. Ideally, when employees themselves have been involved with the goal-setting and choosing the course of action to be followed by them, they are more likely to fulfill their responsibilities.According to George S. Odiorne, the system of _____ can be described as a process whereby the superior and subordinate jointly identify common goals, define each individual's major areas of responsibility in terms of the results expected of him or her, and use these measures as guides for operating the unit and assessing the contribution of each of its members.

Exam Probability: **Low**

1. *Answer choices:*

(see index for correct answer)

- a. Management by objectives
- b. Bonus payment
- c. Perceived organizational support
- d. Workforce modeling

Guidance: level 1

:: Labor rights ::

A _____ is a wrong or hardship suffered, real or supposed, which forms legitimate grounds of complaint. In the past, the word meant the infliction or cause of hardship.

Exam Probability: **Medium**

2. *Answer choices:*

(see index for correct answer)

- a. Swift raids
- b. Grievance
- c. Kim Bobo
- d. The Hyatt 100

Guidance: level 1

:: Human resource management ::

_____ assesses whether a person performs a job well. _____ , studied academically as part of industrial and organizational psychology, also forms a part of human resources management. Performance is an important criterion for organizational outcomes and success. John P. Campbell describes _____ as an individual-level variable, or something a single person does. This differentiates it from more encompassing constructs such as organizational performance or national performance, which are higher-level variables.

3. *Answer choices:*

(see index for correct answer)

- a. Action alert
- b. Pay in lieu of notice
- c. Job performance
- d. Expense management

Guidance: level 1

:: Employment compensation ::

A _____ is the minimum income necessary for a worker to meet their basic needs. Needs are defined to include food, housing, and other essential needs such as clothing. The goal of a _____ is to allow a worker to afford a basic but decent standard of living. Due to the flexible nature of the term "needs", there is not one universally accepted measure of what a _____ is and as such it varies by location and household type.

4. *Answer choices:*

(see index for correct answer)

- a. Seasonal bonuses
- b. Living wage

- c. Non-wage labour costs
- d. Paid Educational Leave Convention, 1974

Guidance: level 1

:: ::

_____ is the means to see, hear, or become aware of something or someone through our fundamental senses. The term _____ derives from the Latin word perceptio, and is the organization, identification, and interpretation of sensory information in order to represent and understand the presented information, or the environment.

Exam Probability: **Low**

5. *Answer choices:*

(see index for correct answer)

- a. imperative
- b. functional perspective
- c. deep-level diversity
- d. interpersonal communication

Guidance: level 1

:: Human resource management ::

_____ is the application of information technology for both networking and supporting at least two individual or collective actors in their shared performing of HR activities.

Exam Probability: **High**

6. *Answer choices:*

(see index for correct answer)

- a. E-HRM
- b. Turnover
- c. Contractor management
- d. Compensation and benefits

Guidance: level 1

:: Problem solving ::

In other words, _____ is a situation where a group of people meet to generate new ideas and solutions around a specific domain of interest by removing inhibitions. People are able to think more freely and they suggest as many spontaneous new ideas as possible. All the ideas are noted down and those ideas are not criticized and after _____ session the ideas are evaluated. The term was popularized by Alex Faickney Osborn in the 1953 book Applied Imagination.

Exam Probability: **Low**

7. *Answer choices:*

(see index for correct answer)

- a. Brainstorming
- b. Self-organising heuristic
- c. Proof by exhaustion
- d. Creativity techniques

Guidance: level 1

:: Organizational theory ::

Decentralisation is the process by which the activities of an organization, particularly those regarding planning and decision making, are distributed or delegated away from a central, authoritative location or group. Concepts of _____ have been applied to group dynamics and management science in private businesses and organizations, political science, law and public administration, economics, money and technology.

Exam Probability: **High**

8. *Answer choices:*

(see index for correct answer)

- a. City Protocol
- b. Decentralization
- c. Staff augmentation
- d. Organization development

:: Organizational behavior ::

_____ is the state or fact of exclusive rights and control over property, which may be an object, land/real estate or intellectual property. _____ involves multiple rights, collectively referred to as title, which may be separated and held by different parties.

Exam Probability: **Low**

9. *Answer choices:*

(see index for correct answer)

- a. Ownership
- b. Boreout
- c. Self-policing
- d. Behavioral systems analysis

:: Behavior ::

_____ refers to behavior-change procedures that were employed during the 1970s and early 1980s. Based on methodological behaviorism, overt behavior was modified with presumed consequences, including artificial positive and negative reinforcement contingencies to increase desirable behavior, or administering positive and negative punishment and/or extinction to reduce problematic behavior. For the treatment of phobias, habituation and punishment were the basic principles used in flooding, a subcategory of desensitization.

Exam Probability: **Medium**

10. *Answer choices:*

(see index for correct answer)

- a. theory of reasoned action
- b. theory of planned behavior

Guidance: level 1

:: Labour relations ::

_____ is a field of study that can have different meanings depending on the context in which it is used. In an international context, it is a subfield of labor history that studies the human relations with regard to work – in its broadest sense – and how this connects to questions of social inequality. It explicitly encompasses unregulated, historical, and non-Western forms of labor. Here, _____ define "for or with whom one works and under what rules. These rules determine the type of work, type and amount of remuneration, working hours, degrees of physical and psychological strain, as well as the degree of freedom and autonomy associated with the work."

11. *Answer choices:*

(see index for correct answer)

- a. Labor relations
- b. Featherbedding
- c. Acas
- d. Jesse Simons

Guidance: level 1

:: Human resource management ::

_____ means increasing the scope of a job through extending the range of its job duties and responsibilities generally within the same level and periphery. _____ involves combining various activities at the same level in the organization and adding them to the existing job. It is also called the horizontal expansion of job activities. This contradicts the principles of specialisation and the division of labour whereby work is divided into small units, each of which is performed repetitively by an individual worker and the responsibilities are always clear. Some motivational theories suggest that the boredom and alienation caused by the division of labour can actually cause efficiency to fall. Thus, _____ seeks to motivate workers through reversing the process of specialisation. A typical approach might be to replace assembly lines with modular work; instead of an employee repeating the same step on each product, they perform several tasks on a single item. In order for employees to be provided with _____ they will need to be retrained in new fields to understand how each field works.

12. *Answer choices:*

(see index for correct answer)

- a. Job enlargement
- b. Compensation and benefits
- c. Co-determination
- d. Organizational culture

Guidance: level 1

:: Teams ::

A _____ usually refers to a group of individuals who work together from different geographic locations and rely on communication technology such as email, FAX, and video or voice conferencing services in order to collaborate. The term can also refer to groups or teams that work together asynchronously or across organizational levels. Powell, Piccoli and Ives define _____ s as "groups of geographically, organizationally and/or time dispersed workers brought together by information and telecommunication technologies to accomplish one or more organizational tasks." According to Ale Ebrahim et. al. , _____ s can also be defined as "small temporary groups of geographically, organizationally and/or time dispersed knowledge workers who coordinate their work predominantly with electronic information and communication technologies in order to accomplish one or more organization tasks."

13. *Answer choices:*

(see index for correct answer)

- a. team composition
- b. Team-building

Guidance: level 1

:: Business terms ::

Centralisation or _____ is the process by which the activities of an organization, particularly those regarding planning and decision-making, framing strategy and policies become concentrated within a particular geographical location group. This moves the important decision-making and planning powers within the center of the organisation.

Exam Probability: **High**

14. *Answer choices:*

(see index for correct answer)

- a. churn rate
- b. strategic plan
- c. back office
- d. Centralization

Guidance: level 1

:: Employment of foreign-born ::

_____ refers to the international labor pool of workers, including those employed by multinational companies and connected through a global system of networking and production, immigrant workers, transient migrant workers, telecommuting workers, those in export-oriented employment, contingent work or other precarious employment. As of 2012, the global labor pool consisted of approximately 3 billion workers, around 200 million unemployed.

Exam Probability: **Low**

15. *Answer choices:*

(see index for correct answer)

- a. Optional Practical Training
- b. L-2 visa
- c. Human capital flight
- d. L-1 visa

Guidance: level 1

:: Human resource management ::

_____ is a sub-discipline of human resources, focused on employee
_____ policy-making. While _____ are tangible, there are intangible
rewards such as recognition, work-life and development. Combined, these are
referred to as total rewards . The term " _____ " refers to the discipline
as well as the rewards themselves.

Exam Probability: **Medium**

16. *Answer choices:*

(see index for correct answer)

- a. Potential analysis
- b. Compensation and benefits
- c. Human resources
- d. Recruitment process outsourcing

Guidance: level 1

:: Management education ::

_____ refers to simulation games that are used as an educational tool
for teaching business. _____ s may be carried out for various business
training such as: general management, finance, organizational behaviour, human
resources, etc. Often, the term "business simulation" is used with the same
meaning.

Exam Probability: **Medium**

17. *Answer choices:*

(see index for correct answer)

- a. Great Lakes Institute of Management
- b. Master of Commerce
- c. Business game
- d. Fachwirt

Guidance: level 1

:: Human resource management ::

An _____ is a diagram that shows the structure of an organization and the relationships and relative ranks of its parts and positions/jobs. The term is also used for similar diagrams, for example ones showing the different elements of a field of knowledge or a group of languages.

Exam Probability: **Medium**

18. *Answer choices:*

(see index for correct answer)

- a. The war for talent
- b. Organizational chart
- c. Functional job analysis
- d. Recruitment process outsourcing

:: Business ::

_____ is a trade policy that does not restrict imports or exports; it can also be understood as the free market idea applied to international trade. In government, _____ is predominantly advocated by political parties that hold liberal economic positions while economically left-wing and nationalist political parties generally support protectionism, the opposite of _____ .

Exam Probability: **Medium**

19. *Answer choices:*

(see index for correct answer)

- a. Post-transaction marketing
- b. Free Trade
- c. Kingdomality
- d. Employee experience management

:: Belief ::

_____ is an umbrella term of influence. _____ can attempt to influence a person's beliefs, attitudes, intentions, motivations, or behaviors. In business, _____ is a process aimed at changing a person's attitude or behavior toward some event, idea, object, or other person, by using written, spoken words or visual tools to convey information, feelings, or reasoning, or a combination thereof. _____ is also an often used tool in the pursuit of personal gain, such as election campaigning, giving a sales pitch, or in trial advocacy. _____ can also be interpreted as using one's personal or positional resources to change people's behaviors or attitudes.Systematic _____ is the process through which attitudes or beliefs are leveraged by appeals to logic and reason. Heuristic _____ on the other hand is the process through which attitudes or beliefs are leveraged by appeals to habit or emotion.

Exam Probability: **High**

20. *Answer choices:*

(see index for correct answer)

- a. Persuasion
- b. Hold come what may
- c. Disquotational principle
- d. Wish fulfillment

Guidance: level 1

:: Free market ::

Piece work is any type of employment in which a worker is paid a fixed _____ for each unit produced or action performed regardless of time.

Exam Probability: **High**

21. *Answer choices:*

(see index for correct answer)

- a. Piece rate
- b. Regulated market

Guidance: level 1

:: Stochastic processes ::

_____ in its modern meaning is a "new idea, creative thoughts, new imaginations in form of device or method". _____ is often also viewed as the application of better solutions that meet new requirements, unarticulated needs, or existing market needs. Such _____ takes place through the provision of more-effective products, processes, services, technologies, or business models that are made available to markets, governments and society. An _____ is something original and more effective and, as a consequence, new, that "breaks into" the market or society. _____ is related to, but not the same as, invention, as _____ is more apt to involve the practical implementation of an invention to make a meaningful impact in the market or society, and not all _____ s require an invention. _____ often manifests itself via the engineering process, when the problem being solved is of a technical or scientific nature. The opposite of _____ is exnovation.

22. *Answer choices:*

(see index for correct answer)

- a. Lumpability
- b. Renewal theory
- c. Progressively measurable process
- d. Abstract Wiener space

Guidance: level 1

:: ::

A _____ , covering letter, motivation letter, motivational letter or a letter of motivation is a letter of introduction attached to, or accompanying another document such as a résumé or curriculum vitae.

23. *Answer choices:*

(see index for correct answer)

- a. Cover letter
- b. open system
- c. interpersonal communication
- d. imperative

:: Corporate governance ::

An _____ is generally a person responsible for running an organization, although the exact nature of the role varies depending on the organization. In many militaries, an _____ , or "XO," is the second-in-command, reporting to the commanding officer. The XO is typically responsible for the management of day-to-day activities, freeing the commander to concentrate on strategy and planning the unit's next move.

Exam Probability: **High**

24. *Answer choices:*

(see index for correct answer)

- a. Institute of Directors in New Zealand
- b. Model Audit Rule 205
- c. Chief process officer
- d. Standing proxy

:: Human resource management ::

An _____ is a software application that enables the electronic handling of recruitment needs. An ATS can be implemented or accessed online on an enterprise or small business level, depending on the needs of the company and there is also free and open source ATS software available. An ATS is very similar to customer relationship management systems, but are designed for recruitment tracking purposes. In many cases they filter applications automatically based on given criteria such as keywords, skills, former employers, years of experience and schools attended. This has caused many to adapt resume optimization techniques similar to those used in search engine optimization when creating and formatting their résumé.

Exam Probability: **High**

25. *Answer choices:*

(see index for correct answer)

- a. Expense management
- b. Fresh tracks
- c. Applicant tracking system
- d. Occupational burnout

Guidance: level 1

:: Termination of employment ::

The _____ of 1988 is a US labor law which protects employees, their families, and communities by requiring most employers with 100 or more employees to provide 60 calendar-day advance notification of plant closings and mass layoffs of employees, as defined in the Act. In 2001, there were about 2,000 mass layoffs and plant closures which were subject to WARN advance notice requirements and which affected about 660,000 employees.

Exam Probability: **Medium**

26. *Answer choices:*

(see index for correct answer)

- a. Letter of resignation
- b. Worker Adjustment and Retraining Notification Act
- c. Pink slip
- d. Enforced retirement

Guidance: level 1

:: Unemployment benefits ::

_____ are payments made by back authorized bodies to unemployed people. In the United States, benefits are funded by a compulsory governmental insurance system, not taxes on individual citizens. Depending on the jurisdiction and the status of the person, those sums may be small, covering only basic needs, or may compensate the lost time proportionally to the previous earned salary.

27. *Answer choices:*

(see index for correct answer)

- a. National Insurance Act 1911
- b. Unemployment benefits in Spain
- c. Kela
- d. Unemployment benefits in Sweden

Guidance: level 1

:: ::

In production, research, retail, and accounting, a _____ is the value of money that has been used up to produce something or deliver a service, and hence is not available for use anymore. In business, the _____ may be one of acquisition, in which case the amount of money expended to acquire it is counted as _____ . In this case, money is the input that is gone in order to acquire the thing. This acquisition _____ may be the sum of the _____ of production as incurred by the original producer, and further _____ s of transaction as incurred by the acquirer over and above the price paid to the producer. Usually, the price also includes a mark-up for profit over the _____ of production.

Exam Probability: **Low**

28. *Answer choices:*

(see index for correct answer)

- a. similarity-attraction theory
- b. personal values
- c. Cost
- d. process perspective

Guidance: level 1

:: Industrial agreements ::

A _____ , in labor relations, is a group of employees with a clear and identifiable community of interests who are represented by a single labor union in collective bargaining and other dealings with management. Examples would be non-management professors, law enforcement professionals, blue-collar workers, clerical and administrative employees, etc. Geographic location as well as the number of facilities included in _____ s can be at issue during representation cases.

Exam Probability: **Medium**

29. *Answer choices:*

(see index for correct answer)

- a. Industrial arbitration
- b. Australian workplace agreement
- c. Enterprise bargaining agreement
- d. Bargaining unit

Guidance: level 1

A _____ is a research instrument consisting of a series of questions for the purpose of gathering information from respondents. The _____ was invented by the Statistical Society of London in 1838.

Exam Probability: **Low**

30. *Answer choices:*

(see index for correct answer)

- a. surface-level diversity
- b. Questionnaire
- c. Character
- d. similarity-attraction theory

Guidance: level 1

:: Employment compensation ::

_____ refers to various incentive plans introduced by businesses that provide direct or indirect payments to employees that depend on company's profitability in addition to employees' regular salary and bonuses. In publicly traded companies these plans typically amount to allocation of shares to employees. One of the earliest pioneers of _____ was Englishman Theodore Cooke Taylor, who is known to have introduced the practice in his woollen mills during the late 1800s .

Exam Probability: **Low**

31. *Answer choices:*

(see index for correct answer)

- a. Wage regulation
- b. Personal income
- c. Medical Care and Sickness Benefits Convention, 1969
- d. Golden handcuffs

Guidance: level 1

:: ::

A _____ contract is a form of employment that carries fewer hours per week than a full-time job. They work in shifts. The shifts are often rotational. Workers are considered to be _____ if they commonly work fewer than 30 hours per week. According to the International Labour Organization, the number of _____ workers has increased from one-fourth to a half in the past 20 years in most developed countries, excluding the United States. There are many reasons for working _____ , including the desire to do so, having one`s hours cut back by an employer and being unable to find a full-time job. The International Labour Organisation Convention 175 requires that _____ workers be treated no less favourably than full-time workers.

Exam Probability: **Medium**

32. *Answer choices:*

(see index for correct answer)

- a. surface-level diversity
- b. Character
- c. imperative
- d. Sarbanes-Oxley act of 2002

Guidance: level 1

:: Employment compensation ::

_____s and benefits in kind include various types of non-wage compensation provided to employees in addition to their normal wages or salaries. Instances where an employee exchanges wages for some other form of benefit is generally referred to as a "salary packaging" or "salary exchange" arrangement. In most countries, most kinds of _____s are taxable to at least some degree.Examples of these benefits include: housing furnished or not, with or without free utilities; group insurance ; disability income protection; retirement benefits; daycare; tuition reimbursement; sick leave; vacation ; social security; profit sharing; employer student loan contributions; conveyancing; domestic help ; and other specialized benefits.

Exam Probability: **High**

33. *Answer choices:*

(see index for correct answer)

- a. Pay-for-Performance
- b. Employee stock option
- c. Long service leave
- d. Merit pay

Guidance: level 1

:: Labour law ::

A _____ is a "shop-floor" organization representing workers that functions as a local/firm-level complement to trade unions but is independent of these at least in some countries. _____ s exist with different names in a variety of related forms in a number of European countries, including Britain ; Germany and Austria ; Luxembourg ; the Netherlands and Flanders in Belgium ; Italy ; France ; Wallonia in Belgium and Spain .

Exam Probability: **High**

34. *Answer choices:*

(see index for correct answer)

- a. Michele Tiraboschi
- b. Non-compete clause
- c. Conditional dismissal
- d. Vesting

Guidance: level 1

:: ::

An _____ is a period of work experience offered by an organization for a limited period of time. Once confined to medical graduates, the term is now used for a wide range of placements in businesses, non-profit organizations and government agencies. They are typically undertaken by students and graduates looking to gain relevant skills and experience in a particular field. Employers benefit from these placements because they often recruit employees from their best interns, who have known capabilities, thus saving time and money in the long run. _____ s are usually arranged by third-party organizations which recruit interns on behalf of industry groups. Rules vary from country to country about when interns should be regarded as employees. The system can be open to exploitation by unscrupulous employers.

Exam Probability: **Medium**

35. *Answer choices:*

(see index for correct answer)

- a. deep-level diversity
- b. Internship
- c. levels of analysis
- d. functional perspective

Guidance: level 1

:: Human resource management ::

_____ is a core function of human resource management and it is related to the specification of contents, methods and relationship of jobs in order to satisfy technological and organizational requirements as well as the social and personal requirements of the job holder or the employee. Its principles are geared towards how the nature of a person's job affects their attitudes and behavior at work, particularly relating to characteristics such as skill variety and autonomy. The aim of a _____ is to improve job satisfaction, to improve through-put, to improve quality and to reduce employee problems .

Exam Probability: **High**

36. *Answer choices:*

(see index for correct answer)

- a. Job design
- b. Restructuring
- c. Skill mix
- d. Service record

Guidance: level 1

:: Sociological terminology ::

In moral and political philosophy, the _____ is a theory or model that originated during the Age of Enlightenment and usually concerns the legitimacy of the authority of the state over the individual. _____ arguments typically posit that individuals have consented, either explicitly or tacitly, to surrender some of their freedoms and submit to the authority in exchange for protection of their remaining rights or maintenance of the social order. The relation between natural and legal rights is often a topic of _____ theory. The term takes its name from The _____ , a 1762 book by Jean-Jacques Rousseau that discussed this concept. Although the antecedents of _____ theory are found in antiquity, in Greek and Stoic philosophy and Roman and Canon Law, the heyday of the _____ was the mid-17th to early 19th centuries, when it emerged as the leading doctrine of political legitimacy.

Exam Probability: **High**

37. *Answer choices:*

(see index for correct answer)

- a. McDonaldization
- b. Social contract
- c. Disability discrimination
- d. Internalized

Guidance: level 1

:: United States employment discrimination case law ::

_____ , 524 U.S. 775 , is a US labor law case of the United States Supreme Court in which the Court identified the circumstances under which an employer may be held liable under Title VII of the Civil Rights Act of 1964 for the acts of a supervisory employee whose sexual harassment of subordinates has created a hostile work environment amounting to employment discrimination. The court held that "an employer is vicariously liable for actionable discrimination caused by a supervisor, but subject to an affirmative defense looking to the reasonableness of the employer's conduct as well as that of a plaintiff victim."

Exam Probability: **High**

38. *Answer choices:*

(see index for correct answer)

- a. McDonnell Douglas Corp. v. Green
- b. Vance v. Ball State University
- c. Bundy v. Jackson
- d. Shyamala Rajender v. University of Minnesota

Guidance: level 1

:: Industrial agreements ::

_____ is a process of negotiation between employers and a group of employees aimed at agreements to regulate working salaries, working conditions, benefits, and other aspects of workers' compensation and rights for workers. The interests of the employees are commonly presented by representatives of a trade union to which the employees belong. The collective agreements reached by these negotiations usually set out wage scales, working hours, training, health and safety, overtime, grievance mechanisms, and rights to participate in workplace or company affairs.

Exam Probability: **High**

39. *Answer choices:*

(see index for correct answer)

- a. Bargaining unit
- b. Compromise agreement
- c. Common rule awards
- d. McCrone Agreement

Guidance: level 1

:: Recruitment ::

Recruitment refers to the overall process of attracting, shortlisting, selecting and appointing suitable candidates for jobs within an organization. Recruitment can also refer to processes involved in choosing individuals for unpaid roles. Managers, human resource generalists and recruitment specialists may be tasked with carrying out recruitment, but in some cases public-sector employment agencies, commercial recruitment agencies, or specialist search consultancies are used to undertake parts of the process. Internet-based technologies which support all aspects of recruitment have become widespread.

Exam Probability: **Medium**

40. *Answer choices:*

(see index for correct answer)

- a. Probation
- b. Riviera Partners
- c. Jeopardy! audition process
- d. The Select Family of Staffing Companies

Guidance: level 1

:: Labour relations ::

An _____ is a place of employment at which one is not required to join or financially support a union as a condition of hiring or continued employment. _____ is also known as a merit shop.

Exam Probability: **Low**

41. *Answer choices:*

(see index for correct answer)

- a. Scranton Declaration
- b. Worker center
- c. Review Body
- d. Open shop

Guidance: level 1

:: Production and manufacturing ::

_____ consists of organization-wide efforts to "install and make permanent climate where employees continuously improve their ability to provide on demand products and services that customers will find of particular value." "Total" emphasizes that departments in addition to production are obligated to improve their operations; "management" emphasizes that executives are obligated to actively manage quality through funding, training, staffing, and goal setting. While there is no widely agreed-upon approach, TQM efforts typically draw heavily on the previously developed tools and techniques of quality control. TQM enjoyed widespread attention during the late 1980s and early 1990s before being overshadowed by ISO 9000, Lean manufacturing, and Six Sigma.

Exam Probability: **Low**

42. *Answer choices:*

(see index for correct answer)

- a. Division of labour

- b. Total Quality Management
- c. BOMtracker
- d. Back-story

Guidance: level 1

:: Employment compensation ::

_____ is time off from work that workers can use to stay home to address their health and safety needs without losing pay. Paid _____ is a statutory requirement in many nations. Most European, many Latin American, a few African and a few Asian countries have legal requirements for paid _____ .

Exam Probability: **Low**

43. *Answer choices:*

(see index for correct answer)

- a. Lockstep compensation
- b. My Family Care
- c. salary sacrifice
- d. Family wage

Guidance: level 1

:: Employment compensation ::

A _____ is a type of employee benefit plan offered in the United States pursuant to Section 125 of the Internal Revenue Code. Its name comes from the earliest such plans that allowed employees to choose between different types of benefits, similar to the ability of a customer to choose among available items in a cafeteria. Qualified _____ s are excluded from gross income. To qualify, a _____ must allow employees to choose from two or more benefits consisting of cash or qualified benefit plans. The Internal Revenue Code explicitly excludes deferred compensation plans from qualifying as a _____ subject to a gross income exemption. Section 125 also provides two exceptions.

Exam Probability: **Medium**

44. *Answer choices:*

(see index for correct answer)

- a. salary sacrifice
- b. Labour law
- c. Performance-related pay
- d. Profit sharing

Guidance: level 1

:: Employment compensation ::

In government contracting, a _____ is defined as the hourly wage, usual benefits and overtime, paid to the majority of workers, laborers, and mechanics within a particular area. This is usually the union wage.

Exam Probability: **Medium**

45. *Answer choices:*

(see index for correct answer)

- a. Medical Care and Sickness Benefits Convention, 1969
- b. Severance package
- c. Scanlon plan
- d. Salary calculator

Guidance: level 1

:: ::

A _____ seeks to further a particular profession, the interests of individuals engaged in that profession and the public interest. In the United States, such an association is typically a nonprofit organization for tax purposes.

Exam Probability: **Low**

46. *Answer choices:*

(see index for correct answer)

- a. Professional association
- b. hierarchical
- c. functional perspective
- d. process perspective

Guidance: level 1

:: Recruitment ::

A _____, also referred commonly as a career fair or career expo, is an event in which employers, recruiters, and schools give information to potential employees. Job seekers attend these while trying to make a good impression to potential coworkers by speaking face-to-face with one another, filling out résumés, and asking questions in attempt to get a good feel on the work needed. Likewise, online _____ s are held, giving job seekers another way to get in contact with probable employers using the internet.

Exam Probability: **Low**

47. *Answer choices:*

(see index for correct answer)

- a. Referral recruitment
- b. Recession-proof job
- c. Homeworker
- d. Integrity Inventory

:: ::

_____ is the process of collecting, analyzing and/or reporting information regarding the performance of an individual, group, organization, system or component. _____ is not a new concept, some of the earliest records of human activity relate to the counting or recording of activities.

Exam Probability: **High**

48. *Answer choices:*

(see index for correct answer)

- a. Performance measurement
- b. deep-level diversity
- c. co-culture
- d. personal values

:: Workplace ::

A _____ , also referred to as a performance review, performance evaluation, development discussion, or employee appraisal is a method by which the job performance of an employee is documented and evaluated.
_____ s are a part of career development and consist of regular reviews of employee performance within organizations.

Exam Probability: **High**

49. *Answer choices:*

(see index for correct answer)

- a. Workplace violence
- b. Performance appraisal
- c. labour turnover
- d. Discrimination based on hair texture

Guidance: level 1

:: Recruitment ::

_____ is a recruitment strategy that uses mobile technology to attract, engage and convert candidates. Common _____ tactics include mobile career sites, _____ by text, _____ apps and social recruiting. _____ is often cited as a growing opportunity for recruiters to connect with candidates more efficiently with "over 89% of job seekers saying their mobile device will be an important tool and resource for their job search." Traditionally, recruiters have used emails and phone calls to engage candidates, but the increase in mobile usage among job seekers has contributed to _____ `s rising popularity.

50. *Answer choices:*

(see index for correct answer)

- a. Golden hello
- b. Railway Recruitment Control Board
- c. Mobile recruiting
- d. Blind audition

Guidance: level 1

:: Telecommuting ::

_____ , also called telework, teleworking, working from home, mobile work, remote work, and flexible workplace, is a work arrangement in which employees do not commute or travel to a central place of work, such as an office building, warehouse, or store. Teleworkers in the 21st century often use mobile telecommunications technology such as Wi-Fi-equipped laptop or tablet computers and smartphones to work from coffee shops; others may use a desktop computer and a landline phone at their home. According to a Reuters poll, approximately "one in five workers around the globe, particularly employees in the Middle East, Latin America and Asia, telecommute frequently and nearly 10 percent work from home every day." In the 2000s, annual leave or vacation in some organizations was seen as absence from the workplace rather than ceasing work, and some office employees used telework to continue to check work e-mails while on vacation.

Exam Probability: **Medium**

51. *Answer choices:*

(see index for correct answer)

- a. Telecommuting
- b. Home Work Convention, 1996
- c. Remote office center
- d. Asia-Pacific Telecentre Network

Guidance: level 1

:: Workplace ::

A _____ is a process through which feedback from an employee's subordinates, colleagues, and supervisor, as well as a self-evaluation by the employee themselves is gathered. Such feedback can also include, when relevant, feedback from external sources who interact with the employee, such as customers and suppliers or other interested stakeholders. _____ is so named because it solicits feedback regarding an employee's behavior from a variety of points of view . It therefore may be contrasted with "downward feedback" , or "upward feedback" delivered to supervisory or management employees by subordinates only.

Exam Probability: **High**

52. *Answer choices:*

(see index for correct answer)

- a. 360-degree feedback
- b. Workplace aggression

- c. Workplace phobia
- d. Feminisation of the workplace

Guidance: level 1

:: Survey methodology ::

A _____ is the procedure of systematically acquiring and recording information about the members of a given population. The term is used mostly in connection with national population and housing _____ es; other common _____ es include agriculture, business, and traffic _____ es. The United Nations defines the essential features of population and housing _____ es as "individual enumeration, universality within a defined territory, simultaneity and defined periodicity", and recommends that population _____ es be taken at least every 10 years. United Nations recommendations also cover _____ topics to be collected, official definitions, classifications and other useful information to co-ordinate international practice.

Exam Probability: **Medium**

53. *Answer choices:*

(see index for correct answer)

- a. Self-report study
- b. Coverage error
- c. Group concept mapping
- d. Computer-assisted survey information collection

:: Self ::

_____ is a term that has been used in various psychology theories, often in different ways. The term was originally introduced by the organismic theorist Kurt Goldstein for the motive to realize one's full potential. In Goldstein's view, it is the organism's master motive, the only real motive: "the tendency to actualize itself as fully as possible is the basic drive ... the drive of _____ ." Carl Rogers similarly wrote of "the curative force in psychotherapy man's tendency to actualize himself, to become his potentialities ... to express and activate all the capacities of the organism." The concept was brought most fully to prominence in Abraham Maslow's hierarchy of needs theory as the final level of psychological development that can be achieved when all basic and mental needs are essentially fulfilled and the "actualization" of the full personal potential takes place, although he adapted this viewpoint later on in life to be more flexible.

Exam Probability: **High**

54. *Answer choices:*

(see index for correct answer)

- a. Narcissism
- b. Self-presentation
- c. Self-sacrifice
- d. Self-actualization

:: Occupational safety and health ::

A safety data sheet , _____ , or product safety data sheet is a document that lists information relating to occupational safety and health for the use of various substances and products. SDSs are a widely used system for cataloging information on chemicals, chemical compounds, and chemical mixtures. SDS information may include instructions for the safe use and potential hazards associated with a particular material or product, along with spill-handling procedures. SDS formats can vary from source to source within a country depending on national requirements.

Exam Probability: **Medium**

55. *Answer choices:*

(see index for correct answer)

- a. Occupational medicine
- b. Kazutaka Kogi
- c. Contact dermatitis
- d. Material safety data sheet

Guidance: level 1

:: ::

_____ is a method for employees to organize into a labor union in which a majority of employees in a bargaining unit sign authorization forms, or "cards", stating they wish to be represented by the union. Since the National Labor Relations Act became law in 1935, _____ has been an alternative to the National Labor Relations Board's election process. _____ and election are both overseen by the National Labor Relations Board. The difference is that with card sign-up, employees sign authorization cards stating they want a union, the cards are submitted to the NLRB and if more than 50% of the employees submitted cards, the NLRB requires the employer to recognize the union. The NLRA election process is an additional step with the NLRB conducting a secret ballot election after authorization cards are submitted. In both cases the employer never sees the authorization cards or any information that would disclose how individual employees voted.

Exam Probability: **Medium**

56. *Answer choices:*

(see index for correct answer)

- a. imperative
- b. hierarchical
- c. Character
- d. deep-level diversity

Guidance: level 1

:: Parental leave ::

_____ is a type of employment discrimination that occurs when expectant women are fired, not hired, or otherwise discriminated against due to their pregnancy or intention to become pregnant. Common forms of _____ include not being hired due to visible pregnancy or likelihood of becoming pregnant, being fired after informing an employer of one's pregnancy, being fired after maternity leave, and receiving a pay dock due to pregnancy. Convention on the Elimination of All Forms of Discrimination against Women prohibits dismissal on the grounds of maternity or pregnancy and ensures right to maternity leave or comparable social benefits. The Maternity Protection Convention C 183 proclaims adequate protection for pregnancy as well. Though women have some protection in the United States because of the _____ Act of 1978, it has not completely curbed the incidence of _____ . The Equal Rights Amendment could ensure more robust sex equality ensuring that women and men could both work and have children at the same time.

Exam Probability: **Medium**

57. *Answer choices:*

(see index for correct answer)

- a. Additional Paternity Leave Regulations 2010
- b. Pregnancy discrimination
- c. Motherhood penalty
- d. Sara Hlupekile Longwe

Guidance: level 1

:: Business law ::

A pre-entry _____ is a form of union security agreement under which the employer agrees to hire union members only, and employees must remain members of the union at all times in order to remain employed. This is different from a post-entry _____ , which is an agreement requiring all employees to join the union if they are not already members. In a union shop, the union must accept as a member any person hired by the employer.

Exam Probability: **Medium**

58. *Answer choices:*

(see index for correct answer)

- a. Closed shop
- b. Managed service company
- c. Refusal to deal
- d. Operating lease

Guidance: level 1

:: Income ::

In business and accounting, net income is an entity's income minus cost of goods sold, expenses and taxes for an accounting period. It is computed as the residual of all revenues and gains over all expenses and losses for the period, and has also been defined as the net increase in shareholders' equity that results from a company's operations. In the context of the presentation of financial statements, the IFRS Foundation defines net income as synonymous with profit and loss. The difference between revenue and the cost of making a product or providing a service, before deducting overheads, payroll, taxation, and interest payments. This is different from operating income .

Exam Probability: **Medium**

59. *Answer choices:*

(see index for correct answer)

- a. Imputed income
- b. Aggregate expenditure
- c. Bottom line
- d. Windfall gain

Guidance: level 1

Information systems

Information systems (IS) are formal, sociotechnical, organizational systems designed to collect, process, store, and distribute information. In a sociotechnical perspective Information Systems are composed by four components: technology, process, people and organizational structure.

:: History of human–computer interaction ::

A _____ , plural mice, is a small rodent characteristically having a pointed snout, small rounded ears, a body-length scaly tail and a high breeding rate. The best known _____ species is the common house _____ . It is also a popular pet. In some places, certain kinds of field mice are locally common. They are known to invade homes for food and shelter.

Exam Probability: **High**

1. *Answer choices:*

(see index for correct answer)

- a. Mouse
- b. Docuverse
- c. Block-oriented terminal
- d. IBM 2260

Guidance: level 1

:: Security compliance ::

A _____ is a communicated intent to inflict harm or loss on another person. A _____ is considered an act of coercion. _____ s are widely observed in animal behavior, particularly in a ritualized form, chiefly in order to avoid the unnecessary physical violence that can lead to physical damage or the death of both conflicting parties.

Exam Probability: **Medium**

2. *Answer choices:*

(see index for correct answer)

- a. Federal Information Security Management Act of 2002
- b. Information assurance vulnerability alert

- c. Threat
- d. Vulnerability

:: ::

A _____ is a computer network that interconnects computers within a limited area such as a residence, school, laboratory, university campus or office building. By contrast, a wide area network not only covers a larger geographic distance, but also generally involves leased telecommunication circuits.

Exam Probability: **High**

3. *Answer choices:*

(see index for correct answer)

- a. empathy
- b. deep-level diversity
- c. Sarbanes-Oxley act of 2002
- d. Local Area Network

:: Payment systems ::

A _____ is any system used to settle financial transactions through the transfer of monetary value. This includes the institutions, instruments, people, rules, procedures, standards, and technologies that make it exchange possible. A common type of _____ is called an operational network that links bank accounts and provides for monetary exchange using bank deposits. Some _____ s also include credit mechanisms, which are essentially a different aspect of payment.

Exam Probability: **Low**

4. *Answer choices:*

(see index for correct answer)

- a. OneVu
- b. TSYS
- c. Electronic Benefit Transfer
- d. Payment system

Guidance: level 1

:: Procurement practices ::

_____ or commercially available off-the-shelf products are packaged solutions which are then adapted to satisfy the needs of the purchasing organization, rather than the commissioning of custom-made, or bespoke, solutions. A related term, Mil-COTS, refers to COTS products for use by the U.S. military.

5. *Answer choices:*

(see index for correct answer)

- a. Construction by configuration
- b. Syndicated procurement

Guidance: level 1

:: Financial markets ::

The _____ business model is a business model in which a customer must pay a recurring price at regular intervals for access to a product or service.
The model was pioneered by publishers of books and periodicals in the 17th century, and is now used by many businesses and websites.

Exam Probability: **Low**

6. *Answer choices:*

(see index for correct answer)

- a. Post earnings announcement drift
- b. Subscription
- c. Lit pool
- d. Market impact

:: Domain name system ::

The _____ is a hierarchical and decentralized naming system for computers, services, or other resources connected to the Internet or a private network. It associates various information with domain names assigned to each of the participating entities. Most prominently, it translates more readily memorized domain names to the numerical IP addresses needed for locating and identifying computer services and devices with the underlying network protocols. By providing a worldwide, distributed directory service, the _____ has been an essential component of the functionality of the Internet since 1985.

Exam Probability: **High**

7. *Answer choices:*

(see index for correct answer)

- a. OpenDNSSEC
- b. Domain Name System
- c. CNAME record
- d. Domain name auction

:: Payment systems ::

_____ is a mobile phone-based money transfer, financing and microfinancing service, launched in 2007 by Vodafone for Safaricom and Vodacom, the largest mobile network operators in Kenya and Tanzania. It has since expanded to Afghanistan, South Africa, India and in 2014 to Romania and in 2015 to Albania. _____ allows users to deposit, withdraw, transfer money and pay for goods and services easily with a mobile device.

Exam Probability: **Medium**

8. *Answer choices:*

(see index for correct answer)

- a. Square, Inc.
- b. Express Payment System
- c. Freedompay
- d. M-Pesa

Guidance: level 1

:: Business process ::

Business process re-engineering is a business management strategy, originally pioneered in the early 1990s, focusing on the analysis and design of workflows and business processes within an organization. BPR aimed to help organizations fundamentally rethink how they do their work in order to improve customer service, cut operational costs, and become world-class competitors.

Exam Probability: **Medium**

9. *Answer choices:*

(see index for correct answer)

- a. Software Ideas Modeler
- b. Business process reengineering
- c. Intention mining
- d. Captive service

Guidance: level 1

:: Production economics ::

_____ is a way of producing goods and services that relies on self-organizing communities of individuals. In such communities, the labor of a large number of people is coordinated towards a shared outcome.

Exam Probability: **High**

10. *Answer choices:*

(see index for correct answer)

- a. Learning-by-doing
- b. Split-off point
- c. Peer production
- d. Fragmentation

Guidance: level 1

:: Intrusion detection systems ::

An _____ is a device or software application that monitors a network or systems for malicious activity or policy violations. Any malicious activity or violation is typically reported either to an administrator or collected centrally using a security information and event management system. A SIEM system combines outputs from multiple sources, and uses alarm filtering techniques to distinguish malicious activity from false alarms.

Exam Probability: **High**

11. *Answer choices:*

(see index for correct answer)

- a. Samhain
- b. Intrusion detection system
- c. Application protocol-based intrusion detection system
- d. Boundaries of Security Report

Guidance: level 1

:: ::

A _____ is a control panel usually located directly ahead of a vehicle's driver, displaying instrumentation and controls for the vehicle's operation.

12. *Answer choices:*

(see index for correct answer)

- a. hierarchical
- b. information systems assessment
- c. hierarchical perspective
- d. Dashboard

Guidance: level 1

:: ::

A _____ or data centre is a building, dedicated space within a building, or a group of buildings used to house computer systems and associated components, such as telecommunications and storage systems.

13. *Answer choices:*

(see index for correct answer)

- a. hierarchical perspective
- b. Data center
- c. corporate values
- d. cultural

:: Finance ::

_____ is a financial estimate intended to help buyers and owners determine the direct and indirect costs of a product or system. It is a management accounting concept that can be used in full cost accounting or even ecological economics where it includes social costs.

Exam Probability: **Medium**

14. *Answer choices:*

(see index for correct answer)

- a. Wrap account
- b. Quantitative easing
- c. Total cost of ownership
- d. Gross up clause

:: Service-oriented (business computing) ::

_____ is a style of software design where services are provided to the other components by application components, through a communication protocol over a network. The basic principles of _____ are independent of vendors, products and technologies.A service is a discrete unit of functionality that can be accessed remotely and acted upon and updated independently, such as retrieving a credit card statement online.

Exam Probability: **High**

15. *Answer choices:*

(see index for correct answer)

- a. SAP Enterprise Architecture Framework
- b. Differentiated service
- c. Service-oriented architecture
- d. Event-Driven Messaging

Guidance: level 1

:: Data analysis ::

_____ is a process of inspecting, cleansing, transforming, and modeling data with the goal of discovering useful information, informing conclusions, and supporting decision-making. _____ has multiple facets and approaches, encompassing diverse techniques under a variety of names, and is used in different business, science, and social science domains. In today's business world, _____ plays a role in making decisions more scientific and helping businesses operate more effectively.

16. *Answer choices:*

(see index for correct answer)

- a. LISREL
- b. Post-hoc analysis
- c. Data Discovery and Query Builder
- d. Data analysis

Guidance: level 1

:: Data management ::

_____ is "data [information] that provides information about other data". Many distinct types of _____ exist, among these descriptive _____ , structural _____ , administrative _____ , reference _____ and statistical _____ .

17. *Answer choices:*

(see index for correct answer)

- a. Single customer view
- b. Metadata
- c. Data binding

- d. Data profiling

Guidance: level 1

:: Network performance ::

_____ is a distributed computing paradigm which brings computer data storage closer to the location where it is needed. Computation is largely or completely performed on distributed device nodes. _____ pushes applications, data and computing power away from centralized points to locations closer to the user. The target of _____ is any application or general functionality needing to be closer to the source of the action where distributed systems technology interacts with the physical world. _____ does not need contact with any centralized cloud, although it may interact with one. In contrast to cloud computing, _____ refers to decentralized data processing at the edge of the network.

Exam Probability: **High**

18. *Answer choices:*
(see index for correct answer)

- a. Network congestion
- b. Switching loop
- c. Edge computing
- d. Weighted random early detection

Guidance: level 1

:: Information systems ::

_____ s are information systems that are developed in response to corporate business initiative. They are intended to give competitive advantage to the organization. They may deliver a product or service that is at a lower cost, that is differentiated, that focuses on a particular market segment, or is innovative.

Exam Probability: **High**

19. *Answer choices:*

(see index for correct answer)

- a. Chief information officer
- b. CIMACT
- c. Field force automation
- d. Information engineering

Guidance: level 1

:: ::

_____ Holdings, Inc. is an American company operating a worldwide online payments system that supports online money transfers and serves as an electronic alternative to traditional paper methods like checks and money orders. The company operates as a payment processor for online vendors, auction sites, and many other commercial users, for which it charges a fee in exchange for benefits such as one-click transactions and password memory. _____ 's payment system, also called _____ , is considered a type of payment rail.

Exam Probability: **Medium**

20. *Answer choices:*

(see index for correct answer)

- a. interpersonal communication
- b. levels of analysis
- c. PayPal
- d. functional perspective

Guidance: level 1

:: Online companies ::

_____ is a business directory service and crowd-sourced review forum, and a public company of the same name that is headquartered in San Francisco, California. The company develops, hosts and markets the _____ .com website and the _____ mobile app, which publish crowd-sourced reviews about businesses. It also operates an online reservation service called _____ Reservations.

21. *Answer choices:*

(see index for correct answer)

- a. Lenddo
- b. We Heart It
- c. High Gear Media
- d. Hangsen

Guidance: level 1

:: ::

Sustainability is the process of people maintaining change in a balanced environment, in which the exploitation of resources, the direction of investments, the orientation of technological development and institutional change are all in harmony and enhance both current and future potential to meet human needs and aspirations. For many in the field, sustainability is defined through the following interconnected domains or pillars: environment, economic and social, which according to Fritjof Capra is based on the principles of Systems Thinking. Sub-domains of _____ development have been considered also: cultural, technological and political. While _____ development may be the organizing principle for sustainability for some, for others, the two terms are paradoxical . _____ development is the development that meets the needs of the present without compromising the ability of future generations to meet their own needs. Brundtland Report for the World Commission on Environment and Development introduced the term of _____ development.

22. *Answer choices:*

(see index for correct answer)

- a. Sustainable
- b. Sarbanes-Oxley act of 2002
- c. co-culture
- d. process perspective

Guidance: level 1

:: Supply chain management terms ::

In business and finance, _____ is a system of organizations, people, activities, information, and resources involved in moving a product or service from supplier to customer. _____ activities involve the transformation of natural resources, raw materials, and components into a finished product that is delivered to the end customer. In sophisticated _____ systems, used products may re-enter the _____ at any point where residual value is recyclable. _____ s link value chains.

Exam Probability: **Low**

23. *Answer choices:*

(see index for correct answer)

- a. Supply-chain management
- b. Supply chain
- c. Cool Chain Quality Indicator

- d. Final assembly schedule

Guidance: level 1

:: Information technology management ::

_____ concerns a cycle of organizational activity: the acquisition of information from one or more sources, the custodianship and the distribution of that information to those who need it, and its ultimate disposition through archiving or deletion.

Exam Probability: **High**

24. *Answer choices:*

(see index for correct answer)

- a. Autonomic networking
- b. Software asset management
- c. Information management
- d. Pop-up ad

Guidance: level 1

:: Survey methodology ::

An _____ is a conversation where questions are asked and answers are given. In common parlance, the word " _____ " refers to a one-on-one conversation between an _____ er and an _____ ee. The _____ er asks questions to which the _____ ee responds, usually so information may be transferred from _____ ee to _____ er . Sometimes, information can be transferred in both directions. It is a communication, unlike a speech, which produces a one-way flow of information.

Exam Probability: **Low**

25. *Answer choices:*

(see index for correct answer)

- a. Coverage error
- b. Group concept mapping
- c. National Health Interview Survey
- d. Interview

Guidance: level 1

:: Business models ::

_____ , or The Computer Utility, is a service provisioning model in which a service provider makes computing resources and infrastructure management available to the customer as needed, and charges them for specific usage rather than a flat rate. Like other types of on-demand computing , the utility model seeks to maximize the efficient use of resources and/or minimize associated costs. Utility is the packaging of system resources, such as computation, storage and services, as a metered service. This model has the advantage of a low or no initial cost to acquire computer resources; instead, resources are essentially rented.

Exam Probability: **High**

26. *Answer choices:*

(see index for correct answer)

- a. Product-service system
- b. Trade printing
- c. Open Music Model
- d. Paid To Click

Guidance: level 1

:: ::

The _____ , commonly known as the Web, is an information system where documents and other web resources are identified by Uniform Resource Locators , which may be interlinked by hypertext, and are accessible over the Internet. The resources of the WWW may be accessed by users by a software application called a web browser.

27. *Answer choices:*

(see index for correct answer)

- a. functional perspective
- b. corporate values
- c. deep-level diversity
- d. hierarchical perspective

Guidance: level 1

:: Mereology ::

_____ , in the abstract, is what belongs to or with something, whether as an attribute or as a component of said thing. In the context of this article, it is one or more components , whether physical or incorporeal, of a person's estate; or so belonging to, as in being owned by, a person or jointly a group of people or a legal entity like a corporation or even a society. Depending on the nature of the _____ , an owner of _____ has the right to consume, alter, share, redefine, rent, mortgage, pawn, sell, exchange, transfer, give away or destroy it, or to exclude others from doing these things, as well as to perhaps abandon it; whereas regardless of the nature of the _____ , the owner thereof has the right to properly use it , or at the very least exclusively keep it.

Exam Probability: **Low**

28. *Answer choices:*

- a. Non-wellfounded mereology
- b. Gunk
- c. Property
- d. Mereology

Guidance: level 1

:: Types of marketing ::

In microeconomics and management, _____ is an arrangement in which the supply chain of a company is owned by that company. Usually each member of the supply chain produces a different product or service, and the products combine to satisfy a common need. It is contrasted with horizontal integration, wherein a company produces several items which are related to one another. _____ has also described management styles that bring large portions of the supply chain not only under a common ownership, but also into one corporation .

Exam Probability: **Low**

29. *Answer choices:*

- a. Consumer Generated Advertising
- b. Multi-domestic strategy
- c. Customerization
- d. Vertical integration

:: Marketing ::

_____ , in marketing, manufacturing, call centres and management, is the use of flexible computer-aided manufacturing systems to produce custom output. Such systems combine the low unit costs of mass production processes with the flexibility of individual customization.

Exam Probability: **Medium**

30. *Answer choices:*

(see index for correct answer)

- a. Mass customization
- b. Ameritest
- c. Leverage
- d. Marketing communications

:: Information technology management ::

An _____ , acceptable usage policy or fair use policy, is a set of rules applied by the owner, creator or administrator of a network, website, or service, that restrict the ways in which the network, website or system may be used and sets guidelines as to how it should be used. AUP documents are written for corporations, businesses, universities, schools, internet service providers , and website owners, often to reduce the potential for legal action that may be taken by a user, and often with little prospect of enforcement.

Exam Probability: **Medium**

31. *Answer choices:*

(see index for correct answer)

- a. E-Booking
- b. Imaging for Windows
- c. Battle command knowledge system
- d. Operations architecture

Guidance: level 1

:: ::

The _____ of 1996 was enacted by the 104th United States Congress and signed by President Bill Clinton in 1996. It was created primarily to modernize the flow of healthcare information, stipulate how Personally Identifiable Information maintained by the healthcare and healthcare insurance industries should be protected from fraud and theft, and address limitations on healthcare insurance coverage.

Exam Probability: **Low**

32. *Answer choices:*

(see index for correct answer)

- a. functional perspective
- b. surface-level diversity
- c. Health Insurance Portability and Accountability Act
- d. open system

Guidance: level 1

:: Telecommunication theory ::

In reliability theory and reliability engineering, the term _____ has the following meanings.

Exam Probability: **Low**

33. *Answer choices:*

(see index for correct answer)

- a. Digital signal processing
- b. Propagation constant
- c. Signal processing
- d. Availability

:: Internet marketing ::

_____ is the process of increasing the quality and quantity of website traffic, increasing visibility of a website or a web page to users of a web search engine. SEO refers to the improvement of unpaid results , and excludes the purchase of paid placement.

Exam Probability: **Medium**

34. *Answer choices:*

(see index for correct answer)

- a. Social media optimization
- b. Seperia
- c. Search engine optimization
- d. Interactive advertising

:: Data management ::

Data aggregation is the compiling of information from databases with intent to prepare combined datasets for data processing.

35. *Answer choices:*

(see index for correct answer)

- a. Database-centric architecture
- b. Content inventory
- c. Storage model
- d. Nested transaction

Guidance: level 1

:: Transaction processing ::

In _____ , information systems typically facilitate and manage transaction-oriented applications.

36. *Answer choices:*

(see index for correct answer)

- a. Online transaction processing
- b. Tuxedo
- c. Consistency model
- d. Quorum

:: Supply chain management ::

_____ is the removal of intermediaries in economics from a supply chain, or cutting out the middlemen in connection with a transaction or a series of transactions. Instead of going through traditional distribution channels, which had some type of intermediary , companies may now deal with customers directly, for example via the Internet. Hence, the use of factory direct and direct from the factory to mean the same thing.

Exam Probability: **Low**

37. *Answer choices:*

(see index for correct answer)

- a. Vendor-managed inventory
- b. Design for logistics
- c. DIFOT
- d. Disintermediation

:: Marketing ::

_____ is the percentage of a market accounted for by a specific entity. In a survey of nearly 200 senior marketing managers, 67% responded that they found the revenue- "dollar _____ " metric very useful, while 61% found "unit _____ " very useful.

Exam Probability: **Medium**

38. *Answer choices:*

(see index for correct answer)

- a. Need
- b. Market share
- c. Aftersales
- d. Art Infusion

Guidance: level 1

:: Data management ::

In business, _____ is a method used to define and manage the critical data of an organization to provide, with data integration, a single point of reference. The data that is mastered may include reference data- the set of permissible values, and the analytical data that supports decision making.

Exam Probability: **Medium**

39. *Answer choices:*

(see index for correct answer)

- a. Data library
- b. Consumer relationship system
- c. CommVault Systems
- d. Master data management

Guidance: level 1

:: Google services ::

_____ is a time-management and scheduling calendar service developed by Google. It became available in beta release April 13, 2006, and in general release in July 2009, on the web and as mobile apps for the Android and iOS platforms.

Exam Probability: **Medium**

40. *Answer choices:*

(see index for correct answer)

- a. Google Flu Trends
- b. Google Cloud Print
- c. Google Patents
- d. Google Helpouts

Guidance: level 1

:: Data collection ::

_____ is the application of data mining techniques to discover patterns from the World Wide Web. As the name proposes, this is information gathered by mining the web. It makes utilization of automated apparatuses to reveal and extricate data from servers and web2 reports, and it permits organizations to get to both organized and unstructured information from browser activities, server logs, website and link structure, page content and different sources.

Exam Probability: **Medium**

41. *Answer choices:*

(see index for correct answer)

- a. Flow tracer
- b. Synthetic Environment for Analysis and Simulations
- c. Web mining
- d. ScraperWiki

Guidance: level 1

:: Outsourcing ::

A service-level agreement is a commitment between a service provider and a client. Particular aspects of the service – quality, availability, responsibilities – are agreed between the service provider and the service user. The most common component of SLA is that the services should be provided to the customer as agreed upon in the contract. As an example, Internet service providers and telcos will commonly include _____ s within the terms of their contracts with customers to define the level of service being sold in plain language terms. In this case the SLA will typically have a technical definition in mean time between failures , mean time to repair or mean time to recovery ; identifying which party is responsible for reporting faults or paying fees; responsibility for various data rates; throughput; jitter; or similar measurable details.

Exam Probability: **Medium**

42. *Answer choices:*

(see index for correct answer)

- a. Service level agreement
- b. Virtual Staff Finder
- c. Managed VoIP Service
- d. PFSweb

Guidance: level 1

:: Information and communication technologies for development ::

_____ is a non-profit initiative established with the goal of transforming education for children around the world; this goal was to be achieved by creating and distributing educational devices for the developing world, and by creating software and content for those devices.

Exam Probability: **High**

43. *Answer choices:*

(see index for correct answer)

- a. Simputer
- b. SITIA
- c. Web 2.0 for development
- d. One Laptop per Child

Guidance: level 1

:: ::

_____ LLC is an American multinational technology company that specializes in Internet-related services and products, which include online advertising technologies, search engine, cloud computing, software, and hardware. It is considered one of the Big Four technology companies, alongside Amazon, Apple and Facebook.

Exam Probability: **Low**

44. *Answer choices:*

- a. information systems assessment
- b. Google
- c. personal values
- d. process perspective

Guidance: level 1

:: Geographic information systems ::

_____ is the computational process of transforming a physical address description to a location on the Earth's surface . Reverse _____ , on the other hand, converts geographic coordinates to a description of a location, usually the name of a place or an addressable location. _____ relies on a computer representation of address points, the street / road network, together with postal and administrative boundaries.

Exam Probability: **Low**

45. *Answer choices:*

- a. SRTM Water Body Data
- b. Geocoding
- c. ISO/TC 211
- d. Participatory 3D modelling

:: ::

_____ are electronic transfer of money from one bank account to another, either within a single financial institution or across multiple institutions, via computer-based systems, without the direct intervention of bank staff.

Exam Probability: **High**

46. *Answer choices:*

(see index for correct answer)

- a. Character
- b. Electronic funds transfer
- c. open system
- d. Sarbanes-Oxley act of 2002

:: Information systems ::

_____ are formal, sociotechnical, organizational systems designed to collect, process, store, and distribute information. In a sociotechnical perspective, _____ are composed by four components: task, people, structure , and technology.

Exam Probability: **High**

47. *Answer choices:*

(see index for correct answer)

- a. Information Systems Journal
- b. Electronic Case Filing System
- c. Information filtering system
- d. Transport standards organisations

Guidance: level 1

:: Policy ::

A _____ is a statement or a legal document that discloses some or all of the ways a party gathers, uses, discloses, and manages a customer or client's data. It fulfills a legal requirement to protect a customer or client's privacy. Personal information can be anything that can be used to identify an individual, not limited to the person's name, address, date of birth, marital status, contact information, ID issue, and expiry date, financial records, credit information, medical history, where one travels, and intentions to acquire goods and services. In the case of a business it is often a statement that declares a party's policy on how it collects, stores, and releases personal information it collects. It informs the client what specific information is collected, and whether it is kept confidential, shared with partners, or sold to other firms or enterprises. Privacy policies typically represent a broader, more generalized treatment, as opposed to data use statements, which tend to be more detailed and specific.

Exam Probability: **Medium**

48. *Answer choices:*

(see index for correct answer)

- a. Privacy policy
- b. Science policy
- c. Veterinary Feed Directive
- d. Security policy

Guidance: level 1

:: Information science ::

In discourse-based grammatical theory, _____ is any tracking of referential information by speakers. Information may be new, just introduced into the conversation; given, already active in the speakers' consciousness; or old, no longer active. The various types of activation, and how these are defined, are model-dependent.

Exam Probability: **High**

49. *Answer choices:*

(see index for correct answer)

- a. Browsing
- b. Source criticism
- c. Toy problem
- d. Upper ontology

Guidance: level 1

:: History of human–computer interaction ::

_____ is a line of motion sensing input devices produced by Microsoft. Initially, the _____ was developed as a gaming accessory for Xbox 360 and Xbox One video game consoles and Microsoft Windows PCs. Based around a webcam-style add-on peripheral, it enabled users to control and interact with their console/computer without the need for a game controller, through a natural user interface using gestures and spoken commands. While the gaming line did not gain much traction and eventually discontinued, third-party developers and researches found several after-market uses for _____ 's advanced low-cost sensor features, leading Microsoft to drive the product line towards more application-neutral uses, including integrating the device with Microsoft's cloud computing platform Azure.

Exam Probability: **Low**

50. *Answer choices:*

(see index for correct answer)

- a. Kinect
- b. IBM 2260
- c. Wired glove
- d. The Mother of All Demos

Guidance: level 1

:: ::

_____ is software designed to provide a platform for other software. Examples of _____ include operating systems like macOS, Ubuntu and Microsoft Windows, computational science software, game engines, industrial automation, and software as a service applications.

Exam Probability: **High**

51. *Answer choices:*

(see index for correct answer)

- a. hierarchical perspective
- b. System software
- c. Character
- d. personal values

Guidance: level 1

:: Cryptography ::

In cryptography, _____ is the process of encoding a message or information in such a way that only authorized parties can access it and those who are not authorized cannot. _____ does not itself prevent interference, but denies the intelligible content to a would-be interceptor. In an _____ scheme, the intended information or message, referred to as plaintext, is encrypted using an _____ algorithm – a cipher – generating ciphertext that can be read only if decrypted. For technical reasons, an _____ scheme usually uses a pseudo-random _____ key generated by an algorithm. It is in principle possible to decrypt the message without possessing the key, but, for a well-designed _____ scheme, considerable computational resources and skills are required. An authorized recipient can easily decrypt the message with the key provided by the originator to recipients but not to unauthorized users.

Exam Probability: **High**

52. *Answer choices:*

(see index for correct answer)

- a. Encryption
- b. cryptosystem
- c. plaintext
- d. Anonymous matching

Guidance: level 1

:: ::

Within the Internet, _____ s are formed by the rules and procedures of the _____ System . Any name registered in the DNS is a _____ . _____ s are used in various networking contexts and for application-specific naming and addressing purposes. In general, a _____ represents an Internet Protocol resource, such as a personal computer used to access the Internet, a server computer hosting a web site, or the web site itself or any other service communicated via the Internet. In 2017, 330.6 million _____ s had been registered.

Exam Probability: **High**

53. *Answer choices:*

(see index for correct answer)

- a. deep-level diversity
- b. corporate values
- c. Character
- d. Domain name

Guidance: level 1

:: Remote administration software ::

_____ is a protocol used on the Internet or local area network to provide a bidirectional interactive text-oriented communication facility using a virtual terminal connection. User data is interspersed in-band with _____ control information in an 8-bit byte oriented data connection over the Transmission Control Protocol .

54. *Answer choices:*

(see index for correct answer)

- a. VIA3
- b. Web-based SSH
- c. Remote Utilities
- d. UltraVNC

Guidance: level 1

:: Supply chain management ::

ERP is usually referred to as a category of business management software — typically a suite of integrated applications—that an organization can use to collect, store, manage, and interpret data from these many business activities.

Exam Probability: **Medium**

55. *Answer choices:*

(see index for correct answer)

- a. ThoughtSpeed Corporation
- b. Irancode
- c. Dealer Business System
- d. Enterprise resource planning

:: Google services ::

_____ is a discontinued image organizer and image viewer for organizing and editing digital photos, plus an integrated photo-sharing website, originally created by a company named Lifescape in 2002. In July 2004, Google acquired _____ from Lifescape and began offering it as freeware. " _____ " is a blend of the name of Spanish painter Pablo Picasso, the phrase mi casa and "pic" for pictures.

Exam Probability: **Medium**

56. *Answer choices:*

(see index for correct answer)

- a. Google WiFi
- b. App Inventor for Android
- c. Picasa
- d. Google Translate

:: Strategic management ::

_____ is a management term for an element that is necessary for an organization or project to achieve its mission. Alternative terms are key result area and key success factor .

Exam Probability: **High**

57. *Answer choices:*

(see index for correct answer)

- a. Vitality curve
- b. Critical success factor
- c. Results-based management
- d. Segmenting and positioning

Guidance: level 1

:: ::

In communications and information processing, _____ is a system of rules to convert information—such as a letter, word, sound, image, or gesture—into another form or representation, sometimes shortened or secret, for communication through a communication channel or storage in a storage medium. An early example is the invention of language, which enabled a person, through speech, to communicate what they saw, heard, felt, or thought to others. But speech limits the range of communication to the distance a voice can carry, and limits the audience to those present when the speech is uttered. The invention of writing, which converted spoken language into visual symbols, extended the range of communication across space and time.

58. *Answer choices:*

- a. information systems assessment
- b. corporate values
- c. hierarchical
- d. levels of analysis

Guidance: level 1

:: Industrial automation ::

_____ is the technology by which a process or procedure is performed with minimal human assistance. _____ or automatic control is the use of various control systems for operating equipment such as machinery, processes in factories, boilers and heat treating ovens, switching on telephone networks, steering and stabilization of ships, aircraft and other applications and vehicles with minimal or reduced human intervention.

Exam Probability: **High**

59. *Answer choices:*

- a. Automation
- b. CODESYS

- c. Advanced Plant Management System
- d. IODD

Guidance: level 1

Marketing

Marketing is the study and management of exchange relationships. Marketing is the business process of creating relationships with and satisfying customers. With its focus on the customer, marketing is one of the premier components of business management.

Marketing is defined by the American Marketing Association as "the activity, set of institutions, and processes for creating, communicating, delivering, and exchanging offerings that have value for customers, clients, partners, and society at large."

:: Monopoly (economics) ::

_____ is a category of property that includes intangible creations of the human intellect. _____ encompasses two types of rights: industrial property rights and copyright. It was not until the 19th century that the term " _____ " began to be used, and not until the late 20th century that it became commonplace in the majority of the world.

Exam Probability: **Low**

1. *Answer choices:*

(see index for correct answer)

- a. Sherman Antitrust Act
- b. Public utility
- c. Building block model
- d. Intellectual property

Guidance: level 1

:: Marketing techniques ::

The _____ or unique selling point is a marketing concept first proposed as a theory to explain a pattern in successful advertising campaigns of the early 1940s. The USP states that such campaigns made unique propositions to customers that convinced them to switch brands. The term was developed by television advertising pioneer Rosser Reeves of Ted Bates & Company. Theodore Levitt, a professor at Harvard Business School, suggested that, "Differentiation is one of the most important strategic and tactical activities in which companies must constantly engage." The term has been used to describe one's "personal brand" in the marketplace. Today, the term is used in other fields or just casually to refer to any aspect of an object that differentiates it from similar objects.

Exam Probability: **Low**

2. *Answer choices:*

(see index for correct answer)

- a. Unique selling proposition
- b. Home staging
- c. Relevant space
- d. Real-time marketing

Guidance: level 1

:: ::

Competition arises whenever at least two parties strive for a goal which cannot be shared: where one's gain is the other's loss .

3. *Answer choices:*

(see index for correct answer)

- a. Competitor
- b. empathy
- c. deep-level diversity
- d. functional perspective

Guidance: level 1

:: Materials ::

A _____ , also known as a feedstock, unprocessed material, or primary commodity, is a basic material that is used to produce goods, finished products, energy, or intermediate materials which are feedstock for future finished products. As feedstock, the term connotes these materials are bottleneck assets and are highly important with regard to producing other products. An example of this is crude oil, which is a _____ and a feedstock used in the production of industrial chemicals, fuels, plastics, and pharmaceutical goods; lumber is a _____ used to produce a variety of products including all types of furniture. The term " _____ " denotes materials in minimally processed or unprocessed in states; e.g., raw latex, crude oil, cotton, coal, raw biomass, iron ore, air, logs, or water i.e. "...any product of agriculture, forestry, fishing and any other mineral that is in its natural form or which has undergone the transformation required to prepare it for internationally marketing in substantial volumes."

4. *Answer choices:*

(see index for correct answer)

- a. Raw material
- b. Sealant
- c. Technora
- d. Noil

Guidance: level 1

:: Marketing ::

A _____ is the quantity of payment or compensation given by one party to another in return for one unit of goods or services.. A _____ is influenced by both production costs and demand for the product. A _____ may be determined by a monopolist or may be imposed on the firm by market conditions.

Exam Probability: **Medium**

5. *Answer choices:*

(see index for correct answer)

- a. Interruption marketing
- b. Observatory of prices
- c. Bluetooth advertising
- d. Price

:: International trade ::

In finance, an _____ is the rate at which one currency will be exchanged for another. It is also regarded as the value of one country's currency in relation to another currency. For example, an interbank _____ of 114 Japanese yen to the United States dollar means that ¥114 will be exchanged for each US$1 or that US$1 will be exchanged for each ¥114. In this case it is said that the price of a dollar in relation to yen is ¥114, or equivalently that the price of a yen in relation to dollars is $1/114.

Exam Probability: **Medium**

6. *Answer choices:*

(see index for correct answer)

- a. Intrastat
- b. International Standards of Accounting and Reporting
- c. Intra-industry trade
- d. Exchange rate

:: ::

An _____ , often referred to as a creative agency or an ad agency, is a business dedicated to creating, planning, and handling advertising and sometimes other forms of promotion and marketing for its clients. An ad agency is generally independent from the client; it may be an internal department or agency that provides an outside point of view to the effort of selling the client's products or services, or an outside firm. An agency can also handle overall marketing and branding strategies promotions for its clients, which may include sales as well.

Exam Probability: **High**

7. *Answer choices:*

(see index for correct answer)

- a. Advertising agency
- b. personal values
- c. empathy
- d. cultural

Guidance: level 1

:: Information technology management ::

B2B is often contrasted with business-to-consumer . In B2B commerce, it is often the case that the parties to the relationship have comparable negotiating power, and even when they do not, each party typically involves professional staff and legal counsel in the negotiation of terms, whereas B2C is shaped to a far greater degree by economic implications of information asymmetry. However, within a B2B context, large companies may have many commercial, resource and information advantages over smaller businesses. The United Kingdom government, for example, created the post of Small Business Commissioner under the Enterprise Act 2016 to "enable small businesses to resolve disputes" and "consider complaints by small business suppliers about payment issues with larger businesses that they supply."

Exam Probability: **High**

8. *Answer choices:*

(see index for correct answer)

- a. Business-to-business
- b. GESMES/TS
- c. One-to-one
- d. Soluto

Guidance: level 1

:: Television commercials ::

_____ is a phenomenon whereby something new and somehow valuable is formed. The created item may be intangible or a physical object .

9. *Answer choices:*

(see index for correct answer)

- a. Slim Jeans
- b. Creativity
- c. Batman OnStar commercials
- d. NoitulovE

Guidance: level 1

:: Management ::

_____ is the process of thinking about the activities required to achieve a desired goal. It is the first and foremost activity to achieve desired results. It involves the creation and maintenance of a plan, such as psychological aspects that require conceptual skills. There are even a couple of tests to measure someone's capability of _____ well. As such, _____ is a fundamental property of intelligent behavior. An important further meaning, often just called " _____ " is the legal context of permitted building developments.

Exam Probability: **High**

10. *Answer choices:*

(see index for correct answer)

- a. Management buyout
- b. Certified Project Management Professional
- c. Certified management consultant
- d. Shrinkage

Guidance: level 1

:: Advertising ::

_____ is the behavioral and cognitive process of selectively concentrating on a discrete aspect of information, whether deemed subjective or objective, while ignoring other perceivable information. It is a state of arousal. It is the taking possession by the mind in clear and vivid form of one out of what seem several simultaneous objects or trains of thought. Focalization, the concentration of consciousness, is of its essence. _____ has also been described as the allocation of limited cognitive processing resources.

Exam Probability: **High**

11. *Answer choices:*

(see index for correct answer)

- a. Attention
- b. The Law of Advertising and Mass Communications
- c. Norm of reciprocity
- d. Advertising Producers Association

:: Debt ::

_____ , in finance and economics, is payment from a borrower or deposit-taking financial institution to a lender or depositor of an amount above repayment of the principal sum , at a particular rate. It is distinct from a fee which the borrower may pay the lender or some third party. It is also distinct from dividend which is paid by a company to its shareholders from its profit or reserve, but not at a particular rate decided beforehand, rather on a pro rata basis as a share in the reward gained by risk taking entrepreneurs when the revenue earned exceeds the total costs.

Exam Probability: **Medium**

12. *Answer choices:*

(see index for correct answer)

- a. Money disorders
- b. Museum of Foreign Debt
- c. Interest
- d. Cohort default rate

:: National accounts ::

_____ is a monetary measure of the market value of all the final goods and services produced in a period of time, often annually. GDP per capita does not, however, reflect differences in the cost of living and the inflation rates of the countries; therefore using a basis of GDP per capita at purchasing power parity is arguably more useful when comparing differences in living standards between nations.

Exam Probability: **Low**

13. *Answer choices:*

(see index for correct answer)

- a. Fixed capital
- b. National Income
- c. capital formation

Guidance: level 1

:: ::

_____ s uses different marketing channels and tools in combination: _____ channels focus on any way a business communicates a message to its desired market, or the market in general. A _____ tool can be anything from: advertising, personal selling, direct marketing, sponsorship, communication, and promotion to public relations.

Exam Probability: **Medium**

14. *Answer choices:*

(see index for correct answer)

- a. Character
- b. information systems assessment
- c. Marketing communication
- d. hierarchical perspective

Guidance: level 1

:: Credit cards ::

The _____ Company, also known as Amex, is an American multinational financial services corporation headquartered in Three World Financial Center in New York City. The company was founded in 1850 and is one of the 30 components of the Dow Jones Industrial Average. The company is best known for its charge card, credit card, and traveler's cheque businesses.

Exam Probability: **Medium**

15. *Answer choices:*

(see index for correct answer)

- a. Card scheme
- b. Credit card
- c. InteliSpend Prepaid Solutions
- d. American Express

:: Advertising techniques ::

In promotion and of advertising, a _____ or show consists of a person's written or spoken statement extolling the virtue of a product. The term " _____ " most commonly applies to the sales-pitches attributed to ordinary citizens, whereas the word "endorsement" usually applies to pitches by celebrities. _____ s can be part of communal marketing. Sometimes, the cartoon character can be a _____ in a commercial.

Exam Probability: **Medium**

16. *Answer choices:*

(see index for correct answer)

- a. Repetition variation
- b. FAST marketing
- c. Debranding
- d. Hard sell

:: ::

_____ is the process of making predictions of the future based on past and present data and most commonly by analysis of trends. A commonplace example might be estimation of some variable of interest at some specified future date. Prediction is a similar, but more general term. Both might refer to formal statistical methods employing time series, cross-sectional or longitudinal data, or alternatively to less formal judgmental methods. Usage can differ between areas of application: for example, in hydrology the terms "forecast" and "_____" are sometimes reserved for estimates of values at certain specific future times, while the term "prediction" is used for more general estimates, such as the number of times floods will occur over a long period.

Exam Probability: **Low**

17. *Answer choices:*

(see index for correct answer)

- a. corporate values
- b. Sarbanes-Oxley act of 2002
- c. Forecasting
- d. information systems assessment

Guidance: level 1

:: ::

_____ is the provision of service to customers before, during and after a purchase. The perception of success of such interactions is dependent on employees "who can adjust themselves to the personality of the guest".

_____ concerns the priority an organization assigns to _____ relative to components such as product innovation and pricing. In this sense, an organization that values good _____ may spend more money in training employees than the average organization or may proactively interview customers for feedback.

Exam Probability: **Medium**

18. *Answer choices:*

(see index for correct answer)

- a. deep-level diversity
- b. similarity-attraction theory
- c. Customer service
- d. surface-level diversity

Guidance: level 1

:: ::

The _____ is a U.S. business-focused, English-language international daily newspaper based in New York City. The Journal, along with its Asian and European editions, is published six days a week by Dow Jones & Company, a division of News Corp. The newspaper is published in the broadsheet format and online. The Journal has been printed continuously since its inception on July 8, 1889, by Charles Dow, Edward Jones, and Charles Bergstresser.

19. *Answer choices:*

(see index for correct answer)

- a. Wall Street Journal
- b. imperative
- c. information systems assessment
- d. Character

Guidance: level 1

:: Communication design ::

An _____ is a series of advertisement messages that share a single idea and theme which make up an integrated marketing communication . An IMC is a platform in which a group of people can group their ideas, beliefs, and concepts into one large media base. _____ s utilize diverse media channels over a particular time frame and target identified audiences.

Exam Probability: **High**

20. *Answer choices:*

(see index for correct answer)

- a. Alex Trochut
- b. European Design Award

- c. Ellen Lupton
- d. Advertising campaign

Guidance: level 1

:: Promotion and marketing communications ::

_____ is one of the elements of the promotional mix. . _____ uses both media and non-media marketing communications for a pre-determined, limited time to increase consumer demand, stimulate market demand or improve product availability. Examples include contests, coupons, freebies, loss leaders, point of purchase displays, premiums, prizes, product samples, and rebates.

Exam Probability: **High**

21. *Answer choices:*
(see index for correct answer)

- a. Trade promotion management
- b. The Best Job In The World
- c. Sales letter
- d. Sales promotion

Guidance: level 1

:: ::

A _____ or sample _____ is a single measure of some attribute of a sample . It is calculated by applying a function to the values of the items of the sample, which are known together as a set of data.

Exam Probability: **Low**

22. *Answer choices:*

(see index for correct answer)

- a. imperative
- b. surface-level diversity
- c. Statistic
- d. personal values

Guidance: level 1

:: ::

_____ are interactive computer-mediated technologies that facilitate the creation and sharing of information, ideas, career interests and other forms of expression via virtual communities and networks. The variety of stand-alone and built-in _____ services currently available introduces challenges of definition; however, there are some common features.

Exam Probability: **High**

23. *Answer choices:*

(see index for correct answer)

- a. empathy
- b. Social media
- c. hierarchical
- d. information systems assessment

Guidance: level 1

:: Marketing ::

_____ uses different marketing channels and tools in combination: Marketing communication channels focus on any way a business communicates a message to its desired market, or the market in general. A marketing communication tool can be anything from: advertising, personal selling, direct marketing, sponsorship, communication, and promotion to public relations.

Exam Probability: **High**

24. *Answer choices:*

(see index for correct answer)

- a. Hakan Okay
- b. Blind credential
- c. Servicescape
- d. Marketing communications

:: Management ::

In business, a _____ is the attribute that allows an organization to outperform its competitors. A _____ may include access to natural resources, such as high-grade ores or a low-cost power source, highly skilled labor, geographic location, high entry barriers, and access to new technology.

Exam Probability: **Low**

25. *Answer choices:*

(see index for correct answer)

- a. Certified Energy Manager
- b. Behavioral risk management
- c. Industry or market research
- d. Supply chain network

:: Promotion and marketing communications ::

Advertising mail, also known as _____ , junk mail , mailshot or admail, is the delivery of advertising material to recipients of postal mail. The delivery of advertising mail forms a large and growing service for many postal services, and direct-mail marketing forms a significant portion of the direct marketing industry. Some organizations attempt to help people opt out of receiving advertising mail, in many cases motivated by a concern over its negative environmental impact.

Exam Probability: **High**

26. *Answer choices:*

(see index for correct answer)

- a. Aisle411
- b. Milk Queen
- c. Direct mail
- d. Keep Calm and Carry On

Guidance: level 1

:: Graphic design ::

An _____ is an artifact that depicts visual perception, such as a photograph or other two-dimensional picture, that resembles a subject—usually a physical object—and thus provides a depiction of it. In the context of signal processing, an _____ is a distributed amplitude of color.

Exam Probability: **Medium**

27. *Answer choices:*

(see index for correct answer)

- a. Transformation playing card
- b. Klim Type Foundry
- c. Image
- d. Gestalten

Guidance: level 1

:: Commerce ::

A _____ is a company or individual that purchases goods or services with the intention of selling them rather than consuming or using them. This is usually done for profit . One example can be found in the industry of telecommunications, where companies buy excess amounts of transmission capacity or call time from other carriers and resell it to smaller carriers.

Exam Probability: **High**

28. *Answer choices:*

(see index for correct answer)

- a. Custom house
- b. Reseller
- c. Oxygen bar
- d. Too cheap to meter

:: Management occupations ::

_____ ship is the process of designing, launching and running a new business, which is often initially a small business. The people who create these businesses are called _____ s.

Exam Probability: **High**

29. *Answer choices:*

(see index for correct answer)

- a. Chief business development officer
- b. Legislator
- c. Exempt secretary
- d. Entrepreneur

:: Supply chain management ::

The _____ is a barcode symbology that is widely used in the United States, Canada, United Kingdom, Australia, New Zealand, in Europe and other countries for tracking trade items in stores.

30. *Answer choices:*

(see index for correct answer)

- a. Symphony EYC
- b. Universal Product Code
- c. Dell Theory of Conflict Prevention
- d. Institute for Supply Management

Guidance: level 1

:: Data management ::

In computing, a _____ , also known as an enterprise _____ , is a system used for reporting and data analysis, and is considered a core component of business intelligence. DWs are central repositories of integrated data from one or more disparate sources. They store current and historical data in one single place that are used for creating analytical reports for workers throughout the enterprise.

Exam Probability: **Medium**

31. *Answer choices:*

(see index for correct answer)

- a. Data access
- b. Data warehouse

- c. Junction table
- d. Wiping

Guidance: level 1

:: ::

_____ refers to a diverse array of media technologies that reach a large audience via mass communication. The technologies through which this communication takes place include a variety of outlets.

Exam Probability: **Medium**

32. *Answer choices:*

(see index for correct answer)

- a. personal values
- b. Sarbanes-Oxley act of 2002
- c. Mass media
- d. similarity-attraction theory

Guidance: level 1

:: ::

In business and engineering, new _____ covers the complete process of bringing a new product to market. A central aspect of NPD is product design, along with various business considerations. New _____ is described broadly as the transformation of a market opportunity into a product available for sale. The product can be tangible or intangible , though sometimes services and other processes are distinguished from "products." NPD requires an understanding of customer needs and wants, the competitive environment, and the nature of the market.Cost, time and quality are the main variables that drive customer needs. Aiming at these three variables, innovative companies develop continuous practices and strategies to better satisfy customer requirements and to increase their own market share by a regular development of new products. There are many uncertainties and challenges which companies must face throughout the process. The use of best practices and the elimination of barriers to communication are the main concerns for the management of the NPD .

Exam Probability: **High**

33. *Answer choices:*

(see index for correct answer)

- a. imperative
- b. Product development
- c. deep-level diversity
- d. personal values

Guidance: level 1

:: Marketing ::

A _____ is something that is necessary for an organism to live a healthy life. _____ s are distinguished from wants in that, in the case of a _____ , a deficiency causes a clear adverse outcome: a dysfunction or death. In other words, a _____ is something required for a safe, stable and healthy life while a want is a desire, wish or aspiration. When _____ s or wants are backed by purchasing power, they have the potential to become economic demands.

Exam Probability: **Medium**

34. *Answer choices:*

(see index for correct answer)

- a. Need
- b. All-commodity volume
- c. Digital omnivore
- d. Breakthrough Moments

Guidance: level 1

:: ::

In _____ relations and communication science, _____ s are groups of individual people, and the _____ is the totality of such groupings. This is a different concept to the sociological concept of the Öffentlichkeit or _____ sphere. The concept of a _____ has also been defined in political science, psychology, marketing, and advertising. In _____ relations and communication science, it is one of the more ambiguous concepts in the field. Although it has definitions in the theory of the field that have been formulated from the early 20th century onwards, it has suffered in more recent years from being blurred, as a result of conflation of the idea of a _____ with the notions of audience, market segment, community, constituency, and stakeholder.

Exam Probability: **High**

35. *Answer choices:*

(see index for correct answer)

- a. personal values
- b. interpersonal communication
- c. Public
- d. hierarchical

Guidance: level 1

:: Management accounting ::

_____ s are costs that change as the quantity of the good or service that a business produces changes. _____ s are the sum of marginal costs over all units produced. They can also be considered normal costs. Fixed costs and _____ s make up the two components of total cost. Direct costs are costs that can easily be associated with a particular cost object. However, not all _____ s are direct costs. For example, variable manufacturing overhead costs are _____ s that are indirect costs, not direct costs. _____ s are sometimes called unit-level costs as they vary with the number of units produced.

Exam Probability: **Medium**

36. *Answer choices:*

(see index for correct answer)

- a. Variable cost
- b. Double counting
- c. Fixed cost
- d. Backflush accounting

Guidance: level 1

:: ::

_____ consists of using generic or ad hoc methods in an orderly manner to find solutions to problems. Some of the problem-solving techniques developed and used in philosophy, artificial intelligence, computer science, engineering, mathematics, or medicine are related to mental problem-solving techniques studied in psychology.

37. *Answer choices:*

(see index for correct answer)

- a. similarity-attraction theory
- b. Character
- c. Sarbanes-Oxley act of 2002
- d. Problem Solving

Guidance: level 1

:: Stock market ::

_____ is freedom from, or resilience against, potential harm caused by others. Beneficiaries of _____ may be of persons and social groups, objects and institutions, ecosystems or any other entity or phenomenon vulnerable to unwanted change by its environment.

Exam Probability: **Medium**

38. *Answer choices:*

(see index for correct answer)

- a. Pattern day trader
- b. FTSE Global Equity Index Series
- c. Stock market bubble

- d. French auction

Guidance: level 1

:: ::

_____ is the means to see, hear, or become aware of something or someone through our fundamental senses. The term _____ derives from the Latin word perceptio, and is the organization, identification, and interpretation of sensory information in order to represent and understand the presented information, or the environment.

Exam Probability: **High**

39. *Answer choices:*

(see index for correct answer)

- a. hierarchical
- b. hierarchical perspective
- c. corporate values
- d. levels of analysis

Guidance: level 1

:: ::

In logic and philosophy, an _____ is a series of statements , called the premises or premisses , intended to determine the degree of truth of another statement, the conclusion. The logical form of an _____ in a natural language can be represented in a symbolic formal language, and independently of natural language formally defined " _____ s" can be made in math and computer science.

Exam Probability: **High**

40. *Answer choices:*

(see index for correct answer)

- a. levels of analysis
- b. Argument
- c. interpersonal communication
- d. deep-level diversity

Guidance: level 1

:: ::

An _____ is a contingent motivator. Traditional _____ s are extrinsic motivators which reward actions to yield a desired outcome. The effectiveness of traditional _____ s has changed as the needs of Western society have evolved. While the traditional _____ model is effective when there is a defined procedure and goal for a task, Western society started to require a higher volume of critical thinkers, so the traditional model became less effective. Institutions are now following a trend in implementing strategies that rely on intrinsic motivations rather than the extrinsic motivations that the traditional _____ s foster.

Exam Probability: **Medium**

41. *Answer choices:*

(see index for correct answer)

- a. hierarchical perspective
- b. information systems assessment
- c. Character
- d. Incentive

Guidance: level 1

___

:: Direct marketing ::

_____ is a form of direct marketing using databases of customers or potential customers to generate personalized communications in order to promote a product or service for marketing purposes. The method of communication can be any addressable medium, as in direct marketing.

42. *Answer choices:*

(see index for correct answer)

- a. Forced Free Trial
- b. The Cobra Group
- c. Drayton Bird
- d. Ginsu

Guidance: level 1

:: Direct marketing ::

_____ is a method of direct marketing in which a salesperson solicits prospective customers to buy products or services, either over the phone or through a subsequent face to face or Web conferencing appointment scheduled during the call. _____ can also include recorded sales pitches programmed to be played over the phone via automatic dialing.

Exam Probability: **High**

43. *Answer choices:*

(see index for correct answer)

- a. Flyer
- b. Solo Ads

- c. Forced Free Trial
- d. Telemarketing

:: Marketing ::

_____ is the process of using surveys to evaluate consumer acceptance of a new product idea prior to the introduction of a product to the market. It is important not to confuse _____ with advertising testing, brand testing and packaging testing; as is sometimes done. _____ focuses on the basic product idea, without the embellishments and puffery inherent in advertising.

Exam Probability: **Low**

44. *Answer choices:*

(see index for correct answer)

- a. Jobbing house
- b. Food marketing
- c. Concept testing
- d. Corporate capabilities package

:: ::

_____ is a means of protection from financial loss. It is a form of risk management, primarily used to hedge against the risk of a contingent or uncertain loss

Exam Probability: **High**

45. *Answer choices:*

- a. corporate values
- b. process perspective
- c. surface-level diversity
- d. personal values

Guidance: level 1

:: Basic financial concepts ::

_____ is a sustained increase in the general price level of goods and services in an economy over a period of time. When the general price level rises, each unit of currency buys fewer goods and services; consequently, _____ reflects a reduction in the purchasing power per unit of money a loss of real value in the medium of exchange and unit of account within the economy. The measure of _____ is the _____ rate, the annualized percentage change in a general price index, usually the consumer price index, over time. The opposite of _____ is deflation.

Exam Probability: **Low**

46. *Answer choices:*

(see index for correct answer)

- a. Inflation
- b. Deflation
- c. Tax shield
- d. Future-oriented

Guidance: level 1

:: ::

_____ is a term frequently used in marketing. It is a measure of how products and services supplied by a company meet or surpass customer expectation. _____ is defined as "the number of customers, or percentage of total customers, whose reported experience with a firm, its products, or its services exceeds specified satisfaction goals."

Exam Probability: **Medium**

47. *Answer choices:*

(see index for correct answer)

- a. Customer satisfaction
- b. hierarchical
- c. functional perspective
- d. similarity-attraction theory

:: Business ::

The seller, or the provider of the goods or services, completes a sale in response to an acquisition, appropriation, requisition or a direct interaction with the buyer at the point of sale. There is a passing of title of the item, and the settlement of a price, in which agreement is reached on a price for which transfer of ownership of the item will occur. The seller, not the purchaser typically executes the sale and it may be completed prior to the obligation of payment. In the case of indirect interaction, a person who sells goods or service on behalf of the owner is known as a _____ man or _____ woman or _____ person, but this often refers to someone selling goods in a store/shop, in which case other terms are also common, including _____ clerk, shop assistant, and retail clerk.

Exam Probability: **Low**

48. *Answer choices:*

(see index for correct answer)

- a. Sales
- b. Street marketing
- c. Open-book contract
- d. Business

:: Organizational structure ::

An _____ defines how activities such as task allocation, coordination, and supervision are directed toward the achievement of organizational aims.

Exam Probability: **High**

49. *Answer choices:*

(see index for correct answer)

- a. Unorganisation
- b. Automated Bureaucracy
- c. Organization of the New York City Police Department
- d. Followership

Guidance: level 1

:: ::

_____ is the production of products for use or sale using labour and machines, tools, chemical and biological processing, or formulation. The term may refer to a range of human activity, from handicraft to high tech, but is most commonly applied to industrial design, in which raw materials are transformed into finished goods on a large scale. Such finished goods may be sold to other manufacturers for the production of other, more complex products, such as aircraft, household appliances, furniture, sports equipment or automobiles, or sold to wholesalers, who in turn sell them to retailers, who then sell them to end users and consumers.

50. *Answer choices:*

(see index for correct answer)

- a. open system
- b. surface-level diversity
- c. deep-level diversity
- d. Manufacturing

Guidance: level 1

:: Business planning ::

_____ is an organization's process of defining its strategy, or direction, and making decisions on allocating its resources to pursue this strategy. It may also extend to control mechanisms for guiding the implementation of the strategy. _____ became prominent in corporations during the 1960s and remains an important aspect of strategic management. It is executed by strategic planners or strategists, who involve many parties and research sources in their analysis of the organization and its relationship to the environment in which it competes.

51. *Answer choices:*

(see index for correct answer)

- a. Strategic planning
- b. Community Futures
- c. operational planning
- d. Open Options Corporation

Guidance: level 1

:: Direct selling ::

_____ consists of two main business models: single-level marketing, in which a direct seller makes money by buying products from a parent organization and selling them directly to customers, and multi-level marketing , in which the direct seller may earn money from both direct sales to customers and by sponsoring new direct sellers and potentially earning a commission from their efforts.

Exam Probability: **Medium**

52. *Answer choices:*

(see index for correct answer)

- a. The Longaberger Company
- b. CVSL
- c. Direct selling
- d. Direct Selling Association

Guidance: level 1

:: Direct marketing ::

_____ is a form of advertising where organizations communicate directly to customers through a variety of media including cell phone text messaging, email, websites, online adverts, database marketing, fliers, catalog distribution, promotional letters, targeted television, newspapers, magazine advertisements, and outdoor advertising. Among practitioners, it is also known as direct response marketing.

Exam Probability: **Low**

53. *Answer choices:*

(see index for correct answer)

- a. Mailing list
- b. Book of the Month Club
- c. A Common Reader
- d. Direct marketing

Guidance: level 1

:: ::

_____ , also referred to as orthostasis, is a human position in which the body is held in an upright position and supported only by the feet.

Exam Probability: **Low**

54. *Answer choices:*

(see index for correct answer)

- a. imperative
- b. personal values
- c. surface-level diversity
- d. functional perspective

Guidance: level 1

:: Product management ::

`_____` is a phrase used in the marketing industry which describes the value of having a well-known brand name, based on the idea that the owner of a well-known brand name can generate more revenue simply from brand recognition; that is from products with that brand name than from products with a less well known name, as consumers believe that a product with a well-known name is better than products with less well-known names.

Exam Probability: **High**

55. *Answer choices:*

(see index for correct answer)

- a. Trademark
- b. Product information
- c. Discontinuation
- d. Brand equity

:: Project management ::

_____ is the right to exercise power, which can be formalized by a state and exercised by way of judges, appointed executives of government, or the ecclesiastical or priestly appointed representatives of a God or other deities.

Exam Probability: **Low**

56. *Answer choices:*

(see index for correct answer)

- a. Effort management
- b. Cost-benefit
- c. Authority
- d. 10,000ft

:: Brokered programming ::

An _____ is a form of television commercial, which generally includes a toll-free telephone number or website. Most often used as a form of direct response television , long-form _____ s are typically 28:30 or 58:30 minutes in length. _____ s are also known as paid programming . This phenomenon started in the United States, where _____ s were typically shown overnight , outside peak prime time hours for commercial broadcasters. Some television stations chose to air _____ s as an alternative to the former practice of signing off. Some channels air _____ s 24 hours. Some stations also choose to air _____ s during the daytime hours mostly on weekends to fill in for unscheduled network or syndicated programming. By 2009, most _____ spending in the U.S. occurred during the early morning, daytime and evening hours, or in the afternoon. Stations in most countries around the world have instituted similar media structures. The _____ industry is worth over $200 billion.

Exam Probability: **High**

57. *Answer choices:*

(see index for correct answer)

- a. One Magnificent Morning
- b. Brokered programming
- c. Toonzai
- d. Leased access

Guidance: level 1

:: ::

_____ is a concept of English common law and is a necessity for simple contracts but not for special contracts . The concept has been adopted by other common law jurisdictions, including the US.

Exam Probability: **Medium**

58. *Answer choices:*

(see index for correct answer)

- a. information systems assessment
- b. open system
- c. Consideration
- d. surface-level diversity

Guidance: level 1

:: Stock market ::

The _____ of a corporation is all of the shares into which ownership of the corporation is divided. In American English, the shares are commonly known as "_____ s". A single share of the _____ represents fractional ownership of the corporation in proportion to the total number of shares. This typically entitles the _____ holder to that fraction of the company's earnings, proceeds from liquidation of assets , or voting power, often dividing these up in proportion to the amount of money each _____ holder has invested. Not all _____ is necessarily equal, as certain classes of _____ may be issued for example without voting rights, with enhanced voting rights, or with a certain priority to receive profits or liquidation proceeds before or after other classes of shareholders.

59. *Answer choices:*

(see index for correct answer)

- a. Microcap
- b. American depositary receipt
- c. Stock
- d. Beneficial ownership

Guidance: level 1

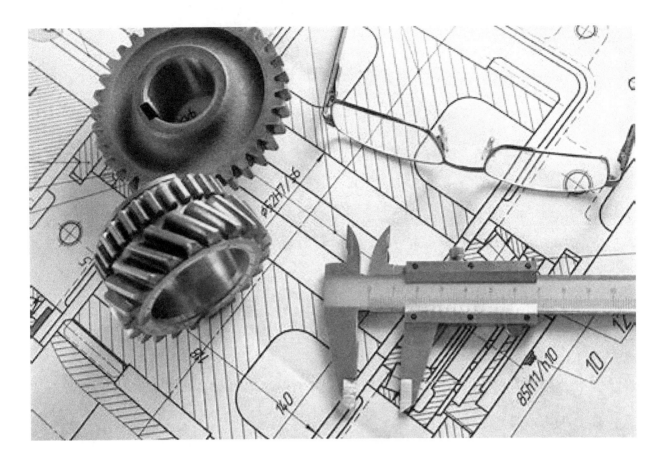

Manufacturing

Manufacturing is the production of merchandise for use or sale using labor and machines, tools, chemical and biological processing, or formulation. The term may refer to a range of human activity, from handicraft to high tech, but is most commonly applied to industrial design , in which raw materials are transformed into finished goods on a large scale. Such finished goods may be sold to other manufacturers for the production of other, more complex products, such as aircraft, household appliances, furniture, sports equipment or automobiles, or sold to wholesalers, who in turn sell them to retailers, who then sell them to end users and consumers.

:: Quality control tools ::

A _____ is a type of diagram that represents an algorithm, workflow or process. _____ can also be defined as a diagramatic representation of an algorithm .

Exam Probability: **High**

1. *Answer choices:*

(see index for correct answer)

- a. EVOP
- b. Flowchart
- c. C-chart
- d. Scatter plot

Guidance: level 1

:: Evaluation ::

_____ is a way of preventing mistakes and defects in manufactured products and avoiding problems when delivering products or services to customers; which ISO 9000 defines as "part of quality management focused on providing confidence that quality requirements will be fulfilled". This defect prevention in _____ differs subtly from defect detection and rejection in quality control and has been referred to as a shift left since it focuses on quality earlier in the process .

Exam Probability: **Low**

2. *Answer choices:*

(see index for correct answer)

- a. Joint Committee on Standards for Educational Evaluation
- b. Educational evaluation
- c. Quality assurance
- d. CESG Claims Tested Mark

Guidance: level 1

:: Knowledge representation ::

_____ s are causal diagrams created by Kaoru Ishikawa that show the causes of a specific event.

Exam Probability: **Medium**

3. *Answer choices:*

(see index for correct answer)

- a. Knowledge integration
- b. Is-a
- c. Yale shooting problem
- d. Ishikawa diagram

Guidance: level 1

:: Time management ::

_____ is the process of planning and exercising conscious control of time spent on specific activities, especially to increase effectiveness, efficiency, and productivity. It involves a juggling act of various demands upon a person relating to work, social life, family, hobbies, personal interests and commitments with the finiteness of time. Using time effectively gives the person "choice" on spending/managing activities at their own time and expediency.

Exam Probability: **Medium**

4. *Answer choices:*

(see index for correct answer)

- a. Time allocation
- b. Getting Things Done
- c. Time management
- d. waiting room

Guidance: level 1

:: Casting (manufacturing) ::

A _____ is a regularity in the world, man-made design, or abstract ideas. As such, the elements of a _____ repeat in a predictable manner. A geometric _____ is a kind of _____ formed of geometric shapes and typically repeated like a wallpaper design.

Exam Probability: **High**

5. *Answer choices:*

(see index for correct answer)

- a. AutoCAST
- b. Permanent mold casting
- c. Full-mold casting
- d. Pattern

Guidance: level 1

:: Lean manufacturing ::

_____ is a scheduling system for lean manufacturing and just-in-time manufacturing . Taiichi Ohno, an industrial engineer at Toyota, developed _____ to improve manufacturing efficiency. _____ is one method to achieve JIT. The system takes its name from the cards that track production within a factory. For many in the automotive sector, _____ is known as the "Toyota nameplate system" and as such the term is not used by some other automakers.

Exam Probability: **Low**

6. *Answer choices:*

(see index for correct answer)

- a. Kanban
- b. Continual improvement process
- c. Statistical thinking
- d. The Machine That Changed the World

Guidance: level 1

:: Quality management ::

_____ ensures that an organization, product or service is consistent. It has four main components: quality planning, quality assurance, quality control and quality improvement. _____ is focused not only on product and service quality, but also on the means to achieve it. _____ , therefore, uses quality assurance and control of processes as well as products to achieve more consistent quality. What a customer wants and is willing to pay for it determines quality. It is written or unwritten commitment to a known or unknown consumer in the market . Thus, quality can be defined as fitness for intended use or, in other words, how well the product performs its intended function

Exam Probability: **Medium**

7. *Answer choices:*

(see index for correct answer)

- a. Quality management
- b. Det Norske Veritas

- c. Good Clinical Laboratory Practice
- d. Bureau Veritas

Guidance: level 1

:: Supply chain management ::

A _____ is a type of auction in which the traditional roles of buyer
and seller are reversed. Thus, there is one buyer and many potential sellers.
In an ordinary auction , buyers compete to obtain goods or services by offering
increasingly higher prices. In contrast, in a _____ , the sellers compete
to obtain business from the buyer and prices will typically decrease as the
sellers underbid each other.

Exam Probability: **High**

8. *Answer choices:*

(see index for correct answer)

- a. Pharmacode
- b. Dealer Business System
- c. Retalix
- d. Cross-border leasing

Guidance: level 1

:: Gas technologies ::

A _____ is a rotary mechanical device that extracts energy from a fluid flow and converts it into useful work. The work produced by a _____ can be used for generating electrical power when combined with a generator. A _____ is a turbomachine with at least one moving part called a rotor assembly, which is a shaft or drum with blades attached. Moving fluid acts on the blades so that they move and impart rotational energy to the rotor. Early _____ examples are windmills and waterwheels.

Exam Probability: **Medium**

9. *Answer choices:*

(see index for correct answer)

- a. Supercritical carbon dioxide
- b. Wet scrubber
- c. Pressure vessel
- d. Turbine

Guidance: level 1

:: Management ::

_____ is an iterative four-step management method used in business for the control and continuous improvement of processes and products. It is also known as the Deming circle/cycle/wheel, the Shewhart cycle, the control circle/cycle, or plan–do–study–act . Another version of this _____ cycle is O _____ . The added "O" stands for observation or as some versions say: "Observe the current condition." This emphasis on observation and current condition has currency with the literature on lean manufacturing and the Toyota Production System. The _____ cycle, with Ishikawa's changes, can be traced back to S. Mizuno of the Tokyo Institute of Technology in 1959.

Exam Probability: **High**

10. *Answer choices:*

(see index for correct answer)

- a. PDCA
- b. Marketing science
- c. Product life-cycle management
- d. Process capability

Guidance: level 1

:: Occupational safety and health ::

_____ is a chemical element with symbol Pb and atomic number 82. It is a heavy metal that is denser than most common materials. _____ is soft and malleable, and also has a relatively low melting point. When freshly cut, _____ is silvery with a hint of blue; it tarnishes to a dull gray color when exposed to air. _____ has the highest atomic number of any stable element and three of its isotopes are endpoints of major nuclear decay chains of heavier elements.

Exam Probability: **Low**

11. *Answer choices:*

(see index for correct answer)

- a. Occupational hygiene
- b. Chromium
- c. Material safety data sheet
- d. Occupational Safety and Health Professional Day

Guidance: level 1

:: E-commerce ::

_____ is the business-to-business or business-to-consumer or business-to-government purchase and sale of supplies, work, and services through the Internet as well as other information and networking systems, such as electronic data interchange and enterprise resource planning.

Exam Probability: **Low**

12. *Answer choices:*

(see index for correct answer)

- a. ICOCA
- b. E-commerce payment system
- c. Very
- d. Extended Validation Certificate

Guidance: level 1

:: Quality ::

The _____ , formerly the _____ Control , is a knowledge-based global community of quality professionals, with nearly 80,000 members dedicated to promoting and advancing quality tools, principles, and practices in their workplaces and communities.

Exam Probability: **High**

13. *Answer choices:*

(see index for correct answer)

- a. Root cause
- b. American Society for Quality
- c. Quality of life
- d. Ringtest

:: Quality assurance ::

Organizations that issue credentials or certify third parties against
official standards are themselves formally accredited by _____ bodies ;
hence they are sometimes known as "accredited certification bodies". The
_____ process ensures that their certification practices are acceptable,
typically meaning that they are competent to test and certify third parties,
behave ethically and employ suitable quality assurance.

Exam Probability: **Medium**

14. *Answer choices:*

(see index for correct answer)

- a. European Association for Quality Assurance in Higher Education
- b. TestLink
- c. Accreditation
- d. Static testing

:: ::

A _____ is a covering that is applied to the surface of an object, usually referred to as the substrate. The purpose of applying the _____ may be decorative, functional, or both. The _____ itself may be an all-over _____ , completely covering the substrate, or it may only cover parts of the substrate. An example of all of these types of _____ is a product label on many drinks bottles- one side has an all-over functional _____ and the other side has one or more decorative _____ s in an appropriate pattern to form the words and images.

Exam Probability: **High**

15. *Answer choices:*

(see index for correct answer)

- a. information systems assessment
- b. surface-level diversity
- c. deep-level diversity
- d. Coating

Guidance: level 1

:: Production and manufacturing ::

_____ is a comprehensive and rigorous industrial process by which a previously sold, leased, used, worn or non-functional product or part is returned to a 'like-new' or 'better-than-new' condition, from both a quality and performance perspective, through a controlled, reproducible and sustainable process.

16. *Answer choices:*

(see index for correct answer)

- a. Fieldbus
- b. Technological theory of social production
- c. Highly accelerated life test
- d. Remanufacturing

Guidance: level 1

:: Metal forming ::

_____ is a type of motion that combines rotation and translation of that object with respect to a surface , such that, if ideal conditions exist, the two are in contact with each other without sliding.

Exam Probability: **Low**

17. *Answer choices:*

(see index for correct answer)

- a. Incremental sheet forming
- b. Draw bench
- c. Knurling
- d. Hemming and seaming

:: Inventory ::

The _____ is the level of inventory which triggers an action to replenish that particular inventory stock. It is a minimum amount of an item which a firm holds in stock, such that, when stock falls to this amount, the item must be reordered. It is normally calculated as the forecast usage during the replenishment lead time plus safety stock. In the EOQ model, it was assumed that there is no time lag between ordering and procuring of materials. Therefore the _____ for replenishing the stocks occurs at that level when the inventory level drops to zero and because instant delivery by suppliers, the stock level bounce back.

Exam Probability: **Low**

18. *Answer choices:*

(see index for correct answer)

- a. Consignment stock
- b. Reorder point
- c. Inventory bounce
- d. Stock obsolescence

:: Sensitivity analysis ::

_____ is the study of how the uncertainty in the output of a mathematical model or system can be divided and allocated to different sources of uncertainty in its inputs. A related practice is uncertainty analysis, which has a greater focus on uncertainty quantification and propagation of uncertainty; ideally, uncertainty and _____ should be run in tandem.

Exam Probability: **Low**

19. *Answer choices:*

(see index for correct answer)

- a. Tornado diagram
- b. Variance-based sensitivity analysis
- c. Fourier amplitude sensitivity testing
- d. Elementary effects method

Guidance: level 1

:: Business planning ::

_____ is an organization's process of defining its strategy, or direction, and making decisions on allocating its resources to pursue this strategy. It may also extend to control mechanisms for guiding the implementation of the strategy. _____ became prominent in corporations during the 1960s and remains an important aspect of strategic management. It is executed by strategic planners or strategists, who involve many parties and research sources in their analysis of the organization and its relationship to the environment in which it competes.

20. *Answer choices:*

(see index for correct answer)

- a. Gap analysis
- b. Exit planning
- c. operational planning
- d. Customer Demand Planning

Guidance: level 1

:: Building materials ::

_____ is an alloy of iron and carbon, and sometimes other elements. Because of its high tensile strength and low cost, it is a major component used in buildings, infrastructure, tools, ships, automobiles, machines, appliances, and weapons.

Exam Probability: **High**

21. *Answer choices:*

(see index for correct answer)

- a. Earthen plaster
- b. Steel
- c. Meleke

- d. Geofoam

Guidance: level 1

:: ::

The _____ is a project plan of how the production budget will be spent over a given timescale, for every phase of a business project.

Exam Probability: **Medium**

22. *Answer choices:*

(see index for correct answer)

- a. Production schedule
- b. functional perspective
- c. interpersonal communication
- d. hierarchical

Guidance: level 1

:: Auditing ::

_____ is the process of systematic examination of a quality system carried out by an internal or external _____ or or an audit team. It is an important part of an organization's quality management system and is a key element in the ISO quality system standard, ISO 9001.

Exam Probability: **Low**

23. *Answer choices:*

(see index for correct answer)

- a. Audit evidence
- b. RSM International
- c. International Register of Certificated Auditors
- d. Quality audit

Guidance: level 1

:: Mereology ::

_____ , in the abstract, is what belongs to or with something, whether as an attribute or as a component of said thing. In the context of this article, it is one or more components , whether physical or incorporeal, of a person's estate; or so belonging to, as in being owned by, a person or jointly a group of people or a legal entity like a corporation or even a society. Depending on the nature of the _____ , an owner of _____ has the right to consume, alter, share, redefine, rent, mortgage, pawn, sell, exchange, transfer, give away or destroy it, or to exclude others from doing these things, as well as to perhaps abandon it; whereas regardless of the nature of the _____ , the owner thereof has the right to properly use it , or at the very least exclusively keep it.

Exam Probability: **High**

24. *Answer choices:*

(see index for correct answer)

- a. Mereotopology
- b. Mereological nihilism
- c. Property
- d. Simple

Guidance: level 1

:: Quality management ::

In quality management system, a _____ is a document developed by management to express the directive of the top management with respect to quality. _____ management is a strategic item.

25. *Answer choices:*

(see index for correct answer)

- a. ISO 9000
- b. Management by wandering around
- c. Regulatory translation
- d. Indian Register Quality Systems

Guidance: level 1

:: Packaging materials ::

_____ is a thin material produced by pressing together moist fibres of cellulose pulp derived from wood, rags or grasses, and drying them into flexible sheets.It is a versatile material with many uses, including writing, printing, packaging, cleaning, decorating, and a number of industrial and construction processes. _____ s are essential in legal or non-legal documentation.

Exam Probability: **High**

26. *Answer choices:*

(see index for correct answer)

- a. EVOH
- b. Glass

- c. Paper
- d. Polymethylpentene

:: Planning ::

_____ is a high level plan to achieve one or more goals under conditions of uncertainty. In the sense of the "art of the general," which included several subsets of skills including tactics, siegecraft, logistics etc., the term came into use in the 6th century C.E. in East Roman terminology, and was translated into Western vernacular languages only in the 18th century. From then until the 20th century, the word " _____ " came to denote "a comprehensive way to try to pursue political ends, including the threat or actual use of force, in a dialectic of wills" in a military conflict, in which both adversaries interact.

Exam Probability: **Low**

27. *Answer choices:*

(see index for correct answer)

- a. Parish plan
- b. Territorialist School
- c. Strategy
- d. Default effect

:: Costs ::

The _____ is computed by dividing the total cost of goods available for sale by the total units available for sale. This gives a weighted-average unit cost that is applied to the units in the ending inventory.

Exam Probability: **High**

28. *Answer choices:*
(see index for correct answer)

- a. Total cost of acquisition
- b. Psychic cost
- c. Average cost
- d. Travel and subsistence

Guidance: level 1

:: Project management ::

A _____ is a type of bar chart that illustrates a project schedule, named after its inventor, Henry Gantt , who designed such a chart around the years 1910–1915. Modern _____ s also show the dependency relationships between activities and current schedule status.

29. *Answer choices:*

(see index for correct answer)

- a. Mandated lead arranger
- b. Gantt chart
- c. Sustainable event management
- d. Trenegy Incorporated

Guidance: level 1

:: Production economics ::

_____ is the joint use of a resource or space. It is also the process of dividing and distributing. In its narrow sense, it refers to joint or alternating use of inherently finite goods, such as a common pasture or a shared residence. Still more loosely, " _____ " can actually mean giving something as an outright gift: for example, to "share" one`s food really means to give some of it as a gift. _____ is a basic component of human interaction, and is responsible for strengthening social ties and ensuring a person`s well-being.

Exam Probability: **High**

30. *Answer choices:*

(see index for correct answer)

- a. Marginal product
- b. Split-off point
- c. Synergy
- d. Sharing

Guidance: level 1

:: Management ::

_____ is the practice of initiating, planning, executing, controlling, and closing the work of a team to achieve specific goals and meet specific success criteria at the specified time.

Exam Probability: **Medium**

31. *Answer choices:*

(see index for correct answer)

- a. Process capability
- b. Project management
- c. Evidence-based management
- d. Local management board

Guidance: level 1

:: Asset ::

In financial accounting, an _____ is any resource owned by the business. Anything tangible or intangible that can be owned or controlled to produce value and that is held by a company to produce positive economic value is an _____ . Simply stated, _____ s represent value of ownership that can be converted into cash . The balance sheet of a firm records the monetary value of the _____ s owned by that firm. It covers money and other valuables belonging to an individual or to a business.

Exam Probability: **Low**

32. *Answer choices:*

(see index for correct answer)

- a. Current asset
- b. Fixed asset

Guidance: level 1

:: Data management ::

_____ refers to a data-driven improvement cycle used for improving, optimizing and stabilizing business processes and designs. The _____ improvement cycle is the core tool used to drive Six Sigma projects. However, _____ is not exclusive to Six Sigma and can be used as the framework for other improvement applications.

Exam Probability: **High**

33. *Answer choices:*

(see index for correct answer)

- a. Automatic data processing equipment
- b. Mobile content management system
- c. Rescentris
- d. Ontology merging

Guidance: level 1

:: Supply chain management ::

_____ is the process of finding and agreeing to terms, and acquiring goods, services, or works from an external source, often via a tendering or competitive bidding process. _____ is used to ensure the buyer receives goods, services, or works at the best possible price when aspects such as quality, quantity, time, and location are compared. Corporations and public bodies often define processes intended to promote fair and open competition for their business while minimizing risks such as exposure to fraud and collusion.

Exam Probability: **High**

34. *Answer choices:*

(see index for correct answer)

- a. Mobile asset management
- b. Channel coordination
- c. Procurement

- d. ERP system

Guidance: level 1

:: Distribution, retailing, and wholesaling ::

The _____ is a distribution channel phenomenon in which forecasts yield supply chain inefficiencies. It refers to increasing swings in inventory in response to shifts in customer demand as one moves further up the supply chain. The concept first appeared in Jay Forrester's Industrial Dynamics and thus it is also known as the Forrester effect. The _____ was named for the way the amplitude of a whip increases down its length. The further from the originating signal, the greater the distortion of the wave pattern. In a similar manner, forecast accuracy decreases as one moves upstream along the supply chain. For example, many consumer goods have fairly consistent consumption at retail but this signal becomes more chaotic and unpredictable as the focus moves away from consumer purchasing behavior.

Exam Probability: **High**

35. *Answer choices:*
(see index for correct answer)

- a. Pallet rack mover
- b. Bullwhip effect
- c. Pallet racking
- d. Key Brand Entertainment

Guidance: level 1

:: Production economics ::

In economics and related disciplines, a _____ is a cost in making any economic trade when participating in a market.

Exam Probability: **Medium**

36. *Answer choices:*

(see index for correct answer)

- a. Industrial production index
- b. Limiting factor
- c. Marginal rate of technical substitution
- d. Transaction cost

Guidance: level 1

:: Monopoly (economics) ::

_____ are "efficiencies formed by variety, not volume". For example, a gas station that sells gasoline can sell soda, milk, baked goods, etc through their customer service representatives and thus achieve gasoline companies _____ .

Exam Probability: **High**

37. *Answer choices:*

(see index for correct answer)

- a. Economies of scope
- b. Public utility
- c. Motion Picture Patents Company
- d. Herfindahl index

Guidance: level 1

:: Production and manufacturing ::

An _____ is a manufacturing process in which parts are added as the semi-finished assembly moves from workstation to workstation where the parts are added in sequence until the final assembly is produced. By mechanically moving the parts to the assembly work and moving the semi-finished assembly from work station to work station, a finished product can be assembled faster and with less labor than by having workers carry parts to a stationary piece for assembly.

Exam Probability: **Medium**

38. *Answer choices:*

(see index for correct answer)

- a. Continuous production
- b. Assembly line
- c. Master production schedule

- d. Verband der Automobilindustrie

Guidance: level 1

:: ::

_____ is the quantity of three-dimensional space enclosed by a closed surface, for example, the space that a substance or shape occupies or contains. _____ is often quantified numerically using the SI derived unit, the cubic metre. The _____ of a container is generally understood to be the capacity of the container; i. e., the amount of fluid that the container could hold, rather than the amount of space the container itself displaces.Three dimensional mathematical shapes are also assigned _____ s. _____ s of some simple shapes, such as regular, straight-edged, and circular shapes can be easily calculated using arithmetic formulas. _____ s of complicated shapes can be calculated with integral calculus if a formula exists for the shape`s boundary. One-dimensional figures and two-dimensional shapes are assigned zero _____ in the three-dimensional space.

Exam Probability: **Medium**

39. *Answer choices:*
(see index for correct answer)

- a. open system
- b. Volume
- c. empathy
- d. levels of analysis

Guidance: level 1

:: Production and manufacturing ::

_____ consists of organization-wide efforts to "install and make permanent climate where employees continuously improve their ability to provide on demand products and services that customers will find of particular value." "Total" emphasizes that departments in addition to production are obligated to improve their operations; "management" emphasizes that executives are obligated to actively manage quality through funding, training, staffing, and goal setting. While there is no widely agreed-upon approach, TQM efforts typically draw heavily on the previously developed tools and techniques of quality control. TQM enjoyed widespread attention during the late 1980s and early 1990s before being overshadowed by ISO 9000, Lean manufacturing, and Six Sigma.

Exam Probability: **Medium**

40. *Answer choices:*

(see index for correct answer)

- a. SERCOS III
- b. Multi-Point Interface
- c. Common Industrial Protocol
- d. Master production schedule

Guidance: level 1

:: Costs ::

In microeconomic theory, the _____ , or alternative cost, of making a particular choice is the value of the most valuable choice out of those that were not taken. In other words, opportunity that will require sacrifices.

Exam Probability: **High**

41. *Answer choices:*

(see index for correct answer)

- a. Sliding scale
- b. Total cost
- c. Opportunity cost
- d. Manufacturing cost

Guidance: level 1

:: Project management ::

A _____ is a professional in the field of project management. _____ s have the responsibility of the planning, procurement and execution of a project, in any undertaking that has a defined scope, defined start and a defined finish; regardless of industry. _____ s are first point of contact for any issues or discrepancies arising from within the heads of various departments in an organization before the problem escalates to higher authorities. Project management is the responsibility of a _____ . This individual seldom participates directly in the activities that produce the end result, but rather strives to maintain the progress, mutual interaction and tasks of various parties in such a way that reduces the risk of overall failure, maximizes benefits, and minimizes costs.

42. *Answer choices:*

(see index for correct answer)

- a. Theory Z of Ouchi
- b. Work package
- c. Changes clause
- d. Project manager

Guidance: level 1

:: Quality awards ::

The _____ recognizes U.S. organizations in the business, health care, education, and nonprofit sectors for performance excellence. The Baldrige Award is the only formal recognition of the performance excellence of both public and private U.S. organizations given by the President of the United States. It is administered by the Baldrige Performance Excellence Program, which is based at and managed by the National Institute of Standards and Technology , an agency of the U.S. Department of Commerce.

Exam Probability: **Medium**

43. *Answer choices:*

(see index for correct answer)

- a. Canada Awards for Excellence

- b. EFQM Excellence Award
- c. Philippine Quality Award
- d. The Deming Cup

Guidance: level 1

:: Production and manufacturing ::

_____ is a concept in purchasing and project management for securing the quality and timely delivery of goods and components.

Exam Probability: **Low**

44. *Answer choices:*

(see index for correct answer)

- a. Production engineering
- b. production control
- c. Six Sigma
- d. Expediting

Guidance: level 1

:: Computer memory companies ::

_____ Corporation is a Japanese multinational conglomerate headquartered in Tokyo, Japan. Its diversified products and services include information technology and communications equipment and systems, electronic components and materials, power systems, industrial and social infrastructure systems, consumer electronics, household appliances, medical equipment, office equipment, as well as lighting and logistics.

Exam Probability: **Low**

45. *Answer choices:*

(see index for correct answer)

- a. Winbond
- b. Mushkin
- c. Toshiba
- d. Wilk Elektronik

Guidance: level 1

:: Management ::

_____ is the identification, evaluation, and prioritization of risks followed by coordinated and economical application of resources to minimize, monitor, and control the probability or impact of unfortunate events or to maximize the realization of opportunities.

Exam Probability: **Medium**

46. *Answer choices:*

(see index for correct answer)

- a. Jarratt report
- b. Balanced scorecard
- c. Functional management
- d. Central administration

Guidance: level 1

:: Manufacturing ::

A _____ is an object used to extend the ability of an individual to modify features of the surrounding environment. Although many animals use simple _____ s, only human beings, whose use of stone _____ s dates back hundreds of millennia, use _____ s to make other _____ s. The set of _____ s needed to perform different tasks that are part of the same activity is called gear or equipment.

Exam Probability: **Medium**

47. *Answer choices:*

(see index for correct answer)

- a. Tool
- b. ANSI/ISA-95
- c. Can seamer
- d. Priming

:: Information technology management ::

The term _____ is used to refer to periods when a system is
unavailable. _____ or outage duration refers to a period of time that a
system fails to provide or perform its primary function. Reliability,
availability, recovery, and unavailability are related concepts. The
unavailability is the proportion of a time-span that a system is unavailable or
offline. This is usually a result of the system failing to function because of
an unplanned event, or because of routine maintenance .

Exam Probability: **Low**

48. *Answer choices:*

(see index for correct answer)

- a. Performance engineering
- b. Run Book Automation
- c. Downtime
- d. Cmdbuild

:: Project management ::

In economics, _____ is the assignment of available resources to various uses. In the context of an entire economy, resources can be allocated by various means, such as markets or central planning.

Exam Probability: **Low**

49. *Answer choices:*

(see index for correct answer)

- a. American Society of Professional Estimators
- b. Doctor of Project Management
- c. Confluence Project Management
- d. Resource allocation

Guidance: level 1

:: Infographics ::

The _____ is a form used to collect data in real time at the location where the data is generated. The data it captures can be quantitative or qualitative. When the information is quantitative, the _____ is sometimes called a tally sheet.

Exam Probability: **Low**

50. *Answer choices:*

(see index for correct answer)

- a. DOT pictograms
- b. Visual.ly
- c. Check sheet
- d. Creately

Guidance: level 1

:: Teams ::

A _____ usually refers to a group of individuals who work together from different geographic locations and rely on communication technology such as email, FAX, and video or voice conferencing services in order to collaborate. The term can also refer to groups or teams that work together asynchronously or across organizational levels. Powell, Piccoli and Ives define _____ s as "groups of geographically, organizationally and/or time dispersed workers brought together by information and telecommunication technologies to accomplish one or more organizational tasks." According to Ale Ebrahim et. al. , _____ s can also be defined as "small temporary groups of geographically, organizationally and/or time dispersed knowledge workers who coordinate their work predominantly with electronic information and communication technologies in order to accomplish one or more organization tasks."

Exam Probability: **Low**

51. *Answer choices:*

(see index for correct answer)

- a. team composition

- b. Team-building

Guidance: level 1

:: Finance ::

_____ is a financial estimate intended to help buyers and owners determine the direct and indirect costs of a product or system. It is a management accounting concept that can be used in full cost accounting or even ecological economics where it includes social costs.

Exam Probability: **High**

52. *Answer choices:*
(see index for correct answer)

- a. Strategic financial management
- b. Debt restructuring
- c. Chartered Financial Planner
- d. Total cost of ownership

Guidance: level 1

:: Industrial processes ::

_____ is a technique involving the condensation of vapors and the return of this condensate to the system from which it originated. It is used in industrial and laboratory distillations. It is also used in chemistry to supply energy to reactions over a long period of time.

Exam Probability: **High**

53. *Answer choices:*

(see index for correct answer)

- a. Copper slag
- b. Reflux
- c. Hoffmann kiln
- d. Deville process

Guidance: level 1

:: Project management ::

Contemporary business and science treat as a _____ any undertaking, carried out individually or collaboratively and possibly involving research or design, that is carefully planned to achieve a particular aim.

Exam Probability: **High**

54. *Answer choices:*

(see index for correct answer)

- a. Cost database
- b. Starmad
- c. American Society of Professional Estimators
- d. Integrated product team

Guidance: level 1

:: Promotion and marketing communications ::

The _____ of American Manufacturers, now ThomasNet, is an online platform for supplier discovery and product sourcing in the US and Canada. It was once known as the "big green books" and "Thomas Registry", and was a multi-volume directory of industrial product information covering 650,000 distributors, manufacturers and service companies within 67,000-plus industrial categories that is now published on ThomasNet.

Exam Probability: **High**

55. *Answer choices:*
(see index for correct answer)

- a. Thomas Register
- b. Blue Chip Stamps
- c. National Consumer Panel
- d. Promotional merchandise

Guidance: level 1

:: Process management ::

When used in the context of communication networks, such as Ethernet or packet radio, _____ or network _____ is the rate of successful message delivery over a communication channel. The data these messages belong to may be delivered over a physical or logical link, or it can pass through a certain network node. _____ is usually measured in bits per second , and sometimes in data packets per second or data packets per time slot.

Exam Probability: **Low**

56. *Answer choices:*
(see index for correct answer)

- a. Process specification
- b. P and R measures
- c. President%27s Quality Award
- d. Proactive contracting

Guidance: level 1

:: Accounting source documents ::

A _____ is a commercial document and first official offer issued by a buyer to a seller indicating types, quantities, and agreed prices for products or services. It is used to control the purchasing of products and services from external suppliers. _____ s can be an essential part of enterprise resource planning system orders.

Exam Probability: **High**

57. *Answer choices:*

(see index for correct answer)

- a. Invoice
- b. Air waybill
- c. Purchase order
- d. Banknote

Guidance: level 1

:: Project management ::

In economics and business decision-making, a sunk cost is a cost that has already been incurred and cannot be recovered.

Exam Probability: **Medium**

58. *Answer choices:*

(see index for correct answer)

- a. Rolling Wave planning
- b. project triangle
- c. Sunk costs
- d. A Guide to the Project Management Body of Knowledge

Guidance: level 1

:: Packaging ::

In work place, _____ or job _____ means good ranking with the hypothesized conception of requirements of a role. There are two types of job _____ s: contextual and task. Task _____ is related to cognitive ability while contextual _____ is dependent upon personality. Task _____ are behavioral roles that are recognized in job descriptions and by remuneration systems, they are directly related to organizational _____, whereas, contextual _____ are value based and additional behavioral roles that are not recognized in job descriptions and covered by compensation; they are extra roles that are indirectly related to organizational _____.
Citizenship _____ like contextual _____ means a set of individual activity/contribution that supports the organizational culture.

Exam Probability: **Medium**

59. *Answer choices:*
(see index for correct answer)

- a. Self-heating food packaging
- b. Performance

- c. Resealable packaging
- d. Twist tie

Guidance: level 1

Commerce

Commerce relates to "the exchange of goods and services, especially on a large scale." It includes legal, economic, political, social, cultural and technological systems that operate in any country or internationally.

:: Credit cards ::

A _____ is a payment card issued to users to enable the cardholder to pay a merchant for goods and services based on the cardholder's promise to the card issuer to pay them for the amounts plus the other agreed charges. The card issuer creates a revolving account and grants a line of credit to the cardholder, from which the cardholder can borrow money for payment to a merchant or as a cash advance.

1. *Answer choices:*

(see index for correct answer)

- a. Fuel card
- b. Credit card
- c. Credit CARD Act of 2009
- d. Visa Inc.

Guidance: level 1

:: ::

In business, overhead or overhead expense refers to an ongoing expense of operating a business. Overheads are the expenditure which cannot be conveniently traced to or identified with any particular cost unit, unlike operating expenses such as raw material and labor. Therefore, overheads cannot be immediately associated with the products or services being offered, thus do not directly generate profits. However, overheads are still vital to business operations as they provide critical support for the business to carry out profit making activities. For example, _____ s such as the rent for a factory allows workers to manufacture products which can then be sold for a profit. Such expenses are incurred for output generally and not for particular work order; e.g., wages paid to watch and ward staff, heating and lighting expenses of factory, etc. Overheads are also very important cost element along with direct materials and direct labor.

2. *Answer choices:*

(see index for correct answer)

- a. functional perspective
- b. Overhead cost
- c. empathy
- d. corporate values

Guidance: level 1

:: ::

A _____ manages, commands, directs, or regulates the behavior of other devices or systems using control loops. It can range from a single home heating controller using a thermostat controlling a domestic boiler to large Industrial _____ s which are used for controlling processes or machines.

Exam Probability: **Low**

3. *Answer choices:*

(see index for correct answer)

- a. personal values
- b. corporate values
- c. Control system
- d. levels of analysis

:: Land value taxation ::

_____ , sometimes referred to as dry _____ , is the solid surface of Earth that is not permanently covered by water. The vast majority of human activity throughout history has occurred in _____ areas that support agriculture, habitat, and various natural resources. Some life forms have developed from predecessor species that lived in bodies of water.

Exam Probability: **High**

4. *Answer choices:*

(see index for correct answer)

- a. Land
- b. Land value tax
- c. Harry Gunnison Brown
- d. Prosper Australia

:: ::

_____ is the practice of deliberately managing the spread of information between an individual or an organization and the public. _____ may include an organization or individual gaining exposure to their audiences using topics of public interest and news items that do not require direct payment. This differentiates it from advertising as a form of marketing communications. _____ is the idea of creating coverage for clients for free, rather than marketing or advertising. But now, advertising is also a part of greater PR Activities.An example of good _____ would be generating an article featuring a client, rather than paying for the client to be advertised next to the article. The aim of _____ is to inform the public, prospective customers, investors, partners, employees, and other stakeholders and ultimately persuade them to maintain a positive or favorable view about the organization, its leadership, products, or political decisions. _____ professionals typically work for PR and marketing firms, businesses and companies, government, and public officials as PIOs and nongovernmental organizations, and nonprofit organizations. Jobs central to _____ include account coordinator, account executive, account supervisor, and media relations manager.

Exam Probability: **Medium**

5. *Answer choices:*

(see index for correct answer)

- a. deep-level diversity
- b. corporate values
- c. open system
- d. Public relations

Guidance: level 1

_____ , or auditory perception, is the ability to perceive sounds by detecting vibrations, changes in the pressure of the surrounding medium through time, through an organ such as the ear. The academic field concerned with _____ is auditory science.

Exam Probability: **Low**

6. *Answer choices:*

(see index for correct answer)

- a. surface-level diversity
- b. empathy
- c. Hearing
- d. information systems assessment

Guidance: level 1

:: Marketing ::

_____ is a concept introduced in a book of the same name in 1999 by marketing expert Seth Godin. _____ is a non-traditional marketing technique that advertises goods and services when advance consent is given.

Exam Probability: **High**

7. *Answer choices:*

(see index for correct answer)

- a. Performance-based advertising
- b. Need
- c. Nutraceutical
- d. Permission marketing

Guidance: level 1

:: ::

_____ is "property consisting of land and the buildings on it, along with its natural resources such as crops, minerals or water; immovable property of this nature; an interest vested in this an item of real property, buildings or housing in general. Also: the business of _____ ; the profession of buying, selling, or renting land, buildings, or housing." It is a legal term used in jurisdictions whose legal system is derived from English common law, such as India, England, Wales, Northern Ireland, United States, Canada, Pakistan, Australia, and New Zealand.

Exam Probability: **High**

8. *Answer choices:*

(see index for correct answer)

- a. imperative
- b. co-culture

- c. Real estate
- d. deep-level diversity

Guidance: level 1

:: Payment systems ::

_____ s are part of a payment system issued by financial institutions, such as a bank, to a customer that enables its owner to access the funds in the customer's designated bank accounts, or through a credit account and make payments by electronic funds transfer and access automated teller machines . Such cards are known by a variety of names including bank cards, ATM cards, MAC , client cards, key cards or cash cards.

Exam Probability: **High**

9. *Answer choices:*

(see index for correct answer)

- a. Cashless catering
- b. BASE24
- c. TPS Pakistan
- d. Payment card

Guidance: level 1

:: International trade ::

In finance, an _____ is the rate at which one currency will be exchanged for another. It is also regarded as the value of one country's currency in relation to another currency. For example, an interbank _____ of 114 Japanese yen to the United States dollar means that ¥114 will be exchanged for each US$1 or that US$1 will be exchanged for each ¥114. In this case it is said that the price of a dollar in relation to yen is ¥114, or equivalently that the price of a yen in relation to dollars is $1/114.

Exam Probability: **High**

10. *Answer choices:*

(see index for correct answer)

- a. Trans-Atlantic trade
- b. Export-led growth
- c. Low-cost country sourcing
- d. Exchange rate

Guidance: level 1

:: Direct marketing ::

_____ is a form of advertising where organizations communicate directly to customers through a variety of media including cell phone text messaging, email, websites, online adverts, database marketing, fliers, catalog distribution, promotional letters, targeted television, newspapers, magazine advertisements, and outdoor advertising. Among practitioners, it is also known as direct response marketing.

11. *Answer choices:*

(see index for correct answer)

- a. Arthur Schiff
- b. Caging
- c. Synapse Group, Inc.
- d. Robinson list

Guidance: level 1

:: Income ::

_____ is a ratio between the net profit and cost of investment resulting from an investment of some resources. A high ROI means the investment's gains favorably to its cost. As a performance measure, ROI is used to evaluate the efficiency of an investment or to compare the efficiencies of several different investments. In purely economic terms, it is one way of relating profits to capital invested. _____ is a performance measure used by businesses to identify the efficiency of an investment or number of different investments.

Exam Probability: **Medium**

12. *Answer choices:*

(see index for correct answer)

- a. Aggregate income
- b. IRD asset
- c. Total personal income
- d. Real income

Guidance: level 1

:: Marketing analytics ::

_____ is a long-term, forward-looking approach to planning with the fundamental goal of achieving a sustainable competitive advantage. Strategic planning involves an analysis of the company's strategic initial situation prior to the formulation, evaluation and selection of market-oriented competitive position that contributes to the company's goals and marketing objectives.

Exam Probability: **High**

13. *Answer choices:*

(see index for correct answer)

- a. Marketing operations management
- b. Market share analysis
- c. Gross rating point
- d. marketing dashboard

Guidance: level 1

:: Meetings ::

A _____ is a body of one or more persons that is subordinate to a deliberative assembly. Usually, the assembly sends matters into a _____ as a way to explore them more fully than would be possible if the assembly itself were considering them. _____ s may have different functions and their type of work differ depending on the type of the organization and its needs.

Exam Probability: **Low**

14. *Answer choices:*

(see index for correct answer)

- a. W00tstock
- b. Committee
- c. Conference hall
- d. Annual general meeting

Guidance: level 1

:: Workplace ::

_____ is asystematic determination of a subject's merit, worth and significance, using criteria governed by a set of standards. It can assist an organization, program, design, project or any other intervention or initiative to assess any aim, realisable concept/proposal, or any alternative, to help in decision-making; or to ascertain the degree of achievement or value in regard to the aim and objectives and results of any such action that has been completed. The primary purpose of _____, in addition to gaining insight into prior or existing initiatives, is to enable reflection and assist in the identification of future change.

Exam Probability: **Low**

15. *Answer choices:*
(see index for correct answer)

- a. Workplace strategy
- b. Evaluation
- c. Workplace conflict
- d. performance review

Guidance: level 1

:: E-commerce ::

The phrase _____ was originally coined in 1997 by Kevin Duffey at the launch of the Global _____ Forum, to mean "the delivery of electronic commerce capabilities directly into the consumer's hand, anywhere, via wireless technology." Many choose to think of _____ as meaning "a retail outlet in your customer's pocket."

16. *Answer choices:*

(see index for correct answer)

- a. APazari
- b. Spamvertising
- c. Electronic commerce
- d. Transport Layer Security

Guidance: level 1

:: Stock market ::

The _____ of a corporation is all of the shares into which ownership of the corporation is divided. In American English, the shares are commonly known as " _____ s". A single share of the _____ represents fractional ownership of the corporation in proportion to the total number of shares. This typically entitles the _____ holder to that fraction of the company's earnings, proceeds from liquidation of assets , or voting power, often dividing these up in proportion to the amount of money each _____ holder has invested. Not all _____ is necessarily equal, as certain classes of _____ may be issued for example without voting rights, with enhanced voting rights, or with a certain priority to receive profits or liquidation proceeds before or after other classes of shareholders.

Exam Probability: **Medium**

17. *Answer choices:*

(see index for correct answer)

- a. Stock
- b. SPI 200 futures contract
- c. Chi-X Global
- d. Open outcry

Guidance: level 1

:: Banking ::

A _____ is a financial institution that accepts deposits from the public and creates credit. Lending activities can be performed either directly or indirectly through capital markets. Due to their importance in the financial stability of a country, _____ s are highly regulated in most countries. Most nations have institutionalized a system known as fractional reserve _____ ing under which _____ s hold liquid assets equal to only a portion of their current liabilities. In addition to other regulations intended to ensure liquidity, _____ s are generally subject to minimum capital requirements based on an international set of capital standards, known as the Basel Accords.

Exam Probability: **Medium**

18. *Answer choices:*
(see index for correct answer)

- a. International Bank of Azerbaijan-Georgia
- b. Savings account

- c. Universal bank
- d. Highly confident letter

Guidance: level 1

:: Auctioneering ::

_____ are electronic auctions, which can be used by sellers to sell their items to many potential buyers. Sellers and buyers can be individuals, organizations etc.

Exam Probability: **High**

19. *Answer choices:*

(see index for correct answer)

- a. Reppert School of Auctioneering
- b. Auction school
- c. Pie supper
- d. Wine auction

Guidance: level 1

:: ::

_____ is a marketing communication that employs an openly sponsored, non-personal message to promote or sell a product, service or idea. Sponsors of _____ are typically businesses wishing to promote their products or services. _____ is differentiated from public relations in that an advertiser pays for and has control over the message. It differs from personal selling in that the message is non-personal, i.e., not directed to a particular individual. _____ is communicated through various mass media, including traditional media such as newspapers, magazines, television, radio, outdoor _____ or direct mail; and new media such as search results, blogs, social media, websites or text messages. The actual presentation of the message in a medium is referred to as an advertisement, or "ad" or advert for short.

20. *Answer choices:*

(see index for correct answer)

- a. personal values
- b. open system
- c. Advertising
- d. Character

Guidance: level 1

:: Business law ::

The _____ , first published in 1952, is one of a number of Uniform Acts that have been established as law with the goal of harmonizing the laws of sales and other commercial transactions across the United States of America through UCC adoption by all 50 states, the District of Columbia, and the Territories of the United States.

Exam Probability: **High**

21. *Answer choices:*

(see index for correct answer)

- a. Closed shop
- b. Extraordinary resolution
- c. Unfair competition
- d. Time-and-a-half

Guidance: level 1

:: ::

_____ is a qualitative measure used to relate the quality of motor vehicle traffic service. LOS is used to analyze roadways and intersections by categorizing traffic flow and assigning quality levels of traffic based on performance measure like vehicle speed, density, congestion, etc.

Exam Probability: **Medium**

22. *Answer choices:*

- a. Level of service
- b. imperative
- c. functional perspective
- d. process perspective

Guidance: level 1

:: ::

_____ is the exchange of capital, goods, and services across international borders or territories.

Exam Probability: **Medium**

23. *Answer choices:*

- a. process perspective
- b. Character
- c. deep-level diversity
- d. International trade

Guidance: level 1

:: Supply chain management ::

_____ is the process of finding and agreeing to terms, and acquiring goods, services, or works from an external source, often via a tendering or competitive bidding process. _____ is used to ensure the buyer receives goods, services, or works at the best possible price when aspects such as quality, quantity, time, and location are compared. Corporations and public bodies often define processes intended to promote fair and open competition for their business while minimizing risks such as exposure to fraud and collusion.

Exam Probability: **Medium**

24. *Answer choices:*

(see index for correct answer)

- a. Procurement
- b. Revenue Technology Services
- c. Yield management
- d. CSCMP Supply Chain Process Standards

Guidance: level 1

:: Commerce ::

_____ , also known as duty _____ is defined by the United States Customs and Border Protection as the refund of certain duties, internal and revenue taxes and certain fees collected upon the importation of goods. Such refunds are only allowed upon the exportation or destruction of goods under U.S. Customs and Border Protection supervision. Duty _____ is an export promotions program sanctioned by the World Trade Organization and allows the refund of certain duties taxes and fees paid upon importation which was established in 1789 in order to promote U.S. innovation and manufacturing across the global market.

Exam Probability: **Low**

25. *Answer choices:*

(see index for correct answer)

- a. Worldwide Centers of Commerce
- b. Haul video
- c. Trading post
- d. Going concern

Guidance: level 1

:: Export and import control ::

" _____ " means the Government Service which is responsible for the administration of _____ law and the collection of duties and taxes and which also has the responsibility for the application of other laws and regulations relating to the importation, exportation, movement or storage of goods.

26. *Answer choices:*

(see index for correct answer)

- a. Customs
- b. Plant Protection and Quarantine
- c. GOST R Conformity Declaration
- d. Customs valuation

Guidance: level 1

:: ::

A _____ is a structured form of play, usually undertaken for enjoyment and sometimes used as an educational tool. _____ s are distinct from work, which is usually carried out for remuneration, and from art, which is more often an expression of aesthetic or ideological elements. However, the distinction is not clear-cut, and many _____ s are also considered to be work or art .

Exam Probability: **Low**

27. *Answer choices:*

(see index for correct answer)

- a. surface-level diversity
- b. Sarbanes-Oxley act of 2002

- c. hierarchical
- d. Game

Guidance: level 1

:: Information technology management ::

_____ s or pop-ups are forms of online advertising on the World Wide Web. A pop-up is a graphical user interface display area, usually a small window, that suddenly appears in the foreground of the visual interface. The pop-up window containing an advertisement is usually generated by JavaScript that uses cross-site scripting , sometimes with a secondary payload that uses Adobe Flash. They can also be generated by other vulnerabilities/security holes in browser security.

Exam Probability: **Low**

28. *Answer choices:*

(see index for correct answer)

- a. Pop-up ad
- b. Storage virtualization
- c. Configuration management database
- d. Microsoft Operations Framework

Guidance: level 1

Business is the activity of making one's living or making money by producing or buying and selling products . Simply put, it is "any activity or enterprise entered into for profit. It does not mean it is a company, a corporation, partnership, or have any such formal organization, but it can range from a street peddler to General Motors."

Exam Probability: **Low**

29. *Answer choices:*

(see index for correct answer)

- a. Firm
- b. Sarbanes-Oxley act of 2002
- c. corporate values
- d. co-culture

Guidance: level 1

_____ are electronic transfer of money from one bank account to another, either within a single financial institution or across multiple institutions, via computer-based systems, without the direct intervention of bank staff.

30. *Answer choices:*

(see index for correct answer)

- a. deep-level diversity
- b. cultural
- c. hierarchical perspective
- d. Electronic funds transfer

Guidance: level 1

:: Minimum wage ::

A _____ is the lowest remuneration that employers can legally pay their workers—the price floor below which workers may not sell their labor. Most countries had introduced _____ legislation by the end of the 20th century.

Exam Probability: **High**

31. *Answer choices:*

(see index for correct answer)

- a. Working poor
- b. Guaranteed minimum income
- c. Minimum wage

- d. Minimum wage in the United States

Guidance: level 1

:: Public relations ::

_____ is the public visibility or awareness for any product, service or company. It may also refer to the movement of information from its source to the general public, often but not always via the media. The subjects of _____ include people , goods and services, organizations, and works of art or entertainment.

Exam Probability: **Low**

32. *Answer choices:*

(see index for correct answer)

- a. International
- b. Zakazukha
- c. Flaunt
- d. Public affairs

Guidance: level 1

:: Management occupations ::

_____ ship is the process of designing, launching and running a new business, which is often initially a small business. The people who create these businesses are called _____ s.

Exam Probability: **Low**

33. *Answer choices:*

(see index for correct answer)

- a. Vorstandsassistent
- b. Comprador
- c. Financial secretary
- d. Chief sustainability officer

Guidance: level 1

:: International trade ::

_____ involves the transfer of goods or services from one person or entity to another, often in exchange for money. A system or network that allows _____ is called a market.

Exam Probability: **Low**

34. *Answer choices:*

(see index for correct answer)

- a. Intervention stocks
- b. Trade in services
- c. Trade
- d. Monetary hegemony

Guidance: level 1

:: Dot-com bubble ::

_____ is an internet portal launched in 1995 that provides a variety of content including news and weather, a metasearch engine, a web-based email, instant messaging, stock quotes, and a customizable user homepage. It is currently operated by IAC Applications of IAC, and _____ Networks. In the U.S., the main _____ site has long been a personal start page called My _____ . _____ also operates an e-mail service, although it is no longer open for new customers.

Exam Probability: **High**

35. *Answer choices:*
(see index for correct answer)

- a. E-Dreams
- b. Urbanfetch
- c. Dot com party
- d. Paid to surf

Guidance: level 1

:: E-commerce ::

A _____ is a financial transaction involving a very small sum of money and usually one that occurs online. A number of _____ systems were proposed and developed in the mid-to-late 1990s, all of which were ultimately unsuccessful. A second generation of _____ systems emerged in the 2010s.

Exam Probability: **Low**

36. *Answer choices:*

(see index for correct answer)

- a. Wildcard certificate
- b. Ven
- c. Micropayment
- d. Online Revolution

Guidance: level 1

:: Commerce ::

An _____ is a bank that offers card association branded payment cards directly to consumers. The name is derived from the practice of issuing payment to the acquiring bank on behalf of its customer .

37. *Answer choices:*

(see index for correct answer)

- a. Going concern
- b. Bill of sale
- c. Issuing bank
- d. Non-commercial

Guidance: level 1

:: Customs duties ::

A _____ is a tax on imports or exports between sovereign states. It is a form of regulation of foreign trade and a policy that taxes foreign products to encourage or safeguard domestic industry. _____ s are the simplest and oldest instrument of trade policy. Traditionally, states have used them as a source of income. Now, they are among the most widely used instruments of protection, along with import and export quotas.

Exam Probability: **Medium**

38. *Answer choices:*

(see index for correct answer)

- a. Customs area
- b. Customs bond

- c. Morrill Tariff
- d. Tariff

:: Supply chain management terms ::

In business and finance, _____ is a system of organizations, people, activities, information, and resources involved in moving a product or service from supplier to customer. _____ activities involve the transformation of natural resources, raw materials, and components into a finished product that is delivered to the end customer. In sophisticated _____ systems, used products may re-enter the _____ at any point where residual value is recyclable. _____ s link value chains.

Exam Probability: **Low**

39. *Answer choices:*

(see index for correct answer)

- a. Overstock
- b. Supply-chain management
- c. Widget
- d. Last mile

:: Manufacturing ::

A _____ is a building for storing goods. _____ s are used by manufacturers, importers, exporters, wholesalers, transport businesses, customs, etc. They are usually large plain buildings in industrial parks on the outskirts of cities, towns or villages.

Exam Probability: **High**

40. *Answer choices:*

(see index for correct answer)

- a. Priming
- b. Lean production
- c. Warehouse
- d. Molecular assembler

Guidance: level 1

:: ::

_____ is the administration of an organization, whether it is a business, a not-for-profit organization, or government body. _____ includes the activities of setting the strategy of an organization and coordinating the efforts of its employees to accomplish its objectives through the application of available resources, such as financial, natural, technological, and human resources. The term " _____ " may also refer to those people who manage an organization.

41. *Answer choices:*

(see index for correct answer)

- a. surface-level diversity
- b. process perspective
- c. empathy
- d. similarity-attraction theory

Guidance: level 1

:: ::

_____ is a means of protection from financial loss. It is a form of risk management, primarily used to hedge against the risk of a contingent or uncertain loss

Exam Probability: **High**

42. *Answer choices:*

(see index for correct answer)

- a. deep-level diversity
- b. personal values
- c. Insurance
- d. functional perspective

:: Manufacturing ::

A _____ is an object used to extend the ability of an individual to modify features of the surrounding environment. Although many animals use simple _____ s, only human beings, whose use of stone _____ s dates back hundreds of millennia, use _____ s to make other _____ s. The set of _____ s needed to perform different tasks that are part of the same activity is called gear or equipment.

Exam Probability: **Medium**

43. *Answer choices:*

(see index for correct answer)

- a. PackML
- b. Heat number
- c. Concrete plant
- d. Tool

:: Organizational structure ::

An _____ defines how activities such as task allocation, coordination, and supervision are directed toward the achievement of organizational aims.

Exam Probability: **High**

44. *Answer choices:*

(see index for correct answer)

- a. Organization of the New York City Police Department
- b. Unorganisation
- c. Organizational structure
- d. Automated Bureaucracy

Guidance: level 1

:: ::

A _____ is a professional who provides expert advice in a particular area such as security , management, education, accountancy, law, human resources, marketing , finance, engineering, science or any of many other specialized fields.

Exam Probability: **High**

45. *Answer choices:*

(see index for correct answer)

- a. interpersonal communication
- b. similarity-attraction theory
- c. Consultant
- d. open system

Guidance: level 1

:: International trade ::

A _____ is a document issued by a carrier to acknowledge receipt of cargo for shipment. Although the term historically related only to carriage by sea, a _____ may today be used for any type of carriage of goods.

Exam Probability: **High**

46. *Answer choices:*

(see index for correct answer)

- a. UNeDocs
- b. Quota share
- c. Bill of lading
- d. Export function

Guidance: level 1

:: Materials ::

A _____ , also known as a feedstock, unprocessed material, or primary commodity, is a basic material that is used to produce goods, finished products, energy, or intermediate materials which are feedstock for future finished products. As feedstock, the term connotes these materials are bottleneck assets and are highly important with regard to producing other products. An example of this is crude oil, which is a _____ and a feedstock used in the production of industrial chemicals, fuels, plastics, and pharmaceutical goods; lumber is a _____ used to produce a variety of products including all types of furniture. The term " _____ " denotes materials in minimally processed or unprocessed in states; e.g., raw latex, crude oil, cotton, coal, raw biomass, iron ore, air, logs, or water i.e. "...any product of agriculture, forestry, fishing and any other mineral that is in its natural form or which has undergone the transformation required to prepare it for internationally marketing in substantial volumes."

Exam Probability: **High**

47. *Answer choices:*

(see index for correct answer)

- a. Raw material
- b. Materials for use in vacuum
- c. Three-dimensional quartz phenolic
- d. Slurry

Guidance: level 1

:: ::

A _____ or _____ s is a type of footwear and not a specific type of shoe. Most _____ s mainly cover the foot and the ankle, while some also cover some part of the lower calf. Some _____ s extend up the leg, sometimes as far as the knee or even the hip. Most _____ s have a heel that is clearly distinguishable from the rest of the sole, even if the two are made of one piece. Traditionally made of leather or rubber, modern _____ s are made from a variety of materials. _____ s are worn both for their functionality protecting the foot and leg from water, extreme cold, mud or hazards or providing additional ankle support for strenuous activities with added traction requirements , or may have hobnails on their undersides to protect against wear and to get better grip; and for reasons of style and fashion.

Exam Probability: **High**

48. *Answer choices:*

(see index for correct answer)

- a. personal values
- b. imperative
- c. Boot
- d. corporate values

Guidance: level 1

:: ::

A _____ , or also known as foreman, overseer, facilitator, monitor, area coordinator, or sometimes gaffer, is the job title of a low level management position that is primarily based on authority over a worker or charge of a workplace. A _____ can also be one of the most senior in the staff at the place of work, such as a Professor who oversees a PhD dissertation. Supervision, on the other hand, can be performed by people without this formal title, for example by parents. The term _____ itself can be used to refer to any personnel who have this task as part of their job description.

Exam Probability: **Low**

49. *Answer choices:*

(see index for correct answer)

- a. surface-level diversity
- b. information systems assessment
- c. Supervisor
- d. open system

Guidance: level 1

:: E-commerce ::

_____ is the activity of buying or selling of products on online services or over the Internet. Electronic commerce draws on technologies such as mobile commerce, electronic funds transfer, supply chain management, Internet marketing, online transaction processing, electronic data interchange , inventory management systems, and automated data collection systems.

50. *Answer choices:*

(see index for correct answer)

- a. Mobilpenge
- b. Center for the Connected Consumer
- c. Conversion as a service
- d. Optimize Capital Markets

Guidance: level 1

:: ::

_____ is an American restaurant chain and international franchise which was founded in 1958 by Dan and Frank Carney. The company is known for its Italian-American cuisine menu, including pizza and pasta, as well as side dishes and desserts. _____ has 18,431 restaurants worldwide as of December 31, 2018, making it the world's largest pizza chain in terms of locations. It is a subsidiary of Yum! Brands, Inc., one of the world's largest restaurant companies.

51. *Answer choices:*

(see index for correct answer)

- a. Pizza Hut

- b. open system
- c. surface-level diversity
- d. similarity-attraction theory

Guidance: level 1

:: Price fixing convictions ::

_____ is the flag carrier airline of the United Kingdom, headquartered at Waterside, Harmondsworth. It is the second largest airline in the United Kingdom, based on fleet size and passengers carried, behind easyJet. The airline is based in Waterside near its main hub at London Heathrow Airport. In January 2011 BA merged with Iberia, creating the International Airlines Group , a holding company registered in Madrid, Spain. IAG is the world's third-largest airline group in terms of annual revenue and the second-largest in Europe. It is listed on the London Stock Exchange and in the FTSE 100 Index. _____ is the first passenger airline to have generated more than $1 billion on a single air route in a year .

Exam Probability: **Low**

52. *Answer choices:*

(see index for correct answer)

- a. YKK Group
- b. British Airways
- c. Heineken International
- d. High Noon Western Americana

:: ::

In logic and philosophy, an _____ is a series of statements , called the premises or premisses , intended to determine the degree of truth of another statement, the conclusion. The logical form of an _____ in a natural language can be represented in a symbolic formal language, and independently of natural language formally defined " _____ s" can be made in math and computer science.

Exam Probability: **High**

53. *Answer choices:*

(see index for correct answer)

- a. similarity-attraction theory
- b. deep-level diversity
- c. Argument
- d. hierarchical perspective

:: Income ::

In business and accounting, net income is an entity's income minus cost of goods sold, expenses and taxes for an accounting period. It is computed as the residual of all revenues and gains over all expenses and losses for the period, and has also been defined as the net increase in shareholders' equity that results from a company's operations. In the context of the presentation of financial statements, the IFRS Foundation defines net income as synonymous with profit and loss. The difference between revenue and the cost of making a product or providing a service, before deducting overheads, payroll, taxation, and interest payments. This is different from operating income .

Exam Probability: **High**

54. *Answer choices:*

(see index for correct answer)

- a. Giganomics
- b. Family income
- c. Real income
- d. Aggregate expenditure

Guidance: level 1

:: Marketing ::

_____ or stock control can be broadly defined as "the activity of checking a shop's stock." However, a more focused definition takes into account the more science-based, methodical practice of not only verifying a business' inventory but also focusing on the many related facets of inventory management "within an organisation to meet the demand placed upon that business economically." Other facets of _____ include supply chain management, production control, financial flexibility, and customer satisfaction. At the root of _____ , however, is the _____ problem, which involves determining when to order, how much to order, and the logistics of those decisions.

Exam Probability: **Medium**

55. *Answer choices:*

(see index for correct answer)

- a. Macromarketing
- b. Gimmick
- c. Inventory control
- d. Customer dynamics

Guidance: level 1

:: Management ::

_____ is the identification, evaluation, and prioritization of risks followed by coordinated and economical application of resources to minimize, monitor, and control the probability or impact of unfortunate events or to maximize the realization of opportunities.

56. *Answer choices:*

(see index for correct answer)

- • a. Executive compensation
- • b. Risk management
- • c. Oriental management
- • d. Knowledge Based Decision Making

Guidance: level 1

:: Marketing ::

The _____ is a foundation model for businesses. The _____ has been defined as the "set of marketing tools that the firm uses to pursue its marketing objectives in the target market". Thus the _____ refers to four broad levels of marketing decision, namely: product, price, place, and promotion. Marketing practice has been occurring for millennia, but marketing theory emerged in the early twentieth century. The contemporary _____ , or the 4 Ps, which has become the dominant framework for marketing management decisions, was first published in 1960. In services marketing, an extended _____ is used, typically comprising 7 Ps, made up of the original 4 Ps extended by process, people, and physical evidence. Occasionally service marketers will refer to 8 Ps, comprising these 7 Ps plus performance.

Exam Probability: **Medium**

57. *Answer choices:*

(see index for correct answer)

- a. The Cellar
- b. Marketing mix
- c. Immersion marketing
- d. Adobe Target

Guidance: level 1

:: Marketing ::

A _____ is an overall experience of a customer that distinguishes an organization or product from its rivals in the eyes of the customer. _____ s are used in business, marketing, and advertising. Name _____ s are sometimes distinguished from generic or store _____ s.

Exam Probability: **Low**

58. *Answer choices:*

(see index for correct answer)

- a. Geographical pricing
- b. Market sector
- c. Double bottom line
- d. Party plan

Guidance: level 1

:: ::

_____ is an abstract concept of management of complex systems according to a set of rules and trends. In systems theory, these types of rules exist in various fields of biology and society, but the term has slightly different meanings according to context. For example.

Exam Probability: **High**

59. *Answer choices:*

(see index for correct answer)

- a. co-culture
- b. information systems assessment
- c. Regulation
- d. empathy

Guidance: level 1

Business ethics

  Business ethics (also known as corporate ethics) is a form of applied ethics or professional ethics, that examines ethical principles and moral or ethical problems that can arise in a business environment. It applies to all aspects of business conduct and is relevant to the conduct of individuals and entire organizations. These ethics originate from individuals, organizational statements or from the legal system. These norms, values, ethical, and unethical practices are what is used to guide business. They help those businesses maintain a better connection with their stakeholders.

:: Hazard analysis ::

Broadly speaking, a _____ is the combined effort of 1. identifying and analyzing potential events that may negatively impact individuals, assets, and/or the environment ; and 2. making judgments "on the tolerability of the risk on the basis of a risk analysis" while considering influencing factors . Put in simpler terms, a _____ analyzes what can go wrong, how likely it is to happen, what the potential consequences are, and how tolerable the identified risk is. As part of this process, the resulting determination of risk may be expressed in a quantitative or qualitative fashion. The _____ is an inherent part of an overall risk management strategy, which attempts to, after a _____ , "introduce control measures to eliminate or reduce" any potential risk-related consequences.

Exam Probability: **Medium**

1. *Answer choices:*

(see index for correct answer)

- a. Hazard
- b. Hazardous Materials Identification System
- c. Risk assessment
- d. Swiss cheese model

Guidance: level 1

:: ::

A _____ is a proceeding by a party or parties against another in the civil court of law. The archaic term "suit in law" is found in only a small number of laws still in effect today. The term " _____ " is used in reference to a civil action brought in a court of law in which a plaintiff, a party who claims to have incurred loss as a result of a defendant's actions, demands a legal or equitable remedy. The defendant is required to respond to the plaintiff's complaint. If the plaintiff is successful, judgment is in the plaintiff's favor, and a variety of court orders may be issued to enforce a right, award damages, or impose a temporary or permanent injunction to prevent an act or compel an act. A declaratory judgment may be issued to prevent future legal disputes.

Exam Probability: **Medium**

2. *Answer choices:*

(see index for correct answer)

- a. functional perspective
- b. similarity-attraction theory
- c. information systems assessment
- d. empathy

Guidance: level 1

:: Corporate crime ::

_____ LLP, based in Chicago, was an American holding company. Formerly one of the "Big Five" accounting firms , the firm had provided auditing, tax, and consulting services to large corporations. By 2001, it had become one of the world's largest multinational companies.

Exam Probability: **Medium**

3. *Answer choices:*

(see index for correct answer)

- a. State-corporate crime
- b. Equity Funding
- c. New England Compounding Center
- d. Langbar International

Guidance: level 1

:: Advertising techniques ::

The _____ is a story from the Trojan War about the subterfuge that the Greeks used to enter the independent city of Troy and win the war. In the canonical version, after a fruitless 10-year siege, the Greeks constructed a huge wooden horse, and hid a select force of men inside including Odysseus. The Greeks pretended to sail away, and the Trojans pulled the horse into their city as a victory trophy. That night the Greek force crept out of the horse and opened the gates for the rest of the Greek army, which had sailed back under cover of night. The Greeks entered and destroyed the city of Troy, ending the war.

4. *Answer choices:*

(see index for correct answer)

- a. Media clip
- b. Transpromotional
- c. Trojan horse
- d. Inconsistent comparison

Guidance: level 1

:: Management ::

The term _____ refers to measures designed to increase the degree of autonomy and self-determination in people and in communities in order to enable them to represent their interests in a responsible and self-determined way, acting on their own authority. It is the process of becoming stronger and more confident, especially in controlling one's life and claiming one's rights.
_____ as action refers both to the process of self- _____ and to professional support of people, which enables them to overcome their sense of powerlessness and lack of influence, and to recognize and use their resources. To do work with power.

Exam Probability: **High**

5. *Answer choices:*

(see index for correct answer)

- a. Empowerment
- b. Knowledge Based Decision Making
- c. Organizational space
- d. Manager Tools Podcast

Guidance: level 1

:: United States federal labor legislation ::

The _____ of 1988 is a United States federal law that generally prevents employers from using polygraph tests, either for pre-employment screening or during the course of employment, with certain exemptions.

Exam Probability: **Medium**

6. *Answer choices:*

(see index for correct answer)

- a. National Whistleblowers Center
- b. Employee Polygraph Protection Act
- c. Civil Rights Act of 1964
- d. Uniformed Services Employment and Reemployment Rights Act

Guidance: level 1

:: Business ethics ::

_____ is a type of harassment technique that relates to a sexual nature and the unwelcome or inappropriate promise of rewards in exchange for sexual favors. _____ includes a range of actions from mild transgressions to sexual abuse or assault. Harassment can occur in many different social settings such as the workplace, the home, school, churches, etc. Harassers or victims may be of any gender.

Exam Probability: **Low**

7. *Answer choices:*

(see index for correct answer)

- a. Foreign official
- b. Burson-Marsteller
- c. Whistleblower
- d. Sexual harassment

Guidance: level 1

:: Human resource management ::

_____ is the ethics of an organization, and it is how an organization responds to an internal or external stimulus. _____ is interdependent with the organizational culture. Although it is akin to both organizational behavior and industrial and organizational psychology as well as business ethics on the micro and macro levels, _____ is neither OB or I/O psychology, nor is it solely business ethics . _____ express the values of an organization to its employees and/or other entities irrespective of governmental and/or regulatory laws.

8. *Answer choices:*

(see index for correct answer)

- a. Action alert
- b. Vendor management system
- c. Organizational ethics
- d. war for talent

Guidance: level 1

:: ::

Competition law is a law that promotes or seeks to maintain market competition by regulating anti-competitive conduct by companies. Competition law is implemented through public and private enforcement. Competition law is known as " _____ law" in the United States for historical reasons, and as "anti-monopoly law" in China and Russia. In previous years it has been known as trade practices law in the United Kingdom and Australia. In the European Union, it is referred to as both _____ and competition law.

Exam Probability: **High**

9. *Answer choices:*

(see index for correct answer)

- a. Antitrust

- b. hierarchical perspective
- c. similarity-attraction theory
- d. levels of analysis

Guidance: level 1

:: Management ::

_____ is the identification, evaluation, and prioritization of risks followed by coordinated and economical application of resources to minimize, monitor, and control the probability or impact of unfortunate events or to maximize the realization of opportunities.

Exam Probability: **High**

10. *Answer choices:*
(see index for correct answer)

- a. Business economics
- b. Certified Project Management Professional
- c. Risk management
- d. Corporate foresight

Guidance: level 1

:: Industrial ecology ::

_____ is a strategy for reducing the amount of waste created and released into the environment, particularly by industrial facilities, agriculture, or consumers. Many large corporations view P2 as a method of improving the efficiency and profitability of production processes by technology advancements. Legislative bodies have enacted P2 measures, such as the _____ Act of 1990 and the Clean Air Act Amendments of 1990 by the United States Congress.

Exam Probability: **Medium**

11. *Answer choices:*

(see index for correct answer)

- a. Pollution Prevention
- b. Waste minimisation
- c. Avoided burden
- d. Cleaner production

Guidance: level 1

:: Globalization-related theories ::

_____ is an economic system based on the private ownership of the means of production and their operation for profit. Characteristics central to _____ include private property, capital accumulation, wage labor, voluntary exchange, a price system, and competitive markets. In a capitalist market economy, decision-making and investment are determined by every owner of wealth, property or production ability in financial and capital markets, whereas prices and the distribution of goods and services are mainly determined by competition in goods and services markets.

Exam Probability: **Low**

12. *Answer choices:*

(see index for correct answer)

- a. Capitalism
- b. Economic Development
- c. post-industrial

Guidance: level 1

:: Real estate ::

_____ s serve several societal needs – primarily as shelter from weather, security, living space, privacy, to store belongings, and to comfortably live and work. A _____ as a shelter represents a physical division of the human habitat and the outside .

Exam Probability: **Low**

13. *Answer choices:*

(see index for correct answer)

- a. Shea Properties
- b. Blockbusting
- c. Planning and zoning commission
- d. Building

Guidance: level 1

:: Confidence tricks ::

A _____ is a business model that recruits members via a promise of payments or services for enrolling others into the scheme, rather than supplying investments or sale of products. As recruiting multiplies, recruiting becomes quickly impossible, and most members are unable to profit; as such, _____ s are unsustainable and often illegal.

Exam Probability: **Medium**

14. *Answer choices:*

(see index for correct answer)

- a. Cackle-bladder
- b. Moving scam
- c. Hokkani boro
- d. Children of Lieutenant Schmidt

:: Majority–minority relations ::

_____ , also known as reservation in India and Nepal, positive discrimination / action in the United Kingdom, and employment equity in Canada and South Africa, is the policy of promoting the education and employment of members of groups that are known to have previously suffered from discrimination. Historically and internationally, support for _____ has sought to achieve goals such as bridging inequalities in employment and pay, increasing access to education, promoting diversity, and redressing apparent past wrongs, harms, or hindrances.

Exam Probability: **Low**

15. *Answer choices:*

(see index for correct answer)

- a. cultural Relativism
- b. cultural dissonance
- c. Affirmative action

:: Marketing ::

_____ is the marketing of products that are presumed to be environmentally safe. It incorporates a broad range of activities, including product modification, changes to the production process, sustainable packaging, as well as modifying advertising. Yet defining _____ is not a simple task where several meanings intersect and contradict each other; an example of this will be the existence of varying social, environmental and retail definitions attached to this term. Other similar terms used are environmental marketing and ecological marketing.

Exam Probability: **Low**

16. *Answer choices:*

(see index for correct answer)

- a. Marketspace
- b. National brand
- c. Green marketing
- d. Discounting

Guidance: level 1

:: Toxicology ::

_____ or lead-based paint is paint containing lead. As pigment, lead chromate , Lead oxide, , and lead carbonate are the most common forms. Lead is added to paint to accelerate drying, increase durability, maintain a fresh appearance, and resist moisture that causes corrosion. It is one of the main health and environmental hazards associated with paint. In some countries, lead continues to be added to paint intended for domestic use, whereas countries such as the U.S. and the UK have regulations prohibiting this, although _____ may still be found in older properties painted prior to the introduction of such regulations. Although lead has been banned from household paints in the United States since 1978, paint used in road markings may still contain it. Alternatives such as water-based, lead-free traffic paint are readily available, and many states and federal agencies have changed their purchasing contracts to buy these instead.

Exam Probability: **Low**

17. *Answer choices:*

(see index for correct answer)

- a. Lead paint
- b. Bongkrek acid
- c. DCMU
- d. Antagonism

Guidance: level 1

:: Auditing ::

_____ , as defined by accounting and auditing, is a process for assuring of an organization's objectives in operational effectiveness and efficiency, reliable financial reporting, and compliance with laws, regulations and policies. A broad concept, _____ involves everything that controls risks to an organization.

Exam Probability: **Low**

18. *Answer choices:*

(see index for correct answer)

- a. Lease audit
- b. Internal control
- c. Sales tax audit
- d. Continuous auditing

Guidance: level 1

:: Pyramid and Ponzi schemes ::

_____ was an Italian swindler and con artist in the U.S. and Canada. His aliases include Charles Ponci, Carlo, and Charles P. Bianchi. Born and raised in Italy, he became known in the early 1920s as a swindler in North America for his money-making scheme. He promised clients a 50% profit within 45 days or 100% profit within 90 days, by buying discounted postal reply coupons in other countries and redeeming them at face value in the United States as a form of arbitrage. In reality, Ponzi was paying earlier investors using the investments of later investors. While this type of fraudulent investment scheme was not originally invented by Ponzi, it became so identified with him that it now is referred to as a "Ponzi scheme". His scheme ran for over a year before it collapsed, costing his "investors" $20 million.

Exam Probability: **High**

19. *Answer choices:*

(see index for correct answer)

- a. Charles Ponzi
- b. Nicolae Popa
- c. Steven Hoffenberg
- d. Afinsa

Guidance: level 1

:: Workplace ::

In business management, _____ is a management style whereby a manager closely observes and/or controls the work of his/her subordinates or employees.

20. *Answer choices:*

(see index for correct answer)

- a. Open allocation
- b. Workplace conflict
- c. Workplace deviance
- d. Micromanagement

Guidance: level 1

:: ::

The _____ is an 1848 political pamphlet by the German philosophers Karl Marx and Friedrich Engels. Commissioned by the Communist League and originally published in London just as the Revolutions of 1848 began to erupt, the Manifesto was later recognised as one of the world's most influential political documents. It presents an analytical approach to the class struggle and the conflicts of capitalism and the capitalist mode of production, rather than a prediction of communism's potential future forms.

Exam Probability: **Medium**

21. *Answer choices:*

(see index for correct answer)

- a. Character

- b. Communist Manifesto
- c. surface-level diversity
- d. functional perspective

Guidance: level 1

:: ::

The _____ , founded in 1912, is a private, nonprofit organization whose self-described mission is to focus on advancing marketplace trust, consisting of 106 independently incorporated local BBB organizations in the United States and Canada, coordinated under the Council of _____ s in Arlington, Virginia.

Exam Probability: **Low**

22. *Answer choices:*

(see index for correct answer)

- a. corporate values
- b. process perspective
- c. information systems assessment
- d. Better Business Bureau

Guidance: level 1

:: Electronic feedback ::

_____ occurs when outputs of a system are routed back as inputs as part of a chain of cause-and-effect that forms a circuit or loop. The system can then be said to feed back into itself. The notion of cause-and-effect has to be handled carefully when applied to _____ systems.

Exam Probability: **Low**

23. *Answer choices:*

(see index for correct answer)

- a. feedback loop
- b. Positive feedback

Guidance: level 1

:: Progressive Era in the United States ::

The Clayton Antitrust Act of 1914 , was a part of United States antitrust law with the goal of adding further substance to the U.S. antitrust law regime; the _____ sought to prevent anticompetitive practices in their incipiency. That regime started with the Sherman Antitrust Act of 1890, the first Federal law outlawing practices considered harmful to consumers . The _____ specified particular prohibited conduct, the three-level enforcement scheme, the exemptions, and the remedial measures.

Exam Probability: **Low**

24. *Answer choices:*

(see index for correct answer)

- a. Mann Act
- b. Clayton Antitrust Act
- c. Clayton Act

Guidance: level 1

:: ::

A _____ is an organization, usually a group of people or a company, authorized to act as a single entity and recognized as such in law. Early incorporated entities were established by charter . Most jurisdictions now allow the creation of new _____ s through registration.

Exam Probability: **High**

25. *Answer choices:*

(see index for correct answer)

- a. information systems assessment
- b. Corporation
- c. interpersonal communication
- d. levels of analysis

Guidance: level 1

:: Carbon finance ::

The _____ is an international treaty which extends the 1992 United Nations Framework Convention on Climate Change that commits state parties to reduce greenhouse gas emissions, based on the scientific consensus that global warming is occurring and it is extremely likely that human-made CO_2 emissions have predominantly caused it. The _____ was adopted in Kyoto, Japan on 11 December 1997 and entered into force on 16 February 2005. There are currently 192 parties to the Protocol.

Exam Probability: **Low**

26. *Answer choices:*

(see index for correct answer)

- a. Carbon offset
- b. Reducing emissions from deforestation and forest degradation
- c. Western Climate Initiative
- d. EcoAid

Guidance: level 1

:: ::

_____ is the means to see, hear, or become aware of something or someone through our fundamental senses. The term _____ derives from the Latin word perceptio, and is the organization, identification, and interpretation of sensory information in order to represent and understand the presented information, or the environment.

Exam Probability: **Low**

27. *Answer choices:*

(see index for correct answer)

- a. process perspective
- b. Perception
- c. interpersonal communication
- d. corporate values

Guidance: level 1

:: ::

_____ is a naturally occurring, yellowish-black liquid found in geological formations beneath the Earth's surface. It is commonly refined into various types of fuels. Components of _____ are separated using a technique called fractional distillation, i.e. separation of a liquid mixture into fractions differing in boiling point by means of distillation, typically using a fractionating column.

Exam Probability: **Low**

28. *Answer choices:*

(see index for correct answer)

- a. Character
- b. interpersonal communication
- c. Petroleum
- d. corporate values

Guidance: level 1

:: False advertising law ::

The Lanham Act is the primary federal trademark statute of law in the United States. The Act prohibits a number of activities, including trademark infringement, trademark dilution, and false advertising.

Exam Probability: **Low**

29. *Answer choices:*

(see index for correct answer)

- a. POM Wonderful LLC v. Coca-Cola Co.
- b. Rebecca Tushnet

Guidance: level 1

:: Power (social and political) ::

_____ is a form of reverence gained by a leader who has strong interpersonal relationship skills. _____ , as an aspect of personal power, becomes particularly important as organizational leadership becomes increasingly about collaboration and influence, rather than command and control.

Exam Probability: **Medium**

30. *Answer choices:*

(see index for correct answer)

- a. Referent power
- b. Expert power
- c. need for power

Guidance: level 1

:: Euthenics ::

_____ is an ethical framework and suggests that an entity, be it an organization or individual, has an obligation to act for the benefit of society at large. _____ is a duty every individual has to perform so as to maintain a balance between the economy and the ecosystems. A trade-off may exist between economic development, in the material sense, and the welfare of the society and environment, though this has been challenged by many reports over the past decade. _____ means sustaining the equilibrium between the two. It pertains not only to business organizations but also to everyone whose any action impacts the environment. This responsibility can be passive, by avoiding engaging in socially harmful acts, or active, by performing activities that directly advance social goals. _____ must be intergenerational since the actions of one generation have consequences on those following.

Exam Probability: **High**

31. *Answer choices:*

(see index for correct answer)

- a. Euthenics
- b. Minnie Cumnock Blodgett
- c. Social responsibility
- d. Home economics

Guidance: level 1

:: Water law ::

The _____ is the primary federal law in the United States governing water pollution. Its objective is to restore and maintain the chemical, physical, and biological integrity of the nation's waters; recognizing the responsibilities of the states in addressing pollution and providing assistance to states to do so, including funding for publicly owned treatment works for the improvement of wastewater treatment; and maintaining the integrity of wetlands. It is one of the United States' first and most influential modern environmental laws. As with many other major U.S. federal environmental statutes, it is administered by the U.S. Environmental Protection Agency , in coordination with state governments. Its implementing regulations are codified at 40 C.F.R. Subchapters D, N, and O .

Exam Probability: **High**

32. *Answer choices:*

(see index for correct answer)

- a. Return flow
- b. Berlin Rules on Water Resources
- c. Clean Water Act
- d. Correlative rights doctrine

Guidance: level 1

:: ::

_____ is the introduction of contaminants into the natural environment that cause adverse change. _____ can take the form of chemical substances or energy, such as noise, heat or light. Pollutants, the components of _____ , can be either foreign substances/energies or naturally occurring contaminants. _____ is often classed as point source or nonpoint source _____ .In 2015, _____ killed 9 million people in the world.

Exam Probability: **High**

33. *Answer choices:*

(see index for correct answer)

- a. surface-level diversity
- b. hierarchical
- c. imperative
- d. similarity-attraction theory

Guidance: level 1

:: Utilitarianism ::

_____ is a school of thought that argues that the pursuit of pleasure and intrinsic goods are the primary or most important goals of human life. A hedonist strives to maximize net pleasure . However upon finally gaining said pleasure, happiness may remain stationary.

Exam Probability: **Medium**

34. *Answer choices:*

(see index for correct answer)

- a. Hedonism
- b. Preference utilitarianism
- c. Telishment
- d. Informed judge

Guidance: level 1

:: ::

Oriental Nicety, formerly _____, Exxon Mediterranean, SeaRiver Mediterranean, S/R Mediterranean, Mediterranean, and Dong Fang Ocean, was an oil tanker that gained notoriety after running aground in Prince William Sound spilling hundreds of thousands of barrels of crude oil in Alaska. On March 24, 1989, while owned by the former Exxon Shipping Company, and captained by Joseph Hazelwood and First Mate James Kunkel bound for Long Beach, California, the vessel ran aground on the Bligh Reef resulting in the second largest oil spill in United States history. The size of the spill is estimated to have been 40,900 to 120,000 m3 , or 257,000 to 750,000 barrels. In 1989, the _____ oil spill was listed as the 54th largest spill in history.

Exam Probability: **Medium**

35. *Answer choices:*

(see index for correct answer)

- a. deep-level diversity

- b. Sarbanes-Oxley act of 2002
- c. Exxon Valdez
- d. information systems assessment

Guidance: level 1

:: ::

A _____ is an astronomical body orbiting a star or stellar remnant that is massive enough to be rounded by its own gravity, is not massive enough to cause thermonuclear fusion, and has cleared its neighbouring region of _____ esimals.

Exam Probability: **High**

36. *Answer choices:*
(see index for correct answer)

- a. similarity-attraction theory
- b. imperative
- c. levels of analysis
- d. hierarchical perspective

Guidance: level 1

:: Fraud ::

In law, _____ is intentional deception to secure unfair or unlawful gain, or to deprive a victim of a legal right. _____ can violate civil law , a criminal law , or it may cause no loss of money, property or legal right but still be an element of another civil or criminal wrong. The purpose of _____ may be monetary gain or other benefits, for example by obtaining a passport, travel document, or driver's license, or mortgage _____ , where the perpetrator may attempt to qualify for a mortgage by way of false statements.

Exam Probability: **High**

37. *Answer choices:*

(see index for correct answer)

- a. Fraud Alert
- b. Extrinsic fraud
- c. Fraud
- d. Gone in 60 Seconds

Guidance: level 1

:: Environmental economics ::

_____ is an institutional arrangement designed to help producers in developing countries achieve better trading conditions. Members of the _____ movement advocate the payment of higher prices to exporters, as well as improved social and environmental standards. The movement focuses in particular on commodities, or products which are typically exported from developing countries to developed countries, but also consumed in domestic markets most notably handicrafts, coffee, cocoa, wine, sugar, fresh fruit, chocolate, flowers and gold. The movement seeks to promote greater equity in international trading partnerships through dialogue, transparency, and respect. It promotes sustainable development by offering better trading conditions to, and securing the rights of, marginalized producers and workers in developing countries. _____ is grounded in three core beliefs; first, producers have the power to express unity with consumers. Secondly, the world trade practices that currently exist promote the unequal distribution of wealth between nations. Lastly, buying products from producers in developing countries at a fair price is a more efficient way of promoting sustainable development than traditional charity and aid.

Exam Probability: **Low**

38. *Answer choices:*

(see index for correct answer)

- a. Journal of Environmental Economics and Management
- b. Fair trade
- c. Ecotax
- d. Total economic value

Guidance: level 1

:: ::

_____ Ltd. is the world's 2nd largest offshore drilling contractor and is based in Vernier, Switzerland. The company has offices in 20 countries, including Switzerland, Canada, United States, Norway, Scotland, India, Brazil, Singapore, Indonesia and Malaysia.

Exam Probability: **High**

39. *Answer choices:*

(see index for correct answer)

- a. information systems assessment
- b. Transocean
- c. hierarchical perspective
- d. open system

Guidance: level 1

:: ::

The _____ is an institution of the European Union, responsible for proposing legislation, implementing decisions, upholding the EU treaties and managing the day-to-day business of the EU. Commissioners swear an oath at the European Court of Justice in Luxembourg City, pledging to respect the treaties and to be completely independent in carrying out their duties during their mandate. Unlike in the Council of the European Union, where members are directly and indirectly elected, and the European Parliament, where members are directly elected, the Commissioners are proposed by the Council of the European Union, on the basis of suggestions made by the national governments, and then appointed by the European Council after the approval of the European Parliament.

Exam Probability: **Medium**

40. *Answer choices:*

(see index for correct answer)

- a. Sarbanes-Oxley act of 2002
- b. corporate values
- c. European Commission
- d. Character

Guidance: level 1

:: Financial regulatory authorities of the United States ::

The _____ is an agency of the United States government responsible for consumer protection in the financial sector. CFPB's jurisdiction includes banks, credit unions, securities firms, payday lenders, mortgage-servicing operations, foreclosure relief services, debt collectors and other financial companies operating in the United States.

Exam Probability: **High**

41. *Answer choices:*

(see index for correct answer)

- a. Securities Investor Protection Corporation
- b. U.S. Securities and Exchange Commission
- c. Office of Thrift Supervision
- d. Office of the Comptroller of the Currency

Guidance: level 1

:: Monopoly (economics) ::

A _____ is a form of intellectual property that gives its owner the legal right to exclude others from making, using, selling, and importing an invention for a limited period of years, in exchange for publishing an enabling public disclosure of the invention. In most countries _____ rights fall under civil law and the _____ holder needs to sue someone infringing the _____ in order to enforce his or her rights. In some industries _____ s are an essential form of competitive advantage; in others they are irrelevant.

42. *Answer choices:*

(see index for correct answer)

- a. Electricity liberalization
- b. Rate-of-return regulation
- c. Monopoly
- d. Patent

Guidance: level 1

:: United States law ::

The ABA _____ , created by the American Bar Association , are a set of rules that prescribe baseline standards of legal ethics and professional responsibility for lawyers in the United States. They were promulgated by the ABA House of Delegates upon the recommendation of the Kutak Commission in 1983. The rules are merely recommendations, or models, and are not themselves binding. However, having a common set of Model Rules facilitates a common discourse on legal ethics, and simplifies professional responsibility training as well as the day-to-day application of such rules. As of 2015, 49 states and four territories have adopted the rules in whole or in part, of which the most recent to do so was the Commonwealth of the Northern Mariana Islands in March 2015. California is the only state that has not adopted the ABA Model Rules, while Puerto Rico is the only U.S. jurisdiction outside of confederation has not adopted them but instead has its own Código de Ética Profesional.

43. *Answer choices:*

(see index for correct answer)

- a. judgment notwithstanding the verdict
- b. Model Rules of Professional Conduct

Guidance: level 1

:: Commercial crimes ::

_____ is an agreement between participants on the same side in a market to buy or sell a product, service, or commodity only at a fixed price, or maintain the market conditions such that the price is maintained at a given level by controlling supply and demand.

Exam Probability: **High**

44. *Answer choices:*

(see index for correct answer)

- a. Price fixing
- b. Fence
- c. Counterfeit
- d. Sweethearting

Guidance: level 1

Cannabis, also known as _____ among other names, is a psychoactive drug from the Cannabis plant used for medical or recreational purposes. The main psychoactive part of cannabis is tetrahydrocannabinol , one of 483 known compounds in the plant, including at least 65 other cannabinoids. Cannabis can be used by smoking, vaporizing, within food, or as an extract.

Exam Probability: **Medium**

45. *Answer choices:*

(see index for correct answer)

- a. cultural
- b. Marijuana
- c. information systems assessment
- d. deep-level diversity

Guidance: level 1

:: Social enterprise ::

Corporate social responsibility is a type of international private business self-regulation. While once it was possible to describe CSR as an internal organisational policy or a corporate ethic strategy, that time has passed as various international laws have been developed and various organisations have used their authority to push it beyond individual or even industry-wide initiatives. While it has been considered a form of corporate self-regulation for some time, over the last decade or so it has moved considerably from voluntary decisions at the level of individual organisations, to mandatory schemes at regional, national and even transnational levels.

Exam Probability: **High**

46. *Answer choices:*

(see index for correct answer)

- a. Social enterprise
- b. Corporate citizenship

Guidance: level 1

:: Cognitive biases ::

In personality psychology, _____ is the degree to which people believe that they have control over the outcome of events in their lives, as opposed to external forces beyond their control. Understanding of the concept was developed by Julian B. Rotter in 1954, and has since become an aspect of personality studies. A person's "locus" is conceptualized as internal or external .

47. *Answer choices:*

(see index for correct answer)

- a. Locus of control
- b. Affect heuristic
- c. Black dog syndrome
- d. Certainty effect

Guidance: level 1

:: Monopoly (economics) ::

The _____ of 1890 was a United States antitrust law that regulates competition among enterprises, which was passed by Congress under the presidency of Benjamin Harrison.

48. *Answer choices:*

(see index for correct answer)

- a. Monopsony
- b. Private finance initiative
- c. Sherman Antitrust Act
- d. Network effect

:: ::

A _____ is a problem offering two possibilities, neither of which is unambiguously acceptable or preferable. The possibilities are termed the horns of the _____ , a clichéd usage, but distinguishing the _____ from other kinds of predicament as a matter of usage.

Exam Probability: **Medium**

49. *Answer choices:*

(see index for correct answer)

- a. Dilemma
- b. cultural
- c. hierarchical
- d. co-culture

:: Minimum wage ::

A _____ is the lowest remuneration that employers can legally pay their workers—the price floor below which workers may not sell their labor. Most countries had introduced _____ legislation by the end of the 20th century.

Exam Probability: **Medium**

50. *Answer choices:*

(see index for correct answer)

- a. Minimum wage in Taiwan
- b. Working poor
- c. Guaranteed minimum income
- d. Minimum wage

Guidance: level 1

:: Types of marketing ::

_____ is an advertisement strategy in which a company uses surprise and/or unconventional interactions in order to promote a product or service. It is a type of publicity. The term was popularized by Jay Conrad Levinson's 1984 book _____ .

Exam Probability: **Medium**

51. *Answer choices:*

- a. Figure of merit
- b. Pre-installed software
- c. Guerrilla Marketing
- d. Diversity marketing

Guidance: level 1

:: Writs ::

In common law, a writ of _____ is a writ whereby a private individual who assists a prosecution can receive all or part of any penalty imposed. Its name is an abbreviation of the Latin phrase _____ pro domino rege quam pro se ipso in hac parte sequitur, meaning "[he] who sues in this matter for the king as well as for himself."

Exam Probability: **Medium**

52. *Answer choices:*

- a. Writ of execution
- b. Writ of assistance

Guidance: level 1

:: ::

_____ is a private Dominican liberal arts college in Madison,
Wisconsin. The college occupies a 55 acres campus overlooking the shores of
Lake Wingra.

Exam Probability: **High**

53. *Answer choices:*

(see index for correct answer)

- a. interpersonal communication
- b. co-culture
- c. Edgewood College
- d. process perspective

Guidance: level 1

:: Electronic waste ::

_____ or e-waste describes discarded electrical or electronic devices.
Used electronics which are destined for refurbishment, reuse, resale, salvage,
recycling through material recovery, or disposal are also considered e-waste.
Informal processing of e-waste in developing countries can lead to adverse
human health effects and environmental pollution.

Exam Probability: **Low**

54. *Answer choices:*

(see index for correct answer)

- a. World Reuse, Repair and Recycling Association
- b. Electronic waste
- c. Techreturns
- d. Solving the E-waste Problem

Guidance: level 1

:: United States federal defense and national security legislation ::

The USA _____ is an Act of the U.S. Congress that was signed into law by President George W. Bush on October 26, 2001. The title of the Act is a contrived three letter initialism preceding a seven letter acronym , which in combination stand for Uniting and Strengthening America by Providing Appropriate Tools Required to Intercept and Obstruct Terrorism Act of 2001. The acronym was created by a 23 year old Congressional staffer, Chris Kyle.

Exam Probability: **High**

55. *Answer choices:*

(see index for correct answer)

- a. Export Administration Act
- b. USA PATRIOT Act

Guidance: level 1

The Federal National Mortgage Association , commonly known as _____ , is a United States government-sponsored enterprise and, since 1968, a publicly traded company. Founded in 1938 during the Great Depression as part of the New Deal, the corporation's purpose is to expand the secondary mortgage market by securitizing mortgage loans in the form of mortgage-backed securities , allowing lenders to reinvest their assets into more lending and in effect increasing the number of lenders in the mortgage market by reducing the reliance on locally based savings and loan associations . Its brother organization is the Federal Home Loan Mortgage Corporation , better known as Freddie Mac. As of 2018, _____ is ranked #21 on the Fortune 500 rankings of the largest United States corporations by total revenue.

Exam Probability: **Medium**

56. *Answer choices:*

(see index for correct answer)

- a. corporate values
- b. Character
- c. interpersonal communication
- d. functional perspective

Guidance: level 1

:: Law ::

_____ is a body of law which defines the role, powers, and structure of different entities within a state, namely, the executive, the parliament or legislature, and the judiciary; as well as the basic rights of citizens and, in federal countries such as the United States and Canada, the relationship between the central government and state, provincial, or territorial governments.

Exam Probability: **Low**

57. *Answer choices:*

(see index for correct answer)

- a. Constitutional law
- b. Comparative law

Guidance: level 1

:: ::

_____ is a region of India consisting of the Indian states of Bihar, Jharkhand, West Bengal, Odisha and also the union territory Andaman and Nicobar Islands. West Bengal`s capital Kolkata is the largest city of this region. The Kolkata Metropolitan Area is the country`s third largest.

Exam Probability: **Medium**

58. *Answer choices:*

(see index for correct answer)

- a. corporate values
- b. surface-level diversity
- c. East India
- d. levels of analysis

Guidance: level 1

:: Organizational structure ::

An ＿＿＿＿＿ defines how activities such as task allocation, coordination, and supervision are directed toward the achievement of organizational aims.

Exam Probability: **High**

59. *Answer choices:*

(see index for correct answer)

- a. Blessed Unrest
- b. Automated Bureaucracy
- c. Unorganisation
- d. Organizational structure

Guidance: level 1

Accounting

Accounting or accountancy is the measurement, processing, and communication of financial information about economic entities such as businesses and corporations. The modern field was established by the Italian mathematician Luca Pacioli in 1494. Accounting, which has been called the "language of business", measures the results of an organization's economic activities and conveys this information to a variety of users, including investors, creditors, management, and regulators.

:: ::

_____ is capital that is contributed to a corporation by investors by purchase of stock from the corporation, the primary market, not by purchase of stock in the open market from other stockholders . It includes share capital as well as additional _____ .

Exam Probability: **Medium**

1. *Answer choices:*

(see index for correct answer)

- a. deep-level diversity
- b. process perspective
- c. Paid-in capital
- d. levels of analysis

Guidance: level 1

:: Accounting source documents ::

A _____ is a commercial document and first official offer issued by a buyer to a seller indicating types, quantities, and agreed prices for products or services. It is used to control the purchasing of products and services from external suppliers. _____ s can be an essential part of enterprise resource planning system orders.

Exam Probability: **Medium**

2. *Answer choices:*

(see index for correct answer)

- a. Credit memo
- b. Credit memorandum
- c. Bank statement
- d. Purchase order

Guidance: level 1

:: Taxation ::

In a tax system, the _____ is the ratio at which a business or person is taxed. There are several methods used to present a _____ : statutory, average, marginal, and effective. These rates can also be presented using different definitions applied to a tax base: inclusive and exclusive.

Exam Probability: **Low**

3. *Answer choices:*

(see index for correct answer)

- a. Optimal taxation
- b. Tax rate
- c. Tax buoyancy
- d. Steuerberater

:: Labor terms ::

_____ , often called DI or disability income insurance, or income protection, is a form of insurance that insures the beneficiary's earned income against the risk that a disability creates a barrier for a worker to complete the core functions of their work. For example, the worker may suffer from an inability to maintain composure in the case of psychological disorders or an injury, illness or condition that causes physical impairment or incapacity to work. It encompasses paid sick leave, short-term disability benefits , and long-term disability benefits . Statistics show that in the US a disabling accident occurs, on average, once every second. In fact, nearly 18.5% of Americans are currently living with a disability, and 1 out of every 4 persons in the US workforce will suffer a disabling injury before retirement.

Exam Probability: **High**

4. *Answer choices:*
(see index for correct answer)

- a. Civilian workers
- b. Benefit incidence
- c. Disability insurance
- d. Strike action

:: ::

The _____ of 1934 is a law governing the secondary trading of securities in the United States of America. A landmark of wide-ranging legislation, the Act of '34 and related statutes form the basis of regulation of the financial markets and their participants in the United States. The 1934 Act also established the Securities and Exchange Commission , the agency primarily responsible for enforcement of United States federal securities law.

Exam Probability: **Medium**

5. *Answer choices:*

(see index for correct answer)

- a. Securities Exchange Act
- b. Character
- c. empathy
- d. hierarchical

Guidance: level 1

:: Management accounting ::

_____ accounting is a traditional cost accounting method introduced in the 1920s, as an alternative for the traditional cost accounting method based on historical costs.

6. *Answer choices:*

(see index for correct answer)

- a. Institute of Certified Management Accountants
- b. Institute of Management Accountants
- c. Factory overhead
- d. Target income sales

Guidance: level 1

:: Generally Accepted Accounting Principles ::

An _____ or profit and loss account is one of the financial statements of a company and shows the company's revenues and expenses during a particular period.

Exam Probability: **High**

7. *Answer choices:*

(see index for correct answer)

- a. Consolidation
- b. Earnings before interest and taxes
- c. Fin 48
- d. Income statement

:: Financial ratios ::

_____ is a measure of how revenue growth translates into growth in operating income. It is a measure of leverage, and of how risky, or volatile, a company's operating income is.

Exam Probability: **High**

8. *Answer choices:*

(see index for correct answer)

- a. Implied multiple
- b. Cash conversion cycle
- c. Net capital outflow
- d. Price/cash flow ratio

:: Shareholders ::

A _____ is a payment made by a corporation to its shareholders, usually as a distribution of profits. When a corporation earns a profit or surplus, the corporation is able to re-invest the profit in the business and pay a proportion of the profit as a _____ to shareholders. Distribution to shareholders may be in cash or, if the corporation has a _____ reinvestment plan, the amount can be paid by the issue of further shares or share repurchase. When _____ s are paid, shareholders typically must pay income taxes, and the corporation does not receive a corporate income tax deduction for the _____ payments.

Exam Probability: **High**

9. *Answer choices:*

(see index for correct answer)

- a. Dividend
- b. Proxy statement
- c. Shotgun clause
- d. Total shareholder return

Guidance: level 1

:: ::

A _____ , in the word`s original meaning, is a sheet of paper on which one performs work. They come in many forms, most commonly associated with children`s school work assignments, tax forms, and accounting or other business environments. Software is increasingly taking over the paper-based _____ .

10. *Answer choices:*

(see index for correct answer)

- a. Worksheet
- b. hierarchical
- c. interpersonal communication
- d. personal values

Guidance: level 1

:: Management accounting ::

_____ , or dollar contribution per unit, is the selling price per unit minus the variable cost per unit. "Contribution" represents the portion of sales revenue that is not consumed by variable costs and so contributes to the coverage of fixed costs. This concept is one of the key building blocks of break-even analysis.

Exam Probability: **Medium**

11. *Answer choices:*

(see index for correct answer)

- a. Contribution margin
- b. Institute of Certified Management Accountants

- c. Constraints accounting
- d. Resource consumption accounting

Guidance: level 1

:: ::

A _____ is an individual or institution that legally owns one or more shares of stock in a public or private corporation. _____ s may be referred to as members of a corporation. Legally, a person is not a _____ in a corporation until their name and other details are entered in the corporation's register of _____ s or members.

Exam Probability: **Low**

12. *Answer choices:*

(see index for correct answer)

- a. imperative
- b. co-culture
- c. surface-level diversity
- d. corporate values

Guidance: level 1

:: ::

An _____ is a systematic and independent examination of books, accounts, statutory records, documents and vouchers of an organization to ascertain how far the financial statements as well as non-financial disclosures present a true and fair view of the concern. It also attempts to ensure that the books of accounts are properly maintained by the concern as required by law. _____ ing has become such a ubiquitous phenomenon in the corporate and the public sector that academics started identifying an " _____ Society". The _____ or perceives and recognises the propositions before them for examination, obtains evidence, evaluates the same and formulates an opinion on the basis of his judgement which is communicated through their _____ ing report.

Exam Probability: **Medium**

13. *Answer choices:*

(see index for correct answer)

- a. deep-level diversity
- b. Audit
- c. process perspective
- d. interpersonal communication

Guidance: level 1

:: ::

A work order is usually a task or a job for a customer, that can be scheduled or assigned to someone. Such an order may be from a customer request or created internally within the organization. Work orders may also be created as follow ups to Inspections or Audits. A work order may be for products or services.

Exam Probability: **High**

14. *Answer choices:*

(see index for correct answer)

- a. Job order
- b. process perspective
- c. corporate values
- d. levels of analysis

Guidance: level 1

:: Management ::

The _____ is a strategy performance management tool – a semi-standard structured report, that can be used by managers to keep track of the execution of activities by the staff within their control and to monitor the consequences arising from these actions.

Exam Probability: **Medium**

15. *Answer choices:*

(see index for correct answer)

- a. Balanced scorecard
- b. Intelligent customer
- c. Meeting
- d. Infrastructure asset management

Guidance: level 1

:: Accounting in the United States ::

The _____ was formed by the American Institute of Certified Public Accountants in 1972, and developed the Objective of Financial Statements. The committee's goal was to create financial statements that helped external users make decisions about the economics of companies. In 1978, the Financial Accounting Standards Board , whose purpose is to develop generally accepted accounting principles, adopted the key objectives established by the _____

.

Exam Probability: **Low**

16. *Answer choices:*

(see index for correct answer)

- a. Variable interest entity
- b. Clean Energy Bank
- c. Association of Government Accountants
- d. Trueblood Committee

:: Financial regulatory authorities of the United States ::

The _____ is the revenue service of the United States federal government. The government agency is a bureau of the Department of the Treasury, and is under the immediate direction of the Commissioner of Internal Revenue, who is appointed to a five-year term by the President of the United States. The IRS is responsible for collecting taxes and administering the Internal Revenue Code, the main body of federal statutory tax law of the United States. The duties of the IRS include providing tax assistance to taxpayers and pursuing and resolving instances of erroneous or fraudulent tax filings. The IRS has also overseen various benefits programs, and enforces portions of the Affordable Care Act.

Exam Probability: **Medium**

17. *Answer choices:*

(see index for correct answer)

- a. Federal Deposit Insurance Corporation
- b. Office of Thrift Supervision
- c. Internal Revenue Service
- d. Federal Reserve Board

:: Financial ratios ::

_____ or interest coverage ratio is a measure of a company's ability to honor its debt payments. It may be calculated as either EBIT or EBITDA divided by the total interest payable.

Exam Probability: **High**

18. *Answer choices:*

(see index for correct answer)

- a. Debt service ratio
- b. Interest coverage ratio
- c. Times interest earned
- d. Dividend payout ratio

Guidance: level 1

:: Accounting ::

_____ are designed to facilitate the process of journalizing and posting transactions. They are used for the most frequent transactions in a business. For example, in merchandising businesses, companies acquire merchandise from vendors, and then in turn sell the merchandise to individuals or other businesses. Sales and purchases are the most common transactions for the merchandising businesses. A business such as a retail store will record the following transactions many times a day for sales on account and cash sales.

Exam Probability: **Low**

19. *Answer choices:*

- a. Cash sweep
- b. Accounting research
- c. European training programs
- d. Engineering Accounting

Guidance: level 1

:: Financial statements ::

_____ s - are the "Financial statements of a group in which the assets, liabilities, equity, income, expenses and cash flows of the parent company and its subsidiaries are presented as those of a single economic entity", according to International Accounting Standard 27 "Consolidated and separate financial statements", and International Financial Reporting Standard 10 " _____ s".

Exam Probability: **High**

20. *Answer choices:*

- a. Clean surplus accounting
- b. Financial statement
- c. Quarterly finance report
- d. PnL Explained

:: Tax avoidance ::

_____ s are any method of reducing taxable income resulting in a reduction of the payments to tax collecting entities, including state and federal governments. The methodology can vary depending on local and international tax laws.

Exam Probability: **Low**

21. *Answer choices:*

(see index for correct answer)

- a. Window tax
- b. GAAR
- c. Lagarde list
- d. Perpetual traveler

:: Financial statements ::

A Statement of changes in equity and similarly the statement of changes in owner's equity for a sole trader, statement of changes in partners' equity for a partnership, statement of changes in Shareholders' equity for a Company or statement of changes in Taxpayers' equity for Government financial statements is one of the four basic financial statements.

Exam Probability: **High**

22. *Answer choices:*

(see index for correct answer)

- a. Statement of retained earnings
- b. Statements on auditing standards
- c. Clean surplus accounting
- d. Government financial statements

Guidance: level 1

:: ::

An _____ is a contingent motivator. Traditional _____ s are extrinsic motivators which reward actions to yield a desired outcome. The effectiveness of traditional _____ s has changed as the needs of Western society have evolved. While the traditional _____ model is effective when there is a defined procedure and goal for a task, Western society started to require a higher volume of critical thinkers, so the traditional model became less effective. Institutions are now following a trend in implementing strategies that rely on intrinsic motivations rather than the extrinsic motivations that the traditional _____ s foster.

23. *Answer choices:*

(see index for correct answer)

- a. functional perspective
- b. Incentive
- c. similarity-attraction theory
- d. open system

Guidance: level 1

:: Commercial crimes ::

_____ is the act of withholding assets for the purpose of conversion of such assets, by one or more persons to whom the assets were entrusted, either to be held or to be used for specific purposes. _____ is a type of financial fraud. For example, a lawyer might embezzle funds from the trust accounts of their clients; a financial advisor might embezzle the funds of investors; and a husband or a wife might embezzle funds from a bank account jointly held with the spouse.

Exam Probability: **High**

24. *Answer choices:*

(see index for correct answer)

- a. Chiasso financial smuggling case

- b. Price fixing
- c. Wage theft
- d. United States antitrust law

Guidance: level 1

:: Taxation ::

A _____ is a person or organization subject to pay a tax. _____ s have an Identification Number, a reference number issued by a government to its citizens.

Exam Probability: **Low**

25. *Answer choices:*

(see index for correct answer)

- a. African Tax Administration Forum
- b. Inflation tax
- c. Bracket creep
- d. Taxpayer

Guidance: level 1

:: Management accounting ::

_____ is an approach to determine a product's life-cycle cost which should be sufficient to develop specified functionality and quality, while ensuring its desired profit. It involves setting a target cost by subtracting a desired profit margin from a competitive market price. A target cost is the maximum amount of cost that can be incurred on a product, however, the firm can still earn the required profit margin from that product at a particular selling price. _____ decomposes the target cost from product level to component level. Through this decomposition, _____ spreads the competitive pressure faced by the company to product's designers and suppliers. _____ consists of cost planning in the design phase of production as well as cost control throughout the resulting product life cycle. The cardinal rule of _____ is to never exceed the target cost. However, the focus of _____ is not to minimize costs, but to achieve a desired level of cost reduction determined by the _____ process.

Exam Probability: **Low**

26. *Answer choices:*

(see index for correct answer)

- a. Entity-level controls
- b. Environmental full-cost accounting
- c. Management accounting in supply chains
- d. Target costing

Guidance: level 1

:: Management ::

Business _____ is a discipline in operations management in which people use various methods to discover, model, analyze, measure, improve, optimize, and automate business processes. BPM focuses on improving corporate performance by managing business processes. Any combination of methods used to manage a company's business processes is BPM. Processes can be structured and repeatable or unstructured and variable. Though not required, enabling technologies are often used with BPM.

Exam Probability: **Medium**

27. *Answer choices:*

(see index for correct answer)

- a. Certified management consultant
- b. Telescopic observations strategic framework
- c. Communities of innovation
- d. Process Management

Guidance: level 1

:: Investment ::

_____ , and investment appraisal, is the planning process used to determine whether an organization's long term investments such as new machinery, replacement of machinery, new plants, new products, and research development projects are worth the funding of cash through the firm's capitalization structure . It is the process of allocating resources for major capital, or investment, expenditures. One of the primary goals of _____ investments is to increase the value of the firm to the shareholders.

28. *Answer choices:*

(see index for correct answer)

- a. Capital budgeting
- b. Miraclebet
- c. Individual Pension Plan
- d. Emerging market

Guidance: level 1

:: ::

The _____ or just chief executive , is the most senior corporate, executive, or administrative officer in charge of managing an organization especially an independent legal entity such as a company or nonprofit institution. CEOs lead a range of organizations, including public and private corporations, non-profit organizations and even some government organizations . The CEO of a corporation or company typically reports to the board of directors and is charged with maximizing the value of the entity, which may include maximizing the share price, market share, revenues or another element. In the non-profit and government sector, CEOs typically aim at achieving outcomes related to the organization`s mission, such as reducing poverty, increasing literacy, etc.

29. *Answer choices:*

(see index for correct answer)

- a. functional perspective
- b. Sarbanes-Oxley act of 2002
- c. Chief executive officer
- d. deep-level diversity

Guidance: level 1

:: Accounting in the United States ::

The _____ is a private-sector, nonprofit corporation created by the Sarbanes–Oxley Act of 2002 to oversee the audits of public companies and other issuers in order to protect the interests of investors and further the public interest in the preparation of informative, accurate and independent audit reports. The PCAOB also oversees the audits of broker-dealers, including compliance reports filed pursuant to federal securities laws, to promote investor protection. All PCAOB rules and standards must be approved by the U.S. Securities and Exchange Commission .

Exam Probability: **Low**

30. *Answer choices:*

(see index for correct answer)

- a. Public Company Accounting Oversight Board
- b. The Wheat Committee
- c. Cotton Plantation Record and Account Book

- d. Other comprehensive income

Guidance: level 1

:: Finance ::

_____ is a notional asset or liability to reflect corporate income taxation on a basis that is the same or more similar to recognition of profits than the taxation treatment. _____ liabilities can arise as a result of corporate taxation treatment of capital expenditure being more rapid than the accounting depreciation treatment. _____ assets can arise due to net loss carry-overs, which are only recorded as asset if it is deemed more likely than not that the asset will be used in future fiscal periods. Different countries may also allow or require discounting of the assets or particularly liabilities. There are often disclosure requirements for potential liabilities and assets that are not actually recognised as an asset or liability.

Exam Probability: **Medium**

31. *Answer choices:*

(see index for correct answer)

- a. NASDAQ futures
- b. Deferred tax
- c. XBRL assurance
- d. Offshore financial centre

Guidance: level 1

:: Television terminology ::

A nonprofit organization , also known as a non-business entity, _____ organization, or nonprofit institution, is dedicated to furthering a particular social cause or advocating for a shared point of view. In economic terms, it is an organization that uses its surplus of the revenues to further achieve its ultimate objective, rather than distributing its income to the organization`s shareholders, leaders, or members. Nonprofits are tax exempt or charitable, meaning they do not pay income tax on the money that they receive for their organization. They can operate in religious, scientific, research, or educational settings.

Exam Probability: **High**

32. *Answer choices:*

(see index for correct answer)

- a. multiplexing
- b. distance learning
- c. Not-for-profit
- d. nonprofit

Guidance: level 1

:: Accounting terminology ::

In accounting/accountancy, _____ are journal entries usually made at the end of an accounting period to allocate income and expenditure to the period in which they actually occurred. The revenue recognition principle is the basis of making _____ that pertain to unearned and accrued revenues under accrual-basis accounting. They are sometimes called Balance Day adjustments because they are made on balance day.

Exam Probability: **High**

33. *Answer choices:*

(see index for correct answer)

- a. Impairment cost
- b. Record to report
- c. Adjusting entries
- d. double-entry bookkeeping

Guidance: level 1

:: Financial ratios ::

In finance, the _____ , also known as the acid-test ratio is a type of liquidity ratio which measures the ability of a company to use its near cash or quick assets to extinguish or retire its current liabilities immediately. Quick assets include those current assets that presumably can be quickly converted to cash at close to their book values. It is the ratio between quickly available or liquid assets and current liabilities.

34. *Answer choices:*

(see index for correct answer)

- a. price-to-cash flow ratio
- b. CASA ratio
- c. Like for like
- d. Quick ratio

Guidance: level 1

:: Accounting terminology ::

A _____ contains all the accounts for recording transactions relating to a company's assets, liabilities, owners' equity, revenue, and expenses. In modern accounting software or ERP, the _____ works as a central repository for accounting data transferred from all subledgers or modules like accounts payable, accounts receivable, cash management, fixed assets, purchasing and projects. The _____ is the backbone of any accounting system which holds financial and non-financial data for an organization. The collection of all accounts is known as the _____ . Each account is known as a ledger account. In a manual or non-computerized system this may be a large book. The statement of financial position and the statement of income and comprehensive income are both derived from the _____ . Each account in the _____ consists of one or more pages. The _____ is where posting to the accounts occurs. Posting is the process of recording amounts as credits , and amounts as debits , in the pages of the _____ . Additional columns to the right hold a running activity total .

Exam Probability: **Low**

35. *Answer choices:*

(see index for correct answer)

- a. General ledger
- b. double-entry bookkeeping
- c. Accounts payable
- d. Accounts receivable

Guidance: level 1

:: Basic financial concepts ::

_____ is a sustained increase in the general price level of goods and services in an economy over a period of time. When the general price level rises, each unit of currency buys fewer goods and services; consequently, _____ reflects a reduction in the purchasing power per unit of money a loss of real value in the medium of exchange and unit of account within the economy. The measure of _____ is the _____ rate, the annualized percentage change in a general price index, usually the consumer price index, over time. The opposite of _____ is deflation.

Exam Probability: **High**

36. *Answer choices:*

(see index for correct answer)

- a. Leverage cycle
- b. Inflation
- c. Future-oriented
- d. Short interest

Guidance: level 1

:: Management accounting ::

In _____ or managerial accounting, managers use the provisions of accounting information in order to better inform themselves before they decide matters within their organizations, which aids their management and performance of control functions.

Exam Probability: **High**

37. *Answer choices:*
(see index for correct answer)

- a. Construction accounting
- b. Cost driver
- c. Management accounting
- d. RCA open-source application

Guidance: level 1

:: Generally Accepted Accounting Principles ::

In accrual accounting, the revenue recognition principle states that expenses should be recorded during the period in which they are incurred, regardless of when the transfer of cash occurs. Conversely, cash basis accounting calls for the recognition of an expense when the cash is paid, regardless of when the expense was actually incurred.

Exam Probability: **Low**

38. *Answer choices:*

(see index for correct answer)

- a. Trial balance
- b. Operating income before depreciation and amortization
- c. Operating profit
- d. Expense

Guidance: level 1

:: Financial ratios ::

The _____ shows the percentage of how profitable a company's assets are in generating revenue.

Exam Probability: **Medium**

39. *Answer choices:*

(see index for correct answer)

- a. Times interest earned
- b. Return on assets
- c. P/B ratio
- d. Dividend payout ratio

Guidance: level 1

:: Marketing ::

_____ or stock is the goods and materials that a business holds for the ultimate goal of resale .

Exam Probability: **Low**

40. *Answer choices:*

(see index for correct answer)

- a. Inventory
- b. Boston matrix
- c. Next-best-action marketing
- d. Corporate capabilities package

Guidance: level 1

:: United States Generally Accepted Accounting Principles ::

In a companies' financial reporting, _____ "includes all changes in equity during a period except those resulting from investments by owners and distributions to owners". Because that use excludes the effects of changing ownership interest, an economic measure of _____ is necessary for financial analysis from the shareholders' point of view

Exam Probability: **Medium**

41. *Answer choices:*

(see index for correct answer)

- a. Available for sale
- b. Comprehensive income
- c. Working Group on Financial Markets
- d. Asset retirement obligation

Guidance: level 1

:: Generally Accepted Accounting Principles ::

_____ s is an accounting term that refers to groups of accounts serving to express the cost of goods and service allocatable within a business or manufacturing organization. The principle behind the pool is to correlate direct and indirect costs with a specified cost driver, so to find out the total sum of expenses related to the manufacture of a product.

Exam Probability: **High**

42. *Answer choices:*

(see index for correct answer)

- a. Operating statement
- b. Reserve
- c. Cost pool
- d. Cost principle

Guidance: level 1

:: Management accounting ::

A _____ is a part of a business which is expected to make an identifiable contribution to the organization's profits.

Exam Probability: **Medium**

43. *Answer choices:*

(see index for correct answer)

- a. Direct material price variance
- b. Target income sales
- c. Profit center
- d. Accounting management

Guidance: level 1

:: ::

In production, research, retail, and accounting, a _____ is the value of money that has been used up to produce something or deliver a service, and hence is not available for use anymore. In business, the _____ may be one of acquisition, in which case the amount of money expended to acquire it is counted as _____ . In this case, money is the input that is gone in order to acquire the thing. This acquisition _____ may be the sum of the _____ of production as incurred by the original producer, and further _____ s of transaction as incurred by the acquirer over and above the price paid to the producer. Usually, the price also includes a mark-up for profit over the _____ of production.

Exam Probability: **High**

44. *Answer choices:*

(see index for correct answer)

- a. corporate values
- b. cultural
- c. interpersonal communication

- d. similarity-attraction theory

Guidance: level 1

:: Insolvency ::

_____ is the process in accounting by which a company is brought to an end in the United Kingdom, Republic of Ireland and United States. The assets and property of the company are redistributed. _____ is also sometimes referred to as winding-up or dissolution, although dissolution technically refers to the last stage of _____ . The process of _____ also arises when customs, an authority or agency in a country responsible for collecting and safeguarding customs duties, determines the final computation or ascertainment of the duties or drawback accruing on an entry.

Exam Probability: **Medium**

45. *Answer choices:*
(see index for correct answer)

- a. Financial distress
- b. Debt consolidation
- c. Liquidation
- d. Insolvency law of Russia

Guidance: level 1

:: Accounting terminology ::

Double-entry bookkeeping, in accounting, is a system of bookkeeping so named because every entry to an account requires a corresponding and opposite entry to a different account. The double entry has two equal and corresponding sides known as debit and credit. The left-hand side is debit and right-hand side is credit. For instance, recording a sale of $100 might require two entries: a debit of $100 to an account named "Stock" and a credit of $100 to an account named "Revenue."

Exam Probability: **High**

46. *Answer choices:*

(see index for correct answer)

- a. Total absorption costing
- b. Capital appreciation
- c. Statement of financial position
- d. General ledger

Guidance: level 1

:: Supply chain management terms ::

In business and finance, _____ is a system of organizations, people, activities, information, and resources involved inmoving a product or service from supplier to customer. _____ activities involve the transformation of natural resources, raw materials, and components into a finished product that is delivered to the end customer. In sophisticated _____ systems, used products may re-enter the _____ at any point where residual value is recyclable. _____ s link value chains.

Exam Probability: **Low**

47. *Answer choices:*

(see index for correct answer)

- a. Supply chain
- b. Consumable
- c. Final assembly schedule
- d. Will call

Guidance: level 1

:: ::

A _____ is a fund into which a sum of money is added during an employee's employment years, and from which payments are drawn to support the person's retirement from work in the form of periodic payments. A _____ may be a "defined benefit plan" where a fixed sum is paid regularly to a person, or a "defined contribution plan" under which a fixed sum is invested and then becomes available at retirement age. _____s should not be confused with severance pay; the former is usually paid in regular installments for life after retirement, while the latter is typically paid as a fixed amount after involuntary termination of employment prior to retirement.

Exam Probability: **Medium**

48. *Answer choices:*

(see index for correct answer)

- a. Pension
- b. personal values
- c. process perspective
- d. interpersonal communication

Guidance: level 1

:: ::

The _____ is a private, non-profit organization standard-setting body whose primary purpose is to establish and improve Generally Accepted Accounting Principles within the United States in the public's interest. The Securities and Exchange Commission designated the FASB as the organization responsible for setting accounting standards for public companies in the US. The FASB replaced the American Institute of Certified Public Accountants' Accounting Principles Board on July 1, 1973.

Exam Probability: **Medium**

49. *Answer choices:*

(see index for correct answer)

- a. personal values
- b. Character
- c. Financial Accounting Standards Board
- d. open system

Guidance: level 1

:: Management accounting ::

_____ s are costs that change as the quantity of the good or service that a business produces changes. _____ s are the sum of marginal costs over all units produced. They can also be considered normal costs. Fixed costs and _____ s make up the two components of total cost. Direct costs are costs that can easily be associated with a particular cost object. However, not all _____ s are direct costs. For example, variable manufacturing overhead costs are _____ s that are indirect costs, not direct costs. _____ s are sometimes called unit-level costs as they vary with the number of units produced.

Exam Probability: **High**

50. *Answer choices:*

(see index for correct answer)

- a. Resource consumption accounting
- b. Backflush accounting
- c. Semi-variable cost
- d. Variance

Guidance: level 1

:: Generally Accepted Accounting Principles ::

A _____ , in accrual accounting, is any account where the asset or liability is not realized until a future date , e.g. annuities, charges, taxes, income, etc. The deferred item may be carried, dependent on type of _____ , as either an asset or liability. See also accrual.

51. *Answer choices:*

(see index for correct answer)

- a. Operating income
- b. Deferral
- c. Net realizable value
- d. Vendor-specific objective evidence

Guidance: level 1

:: Accounting software ::

_____ is an accounting software package developed and marketed by Intuit. _____ products are geared mainly toward small and medium-sized businesses and offer on-premises accounting applications as well as cloud-based versions that accept business payments, manage and pay bills, and payroll functions.

Exam Probability: **High**

52. *Answer choices:*

(see index for correct answer)

- a. SnapAccounting
- b. ABLE

- c. Digital Insight
- d. TRAVERSE

Guidance: level 1

:: ::

A _____ is a form of public administration which, in a majority of contexts, exists as the lowest tier of administration within a given state. The term is used to contrast with offices at state level, which are referred to as the central government, national government, or federal government and also to supranational government which deals with governing institutions between states. _____ s generally act within powers delegated to them by legislation or directives of the higher level of government. In federal states, _____ generally comprises the third tier of government, whereas in unitary states, _____ usually occupies the second or third tier of government, often with greater powers than higher-level administrative divisions.

Exam Probability: **Low**

53. *Answer choices:*

(see index for correct answer)

- a. corporate values
- b. functional perspective
- c. hierarchical
- d. Local government

:: Pricing ::

_____ is a pricing strategy in which the selling price is determined by adding a specific amount markup to a product's unit cost. An alternative pricing method is value-based pricing.

Exam Probability: **Medium**

54. *Answer choices:*
(see index for correct answer)

- a. The price of milk
- b. Fare
- c. Flat rate
- d. Cost-plus pricing

:: ::

In accounting, the _____ is a measure of the number of times inventory is sold or used in a time period such as a year. It is calculated to see if a business has an excessive inventory in comparison to its sales level. The equation for _____ equals the cost of goods sold divided by the average inventory. _____ is also known as inventory turns, merchandise turnover, stockturn, stock turns, turns, and stock turnover.

Exam Probability: **Low**

55. *Answer choices:*

(see index for correct answer)

- a. process perspective
- b. Character
- c. personal values
- d. Inventory turnover

Guidance: level 1

:: Business models ::

A _____ , _____ company or daughter company is a company that is owned or controlled by another company, which is called the parent company, parent, or holding company. The _____ can be a company, corporation, or limited liability company. In some cases it is a government or state-owned enterprise. In some cases, particularly in the music and book publishing industries, subsidiaries are referred to as imprints.

Exam Probability: **Low**

56. *Answer choices:*

(see index for correct answer)

- a. Dependent growth business model
- b. Small business
- c. Subsidiary
- d. Business model pattern

Guidance: level 1

:: Capital gains taxes ::

A _____ refers to profit that results from a sale of a capital asset, such as stock, bond or real estate, where the sale price exceeds the purchase price. The gain is the difference between a higher selling price and a lower purchase price. Conversely, a capital loss arises if the proceeds from the sale of a capital asset are less than the purchase price.

Exam Probability: **Low**

57. *Answer choices:*

(see index for correct answer)

- a. Capital gain
- b. Capital Cost Allowance

- c. Capital gains tax

Guidance: level 1

:: Generally Accepted Accounting Principles ::

Paid-in capital is capital that is contributed to a corporation by investors by purchase of stock from the corporation, the primary market, not by purchase of stock in the open market from other stockholders . It includes share capital as well as additional paid-in capital.

Exam Probability: **High**

58. *Answer choices:*

(see index for correct answer)

- a. Operating statement
- b. Deprival value
- c. Contributed capital
- d. Engagement letter

Guidance: level 1

:: Manufacturing ::

_____ costs are all manufacturing costs that are related to the cost object but cannot be traced to that cost object in an economically feasible way.

Exam Probability: **High**

59. *Answer choices:*

(see index for correct answer)

- a. Guitar manufacturing
- b. Microfactory
- c. Manufacturing overhead
- d. Advanced planning and scheduling

Guidance: level 1

INDEX: Correct Answers

Foundations of Business

1. d: American Express

2. a: Benchmarking

3. d: Retail

4. d: Limited liability

5. b: Land

6. c: Accounts receivable

7. a: Evaluation

8. b: Insurance

9. b: Capital market

10. a: Variable cost

11. a: Recession

12. c: Brainstorming

13. d: Tariff

14. : Labor relations

15. b: Debt

16. a: Initiative

17. c: Currency

18. a: Regulation

19. c: Federal Trade Commission

20. : Money

21. d: Schedule

22. : Trade agreement

23. b: Common stock

24. b: Interview

25. a: Target market

26. a: Copyright

27. d: Description

28. : Marketing

29. : Specification

30. : Six Sigma

31. c: Reputation

32. a: Outsourcing

33. d: Organizational culture

34. c: Management

35. : Property

36. : Good

37. : Trademark

38. a: Balance sheet

39. a: Project management

40. c: Asset

41. b: Decision-making

42. a: Social security

43. c: Bank

44. d: Health

45. a: Office

46. c: Security

47. b: ITeM

48. : Financial crisis

49. a: Customs

50. : Cultural

51. : Working capital

52. d: Need

53. b: Venture capital

54. a: Entrepreneurship

55. c: Industry

56. a: Trade

57. c: Opportunity cost

58. : Problem

59. b: Buyer

Management

1. : Small business

2. : Initiative

3. a: Empowerment

4. c: Cost

5. c: Linear programming

6. c: Forecasting

7. a: Description

8. : Ratio

9. c: World Trade Organization

10. d: Situational leadership

11. d: Mass customization

12. c: Standard deviation

13. d: Risk management

14. c: Corporate governance

15. : Economies of scale

16. d: Time management

17. c: Innovation

18. a: Employee stock

19. : Goal

20. a: Individualism

21. b: Leadership style

22. b: Arbitration

23. : Reputation

24. c: Standardization

25. b: Emotional intelligence

26. b: Franchising

27. d: Interaction

28. c: Control chart

29. : Chief executive officer

30. d: Revenue

31. c: Performance measurement

32. a: Specification

33. : Scheduling

34. b: Research and development

35. d: Profit sharing

36. a: Senior management

37. d: Organizational commitment

38. : Logistics

39. c: Philosophy

40. : Budget

41. d: European Union

42. c: Quality assurance

43. : Certification

44. c: Overtime

45. b: Justice

46. d: Authority

47. : Sharing

48. a: Training and development

49. b: Statistic

50. a: Performance

51. a: Expatriate

52. d: Transformational leadership

53. c: Career

54. d: Synergy

55. : Bottom line

56. c: Assessment center

57. c: Good

58. a: Raw material

59. a: Job description

Business law

1. a: Duty

2. b: Subsidiary

3. a: Advertisement

4. : Consumer Good

5. : Ford

6. d: Guarantee

7. a: Dividend

8. d: Patent

9. c: Firm offer

10. c: Commercial Paper

11. c: Due diligence

12. c: Duty of care

13. d: Policy

14. d: Security

15. c: Utilitarianism

16. a: Mortgage

17. c: Judicial review

18. d: Personal property

19. c: Lien

20. b: Plaintiff

21. : Welfare

22. d: Good faith

23. d: Adoption

24. c: Insurable interest

25. c: Eminent domain

26. : Mediation

27. a: Manufacturing

28. b: Risk

29. b: Negotiable instrument

30. c: Accounting

31. c: Contract

32. c: Foreclosure

33. d: Property

34. d: Corporation

35. c: Collective bargaining

36. a: Income

37. a: Fee simple

38. c: Presentment

39. a: Utility

40. c: Computer fraud

41. c: Injunction

42. : Market value

43. : Void contract

44. c: Lanham Act

45. b: Perfection

46. d: Incentive

47. c: Wire fraud

48. c: Indictment

49. c: Private law

50. d: Forgery

51. : Appellate Court

52. b: Accord and satisfaction

53. b: Uniform Electronic Transactions Act

54. : Restraint of trade

55. : Amendment

56. b: Advertising

57. b: Security agreement

58. : Sherman Antitrust

59. b: Supreme Court

Finance

1. a: Risk assessment

2. c: Secondary market

3. : Bank

4. b: Insurance

5. c: Standard deviation

6. : Operating leverage

7. b: Long-term liabilities

8. c: Absorption costing

9. c: Land

10. : Bank of America

11. : Good

12. c: Certified Public Accountant

13. c: Compound interest

14. : Debt-to-equity ratio

15. b: Liquidity

16. a: Par value

17. d: Financial accounting

18. c: Fair value

19. d: Double taxation

20. : Accounting method

21. d: Pricing

22. c: Coupon

23. a: Treasury stock

24. d: Stock price

25. : Risk

26. a: Cost

27. a: Public company

28. b: Accrual

29. d: Revenue

30. c: Capital gain

31. b: Liquidation

32. a: Common stock

33. : Shareholder

34. : Underwriting

35. a: Residual value

36. a: Consideration

37. : Opportunity cost

38. a: Loan

39. d: Net profit

40. b: Adjusting entries

41. b: Cost accounting

42. a: Finished good

43. a: Capital lease

44. a: Schedule

45. : Citigroup

46. c: INDEX

47. d: Issuer

48. : Industry

49. c: Free cash flow

50. c: Government bond

51. b: Buyer

52. d: Asset management

53. b: Interest expense

54. a: Return on investment

55. a: Investor

56. c: Arbitrage

57. d: Copyright

58. b: Marketing

59. : Interest

Human resource management

1. a: Management by objectives

2. b: Grievance

3. c: Job performance

4. b: Living wage

5. : Perception

6. a: E-HRM

7. a: Brainstorming

8. b: Decentralization

9. a: Ownership

10. c: Behavior modification

11. a: Labor relations

12. a: Job enlargement

13. c: Virtual team

14. d: Centralization

15. : Global workforce

16. b: Compensation and benefits

17. c: Business game

18. b: Organizational chart

19. b: Free Trade

20. a: Persuasion

21. a: Piece rate

22. : Innovation

23. a: Cover letter

24. : Executive officer

25. c: Applicant tracking system

26. b: Worker Adjustment and Retraining Notification Act

27. : Unemployment benefits

28. c: Cost

29. d: Bargaining unit

30. b: Questionnaire

31. : Profit sharing

32. : Part-time

33. : Employee benefit

34. : Works council

35. b: Internship

36. a: Job design

37. b: Social contract

38. : Faragher v. City of Boca Raton

39. : Collective bargaining

40. : Employee referral

41. d: Open shop

42. b: Total Quality Management

43. : Sick leave

44. : Cafeteria plan

45. : Prevailing wage

46. a: Professional association

47. : Job fair

48. a: Performance measurement

49. b: Performance appraisal

50. c: Mobile recruiting

51. a: Telecommuting

52. a: 360-degree feedback

53. : Census

54. d: Self-actualization

55. d: Material safety data sheet

56. : Card check

57. b: Pregnancy discrimination

58. a: Closed shop

59. c: Bottom line

Information systems

1. a: Mouse

2. c: Threat

3. d: Local Area Network

4. d: Payment system

5. c: Commercial off-the-shelf

6. b: Subscription

7. b: Domain Name System

8. d: M-Pesa

9. b: Business process reengineering

10. c: Peer production

11. b: Intrusion detection system

12. d: Dashboard

13. b: Data center

14. c: Total cost of ownership

15. c: Service-oriented architecture

16. d: Data analysis

17. b: Metadata

18. c: Edge computing

19. : Strategic information system

20. c: PayPal

21. : Yelp

22. a: Sustainable

23. b: Supply chain

24. c: Information management

25. d: Interview

26. : Utility computing

27. : World Wide Web

28. c: Property

29. d: Vertical integration

30. a: Mass customization

31. : Acceptable use policy

32. c: Health Insurance Portability and Accountability Act

33. d: Availability

34. c: Search engine optimization

35. : Data aggregator

36. a: Online transaction processing

37. d: Disintermediation

38. b: Market share

39. d: Master data management

40. : Google Calendar

41. c: Web mining

42. a: Service level agreement

43. d: One Laptop per Child

44. b: Google

45. b: Geocoding

46. b: Electronic funds transfer

47. : Information systems

48. a: Privacy policy

49. : Information flow

50. a: Kinect

51. b: System software

52. a: Encryption

53. d: Domain name

54. : Telnet

55. d: Enterprise resource planning

56. c: Picasa

57. b: Critical success factor

58. : Code

59. a: Automation

Marketing

1. d: Intellectual property

2. a: Unique selling proposition

3. a: Competitor

4. a: Raw material

5. d: Price

6. d: Exchange rate

7. a: Advertising agency

8. a: Business-to-business

9. b: Creativity

10. : Planning

11. a: Attention

12. c: Interest

13. d: Gross domestic product

14. c: Marketing communication

15. d: American Express

16. : Testimonial

17. c: Forecasting

18. c: Customer service

19. a: Wall Street Journal

20. d: Advertising campaign

21. d: Sales promotion

22. c: Statistic

23. b: Social media

24. d: Marketing communications

25. : Competitive advantage

26. c: Direct mail

27. c: Image

28. b: Reseller

29. d: Entrepreneur

30. b: Universal Product Code

31. b: Data warehouse

32. c: Mass media

33. b: Product development

34. a: Need

35. c: Public

36. a: Variable cost

37. d: Problem Solving

38. : Security

39. : Perception

40. b: Argument

41. d: Incentive

42. : Database marketing

43. d: Telemarketing

44. c: Concept testing

45. : Insurance

46. a: Inflation

47. a: Customer satisfaction

48. a: Sales

49. : Organizational structure

50. d: Manufacturing

51. a: Strategic planning

52. c: Direct selling

53. d: Direct marketing

54. : Standing

55. d: Brand equity

56. c: Authority

57. : Infomercial

58. c: Consideration

59. c: Stock

Manufacturing

1. b: Flowchart

2. c: Quality assurance

3. d: Ishikawa diagram

4. c: Time management

5. d: Pattern

6. a: Kanban

7. a: Quality management

8. : Reverse auction

9. d: Turbine

10. a: PDCA

11. : Lead

12. : E-procurement

13. b: American Society for Quality

14. c: Accreditation

15. d: Coating

16. d: Remanufacturing

17. : Rolling

18. b: Reorder point

19. : Sensitivity analysis

20. : Strategic planning

21. b: Steel

22. a: Production schedule

23. d: Quality audit

24. c: Property

25. : Quality policy

26. c: Paper

27. c: Strategy

28. c: Average cost

29. b: Gantt chart

30. d: Sharing

31. b: Project management

32. c: Asset

33. : DMAIC

34. c: Procurement

35. b: Bullwhip effect

36. d: Transaction cost

37. a: Economies of scope

38. b: Assembly line

39. b: Volume

40. : Total quality management

41. c: Opportunity cost

42. d: Project manager

43. : Malcolm Baldrige National Quality Award

44. d: Expediting

45. c: Toshiba

46. : Risk management

47. a: Tool

48. c: Downtime

49. d: Resource allocation

50. c: Check sheet

51. c: Virtual team

52. d: Total cost of ownership

53. b: Reflux

54. : Project

55. a: Thomas Register

56. : Throughput

57. c: Purchase order

58. c: Sunk costs

59. b: Performance

Commerce

1. b: Credit card

2. b: Overhead cost

3. c: Control system

4. a: Land

5. d: Public relations

6. c: Hearing

7. d: Permission marketing

8. c: Real estate

9. d: Payment card

10. d: Exchange rate

11. : Direct marketing

12. : Return on investment

13. : Marketing strategy

14. b: Committee

15. b: Evaluation

16. : Mobile commerce

17. a: Stock

18. : Bank

19. : Forward auction

20. c: Advertising

21. : Uniform Commercial Code

22. a: Level of service

23. d: International trade

24. a: Procurement

25. : Drawback

26. a: Customs

27. d: Game

28. a: Pop-up ad

29. a: Firm

30. d: Electronic funds transfer

31. c: Minimum wage

32. : Publicity

33. : Entrepreneur

34. c: Trade

35. : Excite

36. c: Micropayment

37. c: Issuing bank

38. d: Tariff

39. : Supply chain

40. c: Warehouse

41. : Management

42. c: Insurance

43. d: Tool

44. c: Organizational structure

45. c: Consultant

46. c: Bill of lading

47. a: Raw material

48. c: Boot

49. c: Supervisor

50. : E-commerce

51. a: Pizza Hut

52. b: British Airways

53. c: Argument

54. : Bottom line

55. c: Inventory control

56. b: Risk management

57. b: Marketing mix

58. : Brand

59. c: Regulation

Business ethics

1. c: Risk assessment

2. : Lawsuit

3. : Arthur Andersen

4. c: Trojan horse

5. a: Empowerment

6. b: Employee Polygraph Protection Act

7. d: Sexual harassment

8. c: Organizational ethics

9. a: Antitrust

10. c: Risk management

11. a: Pollution Prevention

12. a: Capitalism

13. d: Building

14. : Pyramid scheme

15. c: Affirmative action

16. c: Green marketing

17. a: Lead paint

18. b: Internal control

19. a: Charles Ponzi

20. d: Micromanagement

21. b: Communist Manifesto

22. d: Better Business Bureau

23. c: Feedback

24. c: Clayton Act

25. b: Corporation

26. : Kyoto Protocol

27. b: Perception

28. c: Petroleum

29. c: Lanham Act

30. a: Referent power

31. c: Social responsibility

32. c: Clean Water Act

33. : Pollution

34. a: Hedonism

35. c: Exxon Valdez

36. : Planet

37. c: Fraud

38. b: Fair trade

39. b: Transocean

40. c: European Commission

41. : Consumer Financial Protection Bureau

42. d: Patent

43. b: Model Rules of Professional Conduct

44. a: Price fixing

45. b: Marijuana

46. b: Corporate citizenship

47. a: Locus of control

48. c: Sherman Antitrust Act

49. a: Dilemma

50. d: Minimum wage

51. c: Guerrilla Marketing

52. c: Qui tam

53. c: Edgewood College

54. b: Electronic waste

55. c: Patriot Act

56. : Fannie Mae

57. a: Constitutional law

58. c: East India

59. d: Organizational structure

Accounting

1. c: Paid-in capital

2. d: Purchase order

3. b: Tax rate

4. c: Disability insurance

5. a: Securities Exchange Act

6. : Standard cost

7. d: Income statement

8. : Operating leverage

9. a: Dividend

10. a: Worksheet

11. a: Contribution margin

12. : Shareholder

13. b: Audit

14. a: Job order

15. a: Balanced scorecard

16. d: Trueblood Committee

17. c: Internal Revenue Service

18. c: Times interest earned

19. : Special journals

20. : Consolidated financial statement

21. : Tax shelter

22. a: Statement of retained earnings

23. b: Incentive

24. : Embezzlement

25. d: Taxpayer

26. d: Target costing

27. d: Process Management

28. a: Capital budgeting

29. c: Chief executive officer

30. a: Public Company Accounting Oversight Board

31. b: Deferred tax

32. c: Not-for-profit

33. c: Adjusting entries

34. d: Quick ratio

35. a: General ledger

36. b: Inflation

37. c: Management accounting

38. : Matching principle

39. b: Return on assets

40. a: Inventory

41. b: Comprehensive income

42. c: Cost pool

43. c: Profit center

44. : Cost

45. c: Liquidation

46. : Double-entry accounting

47. a: Supply chain

48. a: Pension

49. c: Financial Accounting Standards Board

50. : Variable cost

51. b: Deferral

52. : QuickBooks

53. d: Local government

54. d: Cost-plus pricing

55. d: Inventory turnover

56. c: Subsidiary

57. a: Capital gain

58. c: Contributed capital

59. c: Manufacturing overhead